SARAH BERNHARDT

LYSIANE BERNHARDT

SARAH BERNHARDT
MY GRANDMOTHER

Translated by
VYVYAN HOLLAND

37 Illustrations

since 1812

HURST & BLACKETT LTD
LONDON NEW YORK MELBOURNE SYDNEY CAPE TOWN

To my sister
SIMONE BERNHARDT-GROSS
in memory of our Grandmother

CONTENTS

PART III

PART IV

LIST OF ILLUSTRATIONS

PREFACE

ONE summer day, some months before her death, my grandmother, who was then seventy-eight years of age, sent for me to her room in the Manor House of Penhoët, and said to me:

"Lysiane, you are a writer and some day you must write a book about me. So I am going to entrust you with certain objects and certain documents."

"But," I replied, "you have already written your *Memoirs* yourself."

"Yes, but they stop in 1881 and we are now in 1922. Besides," she added with a smile, "perhaps I did not tell everything. In 1881 I felt, as it were, that I was in the centre of things: things were still happening! But from now onwards, if you will come with me, we will make a journey together into the past. It is so amusing to recall the past, particularly when the future can no longer suffer by it. Besides, for me the future only represents a very short way to go."

"Oh!" I cried indignantly. "Haven't you always declared to us, indeed promised us, that you would live to be a hundred and three?"

"Perhaps I was boasting a little. Believe me, we would do well to start our journey at once. As and when they come to my mind, I will tell you tales of my childhood, of my adolescence, of my art, of my travels and even of my love-affairs. But I do not want you to write this book immediately after my death. Let a few years pass first. In that way, my child, you will be more impartial."

Her clear, bright blue eyes turned towards the glittering sea on which rode small fishing-boats with their brown or pink sails.

"The catch must have been good," murmured my grandmother.

I can see her now, lying in her large four-poster bed, already in the grip of the illness that was to carry her off seven months later. She was wearing a white satin nightgown, and her unruly hair, the whiteness of which she no longer sought to disguise, was piled on her head and fastened there with a large blonde tortoiseshell comb. She was waiting, as she did each morning, for my father to bring in the daily catch for her inspection.

"Do you know the Grand-Champs Convent?" she asked me.

"Yes. You pointed it out to me one day when we had been to Versailles."

"One morning," she went on, "at about ten o'clock, a lady rang the bell at the gate of the Grand-Champs Convent . . ."

And our journey had begun.

LYSIANE BERNHARDT.

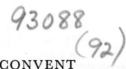

PART ONE

CHAPTER I

THE GRAND-CHAMPS CONVENT

ONE morning, towards ten o'clock, a lady rang the bell at the gate of the Grand-Champs Convent at Versailles. She had two little girls with her. One of them, aged about eleven, was sobbing bitterly, hiding her face in her mother's ample grey cloth skirt. The other little girl looked around her curiously. The high convent wall, the wooden door surmounted by a plain cross, the solemn silence of the Autumn morning only disturbed by the rustling of leaves, struck awe into the child, who, in her turn, snuggled up to her mother.

"Come, Jeanne," said the young woman, gently, "you will frighten your sister. You must both try to be good. Dry your eyes, Sarah, and you, Jeanne, blow your nose." The faint sound of the bell echoed through the convent and presently the portress examined them through the judas.

"I am Madame Judith Bernhardt," said the lady in the grey dress. "I have arranged with the Mother Superior to bring my elder daughter here today."

The portress seemed to be made up of a series of marbles: her eyes, her nose, her rounded lips and chin, and her two high-coloured cheekbones were all like marbles.

"Come in," she said, with a friendly smile.

The visitors were shown into the parlour; but at the sight of the large room in semi-darkness, surrounded by a wrought-iron grille, and of the highly polished floor which was difficult to walk on, the little girl who answered to the name of Sarah clung to her mother and began to cry again.

"I don't want to stay, mama! Take me away!"

"Don't be so silly!"

A nun had just entered the parlour; ignoring Madame Bernhardt, she took the little girl into her arms and spoke to her kindly.

"You must not cry, my child. I am going to show you your little room, the park where you can play, the gymnasium and the orchard, and I am going to introduce you to your little companions. What is your name, dear?"

"Sarah Bernhardt," replied the little girl, in a voice husky with sobbing.

But, more than any words of hers, the blue eyes of Mother Saint-Sophie, Superior of the Grand-Champs Convent, calmed the child's fears.

"Your little girl will be very happy with us, madame," she said. "But I understand her sorrow at leaving her mother and her little sister. What is her sister's name?"

"Jeanne."

But this family scene was not over yet. On hearing her name mentioned, the other child went over to Sarah and, taking advantage of the fact that the Mother Superior was explaining the convent routine to Madame Bernhardt, Jeanne pinched her sister's thin arm and said:

9

"They don't tell you so, but this is a prison. Mother and I are leaving you here because you have such mad ideas and no one can do anything with you."

At this cruel little speech Sarah broke into renewed sobs and tears.

"Why do you say such things to your sister?" asked the Mother Superior, severely. "You're a naughty little girl!"

"Oh," said Madame Bernhardt, hugging her daughter Jeanne passionately to her, "she is so delicate, poor darling, and you mustn't be cross with her."

The Mother Superior was puzzled by all this and looked in amazement from Madame Bernhardt to Jeanne, who tittered and hopped from one foot to the other, and then at Sarah, who had started shaking all over. Then she remembered a letter she had received a fortnight before from Monsieur Bernhardt.

My daughter needs quiet [he wrote]. *Her mother is often away from home and is more interested in her second daughter, Jeanne. I, too, travel a great deal. Sarah is a difficult child, but she has a sweet and a very spontaneous nature. My brother-in-law, Félix Faure, a very good and devout man, agrees with me that it is only by kindness that my child's fits of temper can be controlled. He has advised me to confide her to your care. You may baptize her when she is twelve years old.*

Mother Saint-Sophie, with her quick intuition, understood that little Sarah, jostled from pillar to post, had not even her younger sister's advantage of being able to take refuge in the arms of a capricious mother when assailed by the anguishing sorrows of childhood.

"If you like, madame, I will show you the dormitory."

Judith Bernhardt was a woman of middle height, with regular, slightly semitic features; her clear, short-sighted eyes looked straight at you with a certain insolence; she had fine, lustrous, rather vividly fair hair, which she wore in bandeaux on each side of her head. Her grey cloth dress had lace at the collar and cuffs and over it she wore a black-braided bolero; a toque trimmed with violets completed her costume. She suffered from a weak heart, which frequently made her press her hand to her bosom; a lovely hand with round, tapering fingers.

Both little girls wore plum-coloured dresses with small white collars and low belts, and two rows of buttons as their only ornament. Sarah had fair, reddish hair, a real frizzy mane, parted unevenly down the middle; and this cyclonic hair ended in a mass of twisted strands, curling tightly against the nape of her neck and round her forehead and temples. With her widely-spaced blue eyes, her rather large, well-defined nose and her wide mouth, Madame Bernhardt's daughter was far from being pretty at that age, and would have passed altogether unnoticed but for the strange, far-away, fearless, steady look in her eyes. Her sister Jeanne, on the other hand, was delightful, with her fair golden hair, much tidier than Sarah's and very carefully dressed, and her lovely little delicate face, lit up by two wide grey evasive eyes, which seldom seemed to look one straight in the face.

When Mother Saint-Sophie had finished showing them round Grand-Champs, Sarah had stopped crying. She was fascinated by the trees in the park, the orchard, the refectory, the dormitory, and especially by the children's private gardens: the little girl, now quite calm, thought only of the flowers which she would grow in the Spring. So she gave her mother a rather absent farewell kiss, and it was now the mother who was crying as she embraced her daughter tenderly.

"You had better say good-bye to your little girl here," Mother Saint-Sophie had suggested.

"I'm coming to see you on Sunday," declared Jeanne, giving her sister a peck.

"That's very nice of you," murmured the Mother Superior with a pleased smile.

"Yes," went on the little girl mischievously, "I'll come and trample on your garden!"

.   .   .   .   .

Neither Judith Bernhardt nor Jeanne were to come that Sunday, nor the following Thursday, nor the Sunday after. While Sarah's little companions were rushing into the parlour like a flock of sparrows or were romping in the woods with their parents, she herself was tearing her handkerchief with sorrow and rage. She was now wearing the uniform of Grand-Champs, blue with white braid, and, standing by her garden, she would pull down her hair which she had dressed so carefully that morning.

Her hair—there had been a lot of trouble over that. Madame Bernhardt had asked that her daughter's hair should be combed very gently, as its quality was such that it was apt to get into painful tangles. One morning, however, the nun who was combing it, thinking the process too slow, tugged at it, whereupon Sarah screamed and set upon the nun, biting her and hitting her with her fists, a situation with which only Mother Saint-Sophie was able to cope. And thenceforward she took care to see that Madame Bernhardt's instructions were carried out.

On the second Sunday, when, after the visiting hour was over, the Mother Superior saw the lonely child trampling on her garden and crying bitterly, she took her by the hand and led her to her private study. How warm and comfortable it was there! A fragrant crackling fire was already burning in the fireplace. It was early November and the coolness of Autumn crept through the solid walls of Grand-Champs.

"Come here, my child," said the Mother Superior.

She made Sarah sit beside her and showed the fascinated little girl a richly illuminated *History of the Saints*.

"When we baptize you, according to your father's wishes," she explained, "we will choose a name for you among these saints; because you have not yet been baptized, Sarah. Have you any other names?"

"I'm called Marie Henriette, Reverend Mother."

"Excellent. You have the most beautiful name one could dream of: Marie, the name of Our Most Holy Mother; you will receive the Holy Chrism under that name. And until then, three years from now, we will make you love and understand the religion of Our Lord Jesus Christ."

"I already know the Creed, the Hail Mary and the Lord's Prayer; my Uncle Félix Faure taught me those."

"I know," replied the Mother Superior, patting the child's hand. "Do you love your uncle?"

"Oh yes. But I hate his wife, Aunt Henriette; she is unkind to children, while my Aunt Rosine is so very gentle. I call her Auntie Perfume."

"And how many aunts have you got?"

"Aunt Rosine, Aunt Henriette, Aunt de la Martinique, Aunt Richard, Aunt Bruck and Aunt Betsy. But mama says there may be others in Harlem, because mama is Dutch. My Uncle Faure told me she was born in a tulip."

"And your papa?" asked the Reverend Mother, hiding a smile.

"Oh! He's so handsome!" exclaimed the child. "Look, Reverend Mother!" And the child unfastened a little gold chain which hung round her neck and from which were strung together an enamelled cross and a locket.

"There's my papa. He was a lawyer in Havre; now he travels. Mama's in the other side."

And her blue eyes clouded with sadness.

The Mother Superior could not help thinking that Monsieur and Madame Bernhardt were united in life only upon the frail chest of this child.

.   .   .   .   .

(Eighteen years later I was talking to my grandmother of this book, one day at Belle-Isle, and asked her more about her family. She replied:

"My sister Jeanne, your great-aunt, had a daughter, Saryta, whom you knew and who died very young. My father's brother, a native of Brittany, who was called Ker-Bernhardt, owned a hotel in Valparaiso; this Ker-Bernhardt, whose sons live (or lived) in Chile, had a daughter Louise, who was the mother of your cousin Jacqueline and of her brother Charles Vernay, killed in the 1914 war."

"And my great-grandmother, Judith Bernhardt?"

"She was a van Hard. And now you know as much as I do about our ancestry, and probably more than all those who claim to know a great deal more. An English journalist tried to trace me back to William of Orange; another journalist claimed my descent from Bernadin de Saint-Pierre, who was a native of Havre. The truth is much more simple. My mother, whom I adored, was a flighty young woman from Harlem; my father, who came from a good-class Havre family, abandoned his career as a lawyer to travel about the world. I don't know for whom or for what. Anyway, Lyseron, the family that one has given to one is of no importance. The only people who count are those whom one loves and especially the family that one creates oneself.")

.   .   .   .

On a Sunday about a year later, little Sarah ran into the parlour to embrace her mother and her Aunt Rosine, who smelled of orris-root. The room was lit up by the October sun which played through the window bars on the lace cuffs of the young women. It was three months since Madame Bernhardt had been to Grand-Champs.

"Mama! Aunt Rosine!"

"But, Judy," cried Aunt Rosine, "the child is splendid! And doesn't she look well?"

"We do our best to look after her," murmured Mother Saint-Sophie, who, as usual, had entered unobserved.

"Besides, Reverend Mother, the child adores you, one can see that quite clearly," continued pretty Aunt Rosine mischievously, waving her handkerchief and filling the room with its scent.

"We do our best to make our pupils love us, so that, if necessary, we may take their parents' place," quietly answered the nun, rather shocked by the young woman's affectation. Judy bit her lip and stroked her daughter's hair.

"Are you pleased to see me, darling?"

"Yes, mama," whispered the child, looking solemnly at her mother.

"I've got some news for you."

"Papa has come back?"

"No. But God, no doubt because you have been very good, has sent you another little sister."

"That ought to make you happy, Marie, when you are always asking for a doll," said the Mother Superior, with a smile.

"Marie?" questioned Madame Bernhardt in surprise.

"Yes, we call her Marie to get her used to her baptismal name."

"Another daughter!" exclaimed Sarah in disgust, thinking of Jeanne's spitefulness. "Aren't there any more boys in heaven?"

She snuggled into her mother's arms, against the warm taffeta bodice that smelled of heliotrope, while Aunt Rosine coquettishly studied, through her lorgnette, the portraits of Saint Augustine and of Pius IV which adorned the parlour walls.

"Would you like to come home to see your new sister?"

"I'd rather you brought her here one Sunday, mama. Then I could show her to Louise Buguet, to Dolores, to Pépa and to Amélie Pluche."

"Very well," said Judith Bernhardt sharply, rising abruptly. "Stay here, my child. Reverend Mother, I congratulate you. You have mastered my little wild animal."

"Oh, no!" returned the nun. "I have merely tamed her."

.   .   .   .   .

This was true. Though Sarah had grown tame, thanks to the kindness, the firmness and the sense of justice of the admirable Superior of the Grand-Champs Convent, she was not mastered.

She still often flew into rages, and the sentimental clashes of her life as a schoolgirl, the sympathy of her companions and their petty jealousies, made her either violently angry or exaggeratedly happy, and only the Mother Superior was able to control this emotional and quick-tempered little girl.

For all that, Judy's daughter was happy. Her already strongly marked personality gave her ascendancy over her school companions; they consulted her on the upbringing of the animals in their desks, such as lizards, cockchafers, crickets and frogs; on the colours of the chaplets to be woven for the Virgin Mary, St. Joseph and Saint Anthony; on the embroidery to be made for

Mother Prefect, for Mother Saint-Sophie, and for Sister Marie Tourière. If a quarrel took place between two of the girls, Sarah, majestic as Saint-Louis, would sit in a folding chair beneath an oak tree and would dispense very questionable justice based on her own feelings in the matter.

Life passed quietly and piously and soothed this highly-strung child who was said to be "unbearable", an epithet which is usually applied to the children of impossible parents. Then, one day, an important piece of news disturbed the calm of Grand-Champs. In the refectory, after luncheon, Sister Hélène called for silence, a lay-sister opened the double doors at the end of the room, and the convent staff marched in. At the head came tall, thin, old Mother Saint-Alexis, the doyenne of the convent, then Mother Prefect, Mother Saint-Sophie and Mother Bursar.

"My dear children," said Mother Saint-Alexis breathlessly, "a great joy has been accorded us. The Archbishop of Paris, Monseigneur Sibour, is deigning to honour our devout establishment with a visit. I ask you all to be especially good until then, that is to say in a fortnight's time. Those of you who have already made their first communion will approach the Holy Table on the previous day, so that you may receive the archbishop with due piety. As for my dear 'little ones', baptism is enough for God's children!" ended the doyenne, with a slight smile which disturbed the composure of her mummified features.

And, turning slowly about, supported by Mother Prefect, she left the refectory amid the commotion caused by this sensational announcement. At the moment when the Mother Superior was preparing to leave in her turn, a pale little girl pulled timidly at her sleeve.

"Mother Saint-Sophie! Mother Saint-Sophie!"

"What is it, Amélie?"

"Sarah! Sarah! She's like death, Mother. She's under the table!"

Mother Saint-Sophie hurried over to the long table where the smaller girls sat. When she reached Sarah's place, she saw Louise Buguet, Eugénie Charmel and Pépa Cardanos lifting the tablecloth and peering at an inanimate figure on the floor.

"Quick, Pépa, run and fetch Sister Madeleine."

Helped by the little girls, she dragged Sarah from beneath the table: she had crumpled up like a sawdust doll and showed no signs of life. She was picked up and taken to the infirmary, and so-called "energetic" treatment was given her, namely a drop of melissa cordial on half a lump of sugar, and a few slaps.

After five minutes, Sarah opened her eyes.

"Leave me alone with her," said Mother Saint-Sophie to the bewildered lay-sisters.

Scarcely had Sister Marie des Billes shut the door than Sarah flung her arms round the Mother Superior's neck.

"Mother! Mother Saint-Sophie! I want to die! I am not baptized! I shall never dare approach Monseigneur Sibour like the others. Mother! Mother! Baptize me at once!"

"Little hothead!" whispered Mother Superior, laying the child down again. "I will present you to the Archbishop myself, and I will tell him that a little Jewish child will soon be received into the Church, and that we are doing

14

our utmost to teach the little girl the religion of Our Lord Jesus Christ, so that when she goes to the font she may better understand the sublime beauty of the ceremony. Don't you think, my child, that your case will interest Monseigneur Sibour as much as that of Amélie, Louise or Pépa?"

Poor saintly Mother Saint-Sophie! You unwittingly said the very words to console the child, profane words that awakened in her a need for externalization, an innate longing to be the centre of attraction at any cost; a sentimental need (which later Sarah Bernhardt's enemies described as "self-advertisement"), which enabled the artiste to brave and to dominate crowds, whether hostile or friendly or passionate, and to fight against the other side of her nature: overwhelming shyness.

. . . . .

The great day soon came. Monsiegneur Sibour arrived at Grand-Champs and was present at the performance of a one-act play, *Tobias Recovering His Sight*, played by the best children in the convent, among whom was Sarah.

After this little interlude, Mother Saint-Sophie presented her pupils to the Archbishop of Paris.

When it came to Sarah's turn, Mother Saint-Sophie said to the Archbishop:

"We are baptizing her in the Spring. Her father has promised to be present at the ceremony."

"I will be there too," said the prelate kindly.

"Monseigneur," exclaimed Sarah, on her knees, "if you come back my mother and my sisters will be baptized as well! I promise you that."

. . . . .

Sarah kept her promise. When, in the following May, she received baptism in the Grand-Champs Covent, she implored her mother to embrace the religion of Christ, and Madame Bernhardt, moved by the mysticism of her child, agreed to become a Catholic, together with her two other little girls.

Monseigneur Sibour, himself, was unable to keep his promise. A short time after his visit to Grand-Champs he was assassinated by a homicidal maniac named Verger. Sarah's father also failed her. He died mysteriously in Pisa of a malignant fever, bitterly regretting his inability to embrace his favourite daughter on her baptismal day.

A week after this ceremony, Sarah made her first communion. It was a pale, thin, harassed, ecstatic little girl that approached the Holy Table, a ghost-like apparition, so detached from earthly matters that even the nuns of Grand-Champs were deeply moved.

"We must keep watch over this child," declared Mother Saint-Sophie. "Since she heard of her father's death and since her mother and her sisters have been baptized, she has been so devout that she rather alarms me. I must write to Madame Bernhardt to come and fetch her; a few days in the country will do her good."

. . . . .

It was Sister Marie-Thérèse who, on entering the chapel on the following morning, found Sarah lying prone before the high altar. The nun was bringing a bunch of pinks to lay before the statue of the Virgin Mary, and as she laid the flowers down she caught sight of the child, a crumpled figure on the flagstones, in her nightgown. Sister Marie-Thérèse roused the convent, and Sarah's dormitory neighbours, Louise Buguet and Amélie, were questioned.

"I seemed," said Amélie, "to see Sarah get out of bed and go towards the door, but when I called her she told me that she was going to the church to talk to the Angel Raphael."

"You ought to have told someone, or shouted."

"Sarah's voice sounded so funny that I thought I had been dreaming, so I went to sleep again."

That night Sarah lay on a bed in the infirmary, with bright red patches on her cheeks and haggard eyes. The doctor, hurriedly summoned, looked at Mother Superior and shrugged his shoulders.

"The child has pneumonia, Reverend Mother; she is seriously ill."

"Lord Jesus," whispered Mother Saint-Sophie, crossing herself, "now that this child is Yours, don't take her away from me!"

Copy of Sarah Bernhardt's birth certificate

Mme. Judith Bernhardt, Sarah's mother

Sarah Bernhardt at the beginning of her career

Regina Bernhardt, Sarah's younger sister

Mme. Bernhardt and Sarah

CHAPTER II

CAUTERETS ABOUT 1856

CAUTERETS, huddled round its mountain torrent, gave French people of the Second Empire its sulphurous, alkaline waters, which had been famous since a Roman Emperor had sampled their benefits in his wrought-gold cup. The charming surroundings of the little place, its walks to the Col d'Aubrogue, to Bagnères-de-Bigorre, to Gavarnie, to Lourdes, and the Cauterets specialities, such as caramels and wild-goat *pâtés*, made it a very pleasant watering-place, frequented by a number of Parisians.

In those days, Napoleon III, haunted by the shadow of Napoleon I, reigned over France; the imperial court had restored the glories of the First Empire to the Tuileries, to Fontainebleau and to Compiègne; Princess Mathilde, daughter of Jerome Bonaparte, presided over a literary and political salon in the Rue de Courcelles: there one met both the Dumases, the young Sardou, Théophile Gautier and other writers; Manet was still unknown; Constantin Guys and Daumier were sketching the Parisian life which Offenbach was one day to set to music. Victor Hugo was working in Guernsey; the famous men of the nineteenth century were creating masterpieces in every domain of art.

1856. Women stretched their braided and flounced crinolines over steel hoops; fringed shawls covered their shoulders; there was a craze for bright colours; their saucy little hats were tied beneath the chin by wide ribbons; the dandies wore jackets with short wide sleeves over funnel-shaped cuffs, their trousers widened out until they ended in elephants' feet, and they wore high, cylindrical, narrow-brimmed top hats; a mixture of pretentious good taste and ridiculous affectation.

Towards five o'clock in the evening, an endless procession of vehicles passed down the Champs Élysées: tilburys, victorias, family barouches, hansoms, coupés, four-wheelers. Everything was gay, frivolous, tuneful, trivial. Spring was in the air, and in order not to miss this Spring Judith Bernhardt decided not to protract her visit to Cauterets; now that Sarah had recovered her health, Judy wanted to be back in Paris.

Although Sarah, during this short time away from the gentle influence of Mother Saint-Sophie, had regained her strength and most of her colour, she had lost none of her impetuousness, nor her love of life, nor her yearning to love and to be loved.

"I am coming back to become a nun," she had told the Mother Superior.

However, slowly, through contact with nature and thanks to the easily obtained liberty to run wild over hills and dales, through woods and woodland tracks, Sarah's mysticism vanished in the open air; the little girl's religious ideas scattered like dried leaves, unable to resist the caressing breezes of the valleys and the rushing winds of the plains. During this holiday, Judy made an effort to be affectionate, as her daughter Jeanne had remained in Paris with the baby Regina and the nurse. Madame Guérard, Judith Bernhardt's charming friend, whom Sarah called "my Little Lady", lavished tenderness on the child;

but these two ladies, of whom one dreamed of Paris and the other listened to her dreams, were not enough to distract the turbulent Sarah. Now that she no longer nursed her mysticism, her yearning for affection turned towards God's creatures; and the little house in Cauterets became a menagerie, a refuge for dogs, cats and wounded birds.

("You know, Lysiane, when I left Grand-Champs, and for a long time afterwards, I always thought of Mother Saint-Sophie at the great moments of my life; I missed her kindness, like the daily bread which she had taught me to respect.")

The light was changing. It was now falling on everything that had been in the shade during the afternoon, as was only right. In the Cauterets garden the lizards (which Sarah despised for their laziness) followed the sun on the coping of the garden wall; golden dust rose at the least trembling of a leaf and the sun's rays pierced the shrubbery like golden swords. The house was full of the bustle of departure; the maidservant was hurrying from room to room, and wicker baskets were waiting, on the three steps leading up to the front door, for someone to take them away. Judith Bernhardt, rather pale, put her hand up to her heart.

"I am tired," she exclaimed. "I do hope the storm doesn't start again as it did yesterday evening. And Sarah is late. The child drives me to distraction. It is high time she went back to her convent."

Madame Guérard shrugged her shoulders.

"She can't remain there for ever; she is nearly thirteen."

"She's still only a little girl," replied Madame Bernhardt peevishly. "I've quite enough on my hands with Jeanette and Regina. Heavens! What on earth is that?" And Judith, looking out of the window, gave a scream of horror.

The gate at the end of the little garden had opened and four goats appeared, each with a kid which was trying to suckle its mother. Behind them came Sarah, a birdcage in her right hand, a little basket in the left and a box beneath her arm. And that was not all. She was followed by a horrible spaniel with a mangy tail and a filthy yapping fox-terrier which kept jumping up at the cage.

"Sarah!" cried her outraged mother.

The little girl ran into the drawing-room, followed by the dogs, while the goats began to browse on the nasturtiums, the shrubs, the grass and the nettles, accompanied by their progeny, still groggy on their little soft, white, velvety feet.

Judy's daughter had grown, as children often do during an illness. With her narrow face flushed by her exertions, her healthy, glossy, wind-swept hair, her strange, long, almond-shaped eyes, she was a curious little person, still childish, but so unlike other children that Judith and Madame Guérard gazed at her for a moment in silence with affection, but also with a certain amount of apprehension and pity.

She was wearing a high-necked *broderie-anglaise* dress with a deep collar and short sleeves, leaving her long thin arms bare. She had a wide blue sash round her waist and had tied bluebells and dog violets to her hat-ribbon. A button was off one of her dark brown travelling boots and her white stockings were torn.

"Look at you!" cried Judy. "And we're off in a couple of hours! Call off this horrible dog which is sniffing at me and throw all these animals out of the house!"

"I can't do that, mama. They are presents."

"Presents? You don't imagine that we're going to travel to Paris with this menagerie! Presents for whom?"

"Look, mama," began the child, talking quickly for fear of being interrupted by reproaches which she felt she deserved. "The cat is for Sister Marie-des-Billes; she says there are huge rats under the Assembly Room."

"Oh!" said Madame Bernhardt, relieved. "They're for the convent. Show me."

And she laughed heartily when she saw the ball of black fluff which Sarah pulled triumphantly out of the basket. It was a minute kitten, born that very morning.

"But that cat is smaller than the smallest mouse, and it is bound to die."

"Oh no! I'll bring it up on a bottle. This grocer told me he was going to drown some kittens, so I saved this little one."

"But," interrupted Madame Guérard pityingly, "you ought to have saved its brothers and sisters."

"Guérard!" admonished Judy, severely.

"I was afraid I wouldn't be able to look after them all. Besides, they didn't have a bad death. I persuaded the grocer to warm the water before drowning them."

Again Madame Bernhardt's laugh rang out, thin and clear. Then a hard look came into her eyes.

"So much for the cat. But what's in that box?"

"In that box," cried Sarah triumphantly, "there is Caesar's tortoise. Caesar is the Grand-Champs' dog. Yes, mama, it's a long story. Caesar once had a tortoise which he liked, but it died."

"Get along with you! You're making fun of us. Whoever heard of a dog playing with a tortoise?"

"Yes, mama, because to Caesar a tortoise is an animated stone. So he sits and looks at it all the time, just as you or I would do if we saw the summer-house starting to walk away."

"And that horrible fox-terrier?"

"That's for Amélie Pluche. Her mother will look after it."

"And that other filthy dog?"

"That's for the gardener's little boy."

'And the goats? The two, four, or is it six goats?" went on Judy, working herself into a rage.

"For Mother Saint-Sophie," muttered the child piously. "One day I overheard her saying that she would like a goat, in order to have goat-cheese."

"Yes, but why four?"

"Because Mother Saint-Sophie also told me," and Sarah clasped her hands, " 'whenever anyone asks you for a penny, Sarah, you must always give him two'."

"Very well, then," went on Judith Bernhardt furiously. "I'll tell you something, too; and that is that we are not going to travel with all that menagerie. I don't want to look like a travelling circus. Go and do your hair. What about the birds?"

"For Jeanne," replied Sarah, looking squarely at her mother.

Madame Bernhardt half closed her eyes and went on, more gently:

"I'll let you take the cat for Sister Mary, one goat for Mother Saint-Sophie, and the birds for your sister. As for the rest, you will do me the favour——"

"The rest will go with us too, mama," said Sarah quietly. "I bought the goats with the money my papa gave me, and the other animals were given me by people here."

Judith put her hand to her heart.

"I forbid you to talk to me in that tone, Sarah!"

"Judy," cried Madame Guérard, "don't excite yourself! And you, Sarah, don't defy your mother."

"But, mama, you won't see any of the animals after tomorrow, since you are sending me back to Grand-Champs."

"Sarah!" cried Judy, as the obstinate little girl was about to leave the room.

The child made no further resistance, but buried her face in her mother's bosom, breathing the warm perfume of heliotrope; big tears started into her eyes as she clung to the mother whom she loved so much and who, without any sense of justice, preferred her younger sister.

"Naughty! Naughty!" exclaimed Judy. "You're a naughty little girl."

"I'm sorry, mama! Please forgive me!"

"Come!" said Madame Guérard, thoroughly upset by all this. "We shall be late."

Sarah was laughing now and ran off to her room, after collecting all the animals, and so creating havoc. The spaniel chased the goats, the kids ran after their mothers, the fox-terrier yapped at the tortoise which had laboriously made its way beneath Madame Guérard's armchair; as for the tiny kitten, which, incidentally, died two days later, it looked like a woolly ball forgotten in a basket.

"You know," said Madame Guérard to Judy, "you ought to be more careful with that child. She is devoted to you, and you are not always fair to her."

"I know, I know!" But what Madame Bernhardt did not know was that on the previous evening, Sarah, awakened by the storm, had, from her bed, heard the two women talking together in a whisper in the next room.

"This storm drives me mad! I hope Jeanne is all right."

"Why are you always fretting about Jeanne? What about Regina and Sarah?"

"Oh," said Madame Bernhardt, "I love Sarah better than anyone in the world . . . after Jeanne, of course."

And the drops of water in the sudden downpour on the windows were not more numerous than Sarah's tears on her poor stricken face.

CHAPTER III

JUDITH BERNHARDT'S HOUSE IN PARIS

SARAH remained another ten months at the convent. No doubt she was still obsessed with the idea of offering herself to the Lord, but she always felt a wild desire to exhaust herself physically and mentally, to fly to something new, something which she could not define and which she would never find either inside the walls of Grand-Champs or among the chestnut-trees of Satory. Have you ever noticed certain cats which sleep curled up on a cushion or on a sun-warmed flagstone, completely motionless, lost in far-away dreams? Suddenly their slanting green eyes open, they stretch themselves and bound away towards some unknown destination. Sarah was like one of these, running hither and thither, seeming to want to reach some vague goal. But what goal? Perhaps just simply life itself.

She was almost fourteen years old when her mother, persuaded by Madame Guérard, Régis, Sarah's god-father, and the Duc de Morny, an old family friend of the Bernhardts, decided to remove her from the convent.

That morning Mother Saint-Sophie sent for her. Sarah was finishing an important work of art with her friends the Cardanos; they had built up a large heap of snow and the imposing outline of a human form stood out against a background of shrubbery. A fierce discussion was taking place among the three girls. Should the Snow Man, who was decorated with a moustache and a bristling beard, after the fashion of Napoleon III, have eyes made of blue paper or of coal?

"I know the Emperor has blue eyes; the Duc de Morny told me so!" insisted Sarah.

The discussion was threatening to take a dramatic turn when the voice of Sister Marie-des-Billes floated through the keen air:

"Sarah! Mother Saint-Sophie wants you."

"Don't touch the Emperor!" cried Sarah, dashing off.

Running as fast as she could, slipping and stumbling, she soon caught up with Sister Marie-des-Billes and pulled her cornet as she passed her, making the good sister laugh.

"You sent for me, Reverend Mother?" she asked, as she entered the nun's little study.

"Sit down, my child. Calm yourself and listen to what I'm going to tell you."

"Mother's ill!"

"Your mother isn't ill at all, and will you please not interrupt me."

"I'm sorry," said Sarah, going on her knees before the Mother Superior.

"You see," went on Mother Saint-Sophie, patting Sarah's glowing cheek and stroking her unruly hair, "you will soon be fifteen, and it is time you went home to your family. Your mother wants you."

"Mama?" repeated Sarah incredulously. "Mama wants me?"

She felt intensely happy and at the same time immoderately unhappy at this news. She was going to leave Grand-Champs, the sweet quiet of the convent, her friends, and Mother Saint-Sophie. In the end, the sorrow outweighed the joy and she burst into tears.

"Come, come, dear! A little while ago you confided to me your sorrow that your mother preferred your sister Jeanne to you, and now you cry because Madame Bernhardt sends for you. That's not reasonable, Sarah. You are going out into the great world. Be circumspect, courageous and happy. Each one of us has to bear the burden of his own existence, and it is for each of us to make it as light as he can; but remember that only virtue and loyalty will lighten the load. Remember that evil is always a heavy load to bear. And I shall always be here to help you, my child, if you have need of me. And now, little Sarah, let us pray together."

.   .   .   .   .

Sarah left one fine February morning with her Aunt Rosine, who came for her in a carriage.

"My sister Judy is not very well, Reverend Mother, so I have come to fetch her instead."

Either the orris-root scent, or Rosine's remarkable bonnet with enormous autumn-leaf coloured bows which flapped against her sealskin collar, or her tiny muff to which was pinned a bunch of white violets, or Auntie Perfume's dazzling smile, or Sarah's own school companions in their white-braided uniforms, arranged in order of height—either one or all of these things gave Judith Bernhardt's daughter the impression that she was once more acting on the boards of the Assembly Room, in a play called *Sarah's Good-bye*.

"*Au revoir!* I'll see you soon!" she cried to all the girls, big and little.

She gave Mother Saint-Sophie a last hug and then said, almost impatiently, "I'm ready, auntie; let's go, let's go at once!"

Outside, the coachman tucked the travellers in with an opossum rug. The convent door closed slowly.

"To Paris!" cried the little girl, in a voice husky with excitement.

.   .   .   .   .

"Tell me, Aunt Rosine, am I to have a room to myself?"

"Of course; a lovely little green room, all to yourself. Your sisters Jeanne and Regina will share a large room with Nannie."

Sarah was disappointed. She disliked green.

"My little Auntie Perfume!" said Sarah, laying her head against the young woman's shoulder. Rosine gently untied her pretty bonnet ribbons.

The carriage went clippity-clop beneath the trees of Saint-Cloud. The two roans began to steam. Sarah dozed. Whenever a jolt awoke her, she pictured her arrival in the Rue Saint-Honoré. Her mother would be waiting for her, lying on a yellow plush sofa, her fine hand held up to her heart. Jeanne, rather resentfully, and baby Regina would make a fuss of her. No doubt Monsieur Meydieu, and her god-father Régis would be there too, and the Duc de Morny, of whom Sarah rather stood in awe in those days.

"I'll ask him if the Emperor has blue eyes. He's a friend of his. And My

22

Little Lady will say, 'Good morning, my darling Sarah!' " There! She was forgetting all about her Little Lady! Her dear, exquisite, tender and indulgent Little Lady!

"Wake up!" cried Aunt Rosine. "We're home!"

It was about midday. Carrying her wicker valise, Sarah climbed two storeys of the Saint-Honoré house, followed by Aunt Rosine. Her heart was pounding.

"Mama! Mama! It's me, it's Sarah!" she cried, and tugged at the strip of bead-embroidered cloth which served as a bell-pull. The door opened and a maid took the valise out of the hands of "the little Bernhardt girl".

"Mademoiselle Sarah?" she asked, with a strong Teutonic accent.

"Where's mama?"

"In the drawing-room. I've orders, mademoiselle, to see that you wash your hands and tidy your hair. And madame wants you to put on the blue dress laid out on your bed——"

"But I want to see mama at once!" cried the child, stamping her foot.

The noise brought Madame Guérard on the scene. She kissed Sarah fondly and said:

"Come with me, and I'll explain everything."

"Oh!" cried Sarah in delight, on entering a little room whose blue-green paper was covered with pink peonies.

"I was sure you would like this room. And, mind you, it is yours, and yours only. Your mama chose everything and arranged everything herself."

"I don't like green," said Sarah. "But how pretty and fresh and new it all is; and are the wardrobe and the washstand mine too?"

"Of course. This is your room and this is your furniture."

As a good Flemish woman, Judy had had the Dutch farmhouse chairs painted to match the walls. Actually the whole effect was extremely ugly and pretentious, but to the Grand-Champs schoolgirl it was the prettiest thing in the world.

"Get dressed quickly," went on Madame Guérard, seizing on her little friend's happy mood. "There are some people in the drawing-room who want to see you."

"A reception in my honour?"

"It isn't exactly a reception. It is . . . how shall I say? A sort of family council."

"What?" Sarah scented danger. "A family council? What for?"

"But for you, of course, now that you are grown up."

Oh, she was so tired of people keeping on telling her that she was grown up. Her mother had told her so that day in the parlour when she had broken the news of her father's death to her. Mother Saint-Sophie had also said, "Now you are a big girl." And now her Little Lady was starting the same story.

In short, to be grown up was to have troubles.

"Sarah! Hullo, Sarah!" and Jeanne bounded in, hopping on one foot. "The drawing-room is full of people. It seems they're going to decide at last what to do with you."

"Don't jump on my bed with your dirty boots," replied Sarah, kissing her sister. "And let me get dressed."

"And Regina. Have you seen Regina?"

"Heavens! I forgot all about her!"

Led by Jeanne, Sarah sped like an arrow to the nursery, where a beautiful little girl, with a rather serious expression, was playing with a doll almost as large as herself.

"Hullo, little sister," said Sarah affectionately.

On her way back to her room she passed the drawing-room door, and longed to go in and to enact the scene she had rehearsed that morning, crying, "Here I am, mama!" But her gaiety had left her. Madame Guérard was already holding out to her the sky-blue flounced skirt, with its bodice trimmed with black velvet; and she helped her to tidy her hair.

"I'll go and tell them you are ready, Sarah; they're waiting for you."

"I'm going to make an entry," thought Sarah, and this thought made her feel more cheerful; after all, no doubt all these people really wished her well. She was silly to be so worried about it.

"Here is Sarah," announced Madame Guérard, opening the drawing-room door and standing aside to let Judy's daughter enter.

Judith Bernhardt, stretched on her yellow sofa before the fireplace, opened her arms to the girl.

"Darling! There you are at last!"

Although Judith's voice and gesture were rather affected, Sarah was thrilled by them. Instead of throwing herself on her mother's heliotrope-scented bosom, she walked slowly up to her, knelt down and kissed her ostentatiously. Then she looked around her. The green and yellow drawing-room was ugly but bright. Pots and pans and shining copper bowls held small shrubs, some of which were artificial. All the chairs bore hideous embroidered linen covers, spotlessly clean and embellished, in the case of the armchairs, with green taffeta ribbons. Her entry had been received in respectful silence, and this silence remained unbroken. Finally Judith said, in a low voice:

"My friends, my daughter Sarah is once more among us."

"Good morning, young lady," said the Duc de Morny, jocularly.

The others present were Monsieur Meydieu; her god-father Régis; Maître Clément, the Havre lawyer with the face of a gargoyle, a friend of Sarah's father; Aunt Rosine; Uncle Félix Faure and his wife, the ill-natured Henriette; Aunt Richard; Baron Larrey; General Polhes. Aunt Bruck was absent, being away from Paris, so there were twelve people united in this Council of War, including Judith, the Duc de Morny and Madame Guérard.

Casual remarks now began to follow one after the other. At first they amused Sarah, then they began to annoy her.

"How she's grown! She's a bit pale. She looks like Edouard. The child's too thin. Her hair wants straightening. No, her hair is charming."

Her mother said:

"Come and stand by me, Sarah. Maître Clément, you explain the situation to us."

"It's all quite simple," said the lawyer rather crossly. "Edouard left Sarah a hundred thousand francs for her wedding-day."

"I don't want to be married, mama!"

"Hush!" said several people at once.

"As testamentary executor, I am the trustee of this legacy."

"But," said Madame Bernhardt, "my daughter is only fifteen, and, consequently, from now until her marriage, I have to bring up my three daughters and to feed them." (Here Judith placed her hand on her heart.) "And, alas! I have not sufficient means to do this."

"But, mama——"

"Sh! Sh!"

"So I have brought you together to advise me as to what we should do with Sarah. I am afraid my dear daughter will have to work. But at what? She will, of course, live here. Incidentally, what do you think of your room?"

"I want to go back to Grand-Champs, mama."

"Sh! Sh! Sh!"

"If you find the child a profession, you won't find her a husband," declared god-father Régis, tugging at his moustache, which he wore very long, like a Viking.

"Couldn't we wait a little while before deciding?" suggested Madame Guérard. "Sarah has only just left her convent. Give the child a chance to get used to her new life."

Poor, dear, gentle Madame Guérard! No one even heard what she said, except Sarah, who, stunned by the whole scene, smiled sadly at her.

Aunt Rosine's advice was: "I know the business of 'Charlotte and Daughters', a very fashionable dressmakers in the Rue des Capucines. Sarah could work out her apprenticeship there. Dressmaking pays quite well."

"But one has to have taste and a pretty face," observed Aunt Henriette, looking contemptuously at Sarah.

"You can say what you like, Judy, but personally I see no sense in taking the child away from a convent to shut her up in a sewing-room."

This was Félix Faure's contribution.

"I want to go back to Grand-Champs, mama!"

Everyone started to "hush" her at once.

"At least give the child a profession that will bring her in money," interjected Aunt Richard, whose nose, fortunately for her, was less hooked than were her fingers.

"And a little education, too," added Aunt Henriette. "I am sure my dear niece is a dunce."

"Bah!" said General Polhes. "What the devil does that matter?"

"My dear friend," said Baron Larrey quietly to Judith, "why not simply ask the opinion of the person mainly concerned?"

"Yes," cried Sarah furiously, "I think I might at least be consulted."

"Hush, my child."

"No, mama, I won't hush any more. I won't be a dressmaker, nor married, nor anything at all. If this is the reception I get, I want to go back to Grand-Champs to Mother Saint-Sophie. I want to become a nun. My father left me money to get married. All right! I will be the bride of the Lord and I'll give the hundred thousand francs to Mother Saint-Sophie!"

In vain Madame Guérard tried to calm her. In vain Uncle Faure tried to force her to sit down again.

With her hair on end, her eyes dark with rage, the "Little Bernhardt" held

25

the middle of the drawing-room, standing up to all these people, both friends and enemies.

So that was the way they treated her, trying to get rid of her the moment she came home! All right! They would see! And if her aunt refused to take her to Grand-Champs, she would go alone.

"On foot! Yes, on foot! Because you are all brutes!"

"Really," muttered the loathsome Maître Clément, "you ought to send the girl to a reformatory."

Hardly were the words out of his mouth than Sarah, seizing his cinnamon-coloured waistcoat with one hand, rained a shower of blows on him with the other, striking the lawyer on his chin and on his forehead, while his gargoyle face was made even more hideous by fury. At last Uncle Faure tore the raging little girl from the Officer of the Law, saying to her in a whisper:

"Mother Saint-Sophie wouldn't love you any more if she could see you now, with your claws out like a wildcat."

Sarah let herself be led away; she had lost all her strength, all the fight was gone out of her; she ran to her room and shut herself in, slamming the door with her heel in the secret hope of scratching the paint. Lying on the bed-spread with its pink peonies, she sobbed:

"Mother Saint-Sophie! Mother Saint-Sophie! Why did I ever leave you?"

"You have hurt your mother, my dear!"

Who said that? Sarah bathed her eyes in cold water. She suddenly saw the drawing-room as she had left it: at the moment when she fled to her room her mother had laid her head on the embroidered cushion with her eyes closed and an ashen face. Had she fainted? By a superhuman effort Sarah returned to the drawing-room, and opened the door. People were bustling around the yellow sofa.

"I've killed mama," she thought, and her heart seemed to stop beating; then Judy spoke.

"I feel better, thank you."

Sarah went forward timidly and knelt down.

"I'm sorry. It was wicked of me."

"My little Sarah!" Judith Bernhardt's fine hand left the neighbourhood of her heart for a moment to play with her daughter's hair. "We have misunderstood one another. We will talk matters over quietly between us. And now, my friends, forgive me, and let us go and eat."

But at that moment Charles, Duc de Morny, President of the Legislative Body and friend of the Emperor Napoleon III, took the floor, with the grace and unconcern of a great lord. Raising his hand to call for a moment's attention, he smiled sardonically and uttered this simple little sentence which decided the fate of a famous existence:

"My friends, I have no advice to give you. There are enough of you to decide upon a career for this child, even a career which she does not like. But, apart from marriage, the veil, and fashion, there is one place which is just made for Sarah, namely the Conservatoire."

"The Conservatoire?"

"Certainly. The child has temperament. She will make an excellent actress." And he added in a low voice, gallantly kissing Judy's fingers:

"And so are you, my dear, in your own way."

"Monsieur, what is the Conservatoire?" asked Sarah nervously.

"It is a school of rhetoric, where one is made into a great actress."

"Like Rachel?"

"Like Rachel," replied Morny, quizzically.

"I don't want to be an actress. I want——"

"Yes, we know, Sarah, you want to become a nun," interrupted Morny. "But promise me, first, to go to the theatre, where you have never been. I have a box for the Comédie Française this evening, but unfortunately I cannot go myself. My dear Judy, I earnestly beg of you to take your daughter Sarah to hear *Britannicus*. Your friend Alexandre Dumas will go with you, as he is anxious to see Beauvallet play. And now, little Sarah, give me your arm, because your mother has been good enough to invite us all to luncheon, which must be spoiled by now."

Awed, Sarah accompanied Morny into the dining-room. She could not swallow a single mouthful and dared not open her mouth. The incident was closed. Morny, the man of the *coup d'état* of December 1850, had spoken: the silhouette of Napoleon III haunted the middle classes in the Saint-Honoré quarter. Uncle Félix Faure was silenced; the aunts conversed in low tones; General Polhes held forth on the famous Rachel, as though she were a mare:

"She's got mettle; a bit awkward and skittish. She'll end up broken-winded."

An actress! What had she already heard about this Rachel? Ah, yes! A woman who was always ill. Actress! Something seemed to seize on Sarah's imagination as she pronounced the word "actress". No, it was impossible. Monsieur de Morny was talking nonsense. And by what right, anyway? Raising angry eyes, she met those of the Duc, who was speaking again.

"Indeed, it seems, Sarah, that you gave a remarkable interpretation of the part of the Angel Raphael at the performance in honour of Monseigneur de Sibour. The Mother Superior herself told her friend Anne de Brizolles. Perhaps, after all, you possess talent, my child."

How sweet those words sounded to her ears; they fluttered round her head like butterflies. It was true. Had she not already acted on the stage of the Assembly Room, with the approval, affection and support of her idol, Mother Saint-Sophie?

CHAPTER IV

THE BELOVED MONSTER

THE Comédie Française was filled with a crescendo of applause.

It was warm with a scented warmth, maintained by the lamps and the fashionable perfumes of the moment.

The curtain had just fallen on the second act of *Britannicus*. And now the audience was turning round to look at another scene. The prudish Eugénie de Montijo had launched the fashion of bare shoulders and low *décolletages*, and these shone among the men's dress coats like satin jewel-cases. It was a wonder, by the way these ladies outrageously and delightfully exaggerated the fashion, if a nipple did not appear here and there, springing, coral-tinted, from its prison. Crinolines spread themselves in the boxes like gigantic flowers; the women wore jewellery and feathers in their hair and in some cases perfect imitation fruit, to please the Empress, who adored fruit.

"Look along the first-tier boxes. There's Céleste Mogador, the glory of the Bal Mabille," said a man of about fifty, with crinkly hair and negroid features, who was sitting with Madame Bernhardt and Sarah in a grand-tier box. "And there is Madame d'Hauteville in the box opposite. She's talking to Pauline de Metternich."

"How does she manage to remain so thin?" asked Judith, who was beginning to lose her figure. "She must be like her cigar and burn inside as well. How charming Madame de Gallifet looks tonight in her black and straw gown. A treasure from Worth's. And can you tell me, my dear, who that is with the Baroness Nathaniel de Rothschild? I seem to know her face."

"That's Madame Sand, without her trousers."

"Ah! That's it! I knew there was something about her I didn't recognize."

"Charming! And there, in the eighth row of the stalls, sits our one and only Barbey d'Aurévilly——"

He stopped in the middle of his sentence. For there at his side, Sarah, who had been crying quietly to herself so that her mother should not notice, suddenly broke into loud sobs and, as the parapet of the box hid her slim figure, some of the members of the audience were now craning their necks to catch a glimpse of this small person who, for some time now, had been a prey to such great sorrow.

"You're being idiotic!" cried Madame Bernhardt. "Stop crying at once!"

Judy was angrily scolding her daughter. Fancy working oneself up into such a state!

"I'm crying because of Junie!" sobbed the girl, quite unable to control herself. "I don't want to stay! They're going to kill Britannicus."

Alexandre Dumas was much amused; his face beamed with delight between the points of his high collar.

"What an extraordinary child!"

So far from this unromantic remark calming Sarah's retrospective misery, it made her break into fresh floods of tears. Half the audience was now on its feet, gazing towards Madame Bernhardt's box, while that lady, trying to appear unconcerned, was pinching her daughter's arm.

"You're being perfectly ridiculous! Just look at your dress!"

Between sniffing, blowing her nose and coughing, Sarah dried her eyes; her sky-blue taffeta dress (it was the only one she possessed at the moment) was stained by tears. When people saw that this strange young girl had calmed down they resumed their conversation, while Sarah eyed them through wet lashes. "They're cruel! They're all cruel!" she thought at first. But, as some of the audience were still looking at the box-tier and as Barbey d'Aurévilly himself, for all his superciliousness and exaggerated elegance, deigned to fix his attention on her, Sarah felt a tremor run through her. A strange longing came over her; should she resist it or not? The remainder of the audience was now returning from the foyer.

"I must be quick," she thought.

Could she again attract and hold the attention of all those puppet-like heads, and make the public turn again to stare at that little figure dressed in sky-blue? She wanted to taste the marvellous sweetness of their curiosity, the interest of those common people, those nobles, those artists, those women, old or beautiful, ugly or rich. A magnetic influence linked her, not to each of these splendid or grotesque people, but to all of them—yes, to them all. She seemed to see the public as an irresistible and Beloved Monster. She wanted it for herself.

The trembling child screamed and let her head fall on the parapet of the box, rolling it from side to side; her rebellious fair hair fell all over the velvet ledge. And Sarah waited. For what? A murmur from the Monster, either approving or disapproving, but something that was for herself alone.

The murmur came first from Judith Bernhardt.

"Sarah! Will you stop playing the fool? You'll pay for this."

Sarah paid no attention whatever. She was listening for the other sound. It came and grew in volume: in the form of laughter—laughter at once low and cruel. "Like that of a lover," thought Sarah. "Yes, like the laughter of the young man whom I heard laugh one afternoon with his betrothed, in the Satory woods." And without ceasing to roll her head, Sarah spread her fingers and looked between them at the Monster. There was a little desultory applause.

"Let's go!" decided Judy, beside herself with mortification.

She had already risen to take the intolerable little girl away when Dumas observed in an undertone:

"Don't distress yourself. Morny was quite right. The child will make a marvellous actress."

"She is making a fool of me!" replied Judith acidly.

The warning that the next act was about to begin saved the situation. The lights went out; suddenly calmed, Sarah stealthily put her hand in her mother's and squeezed it.

"I'm sorry, mama dear; I won't do it again."

"Sh!" said Dumas. "Listen to the play, Sarah, and try to understand it."

.   .   .   .   .

With his arm round the young girl's chair, Dumas explained to her the plot of Racine's tragedy. When Beauvallet declaimed a particularly sublime passage, the author of *The Three Musketeers* hugged Sarah's shoulders, as though to carry her with him on the rhythm of the beautiful winged words. Luckily, the actors spoke so loudly that the celebrated novelist's words reached only the girl's ears. She had forgotten the audience. Guided by Dumas, her imagination gripped the stage, bringing to life now the pathetic Junie, now the noble Britannicus, the hypocritic hero or the tragic Agrippine. Actress! She, too, in a white robe concealing her slenderness in carefully designed drapery, might tread the boards, perhaps even these boards, who could tell? Yes! The Comédie Française. Was it not the most beautiful, at any rate the most famous, theatre in Paris? She would love to speak those verses in a loud, clear, resonant voice: the same voice which had at Grand-Champs declared to Tobias, played by her friend Pluche: "Fear nothing. I will lead you!"

And Mother Saint-Sophie? But she would be there, dear, sweet, adored little saint! She would be there in the box with mama, smiling tenderly, and Monsieur Dumas, and the Duc de Morny plucking at his beard, and Jeanne sitting on the parapet. But there was Amélie Pluche in front of her, swaying madly. She was going to fall. She was falling!

And Sarah woke up with a scream and that Monster, the Public, shouted "Sh!" at her.

"Might it please the gods that this should be the last of his crimes!"

And the curtain fell. There was loud and prolonged applause. A few of the audience, before leaving, glanced towards Judith Bernhardt's box to see whether the strange little girl was still in tears. But she was half asleep; shattered by her emotions, she was suffering from a violent headache. Nothing seemed to be able to have any effect upon her; neither the scolding of her mother, nor Morny's idea, nor the Beloved Monster, nor her green room; she longed for one thing only: her bed, and to sleep and sleep. Clinging to Alexandre Dumas, she pressed herself against him, feeling the protection of his broad frame. How nice he was, Monsieur Dumas, with his grey, crinkly hair! How kind he was to her! She would have liked him to put her to bed, to tuck her up, and to go on speaking to her. In the carriage home she slept again, and Dumas carried her up to her room. He helped Judy to unfasten her frock and, bending over her, he whispered, prophetically, into her unhearing ear, "Good night, little star."

.   .   .   .

("Grandmother, why did you never mention Dumas at the beginning of your *Memoirs*? You only quote him in connection with Kean."

"Well, before he died, he had a bitter quarrel with my family, and I promised mama that I would never talk about all that. But now! It's so far away now! More than half a century.")

CHAPTER V

MORNY'S LITTLE IDEA

THE little idea of Morny's, so casually expressed, developed in various ways. In the same way that sweet-pea seeds are scattered through a garden, some in the shade and some in the sun, some developing into beautiful pink or white flowers, and some shrivelling up as soon as they germinate, so the little idea had grown in different ways in the Rue Saint-Honoré coterie. The aunts, except Aunt Rosine, who found it funny, thought the idea preposterous. Actress, indeed! Unless one had talent, it simply implied a loose life. Madame Guérard, a little frightened by the adventurous life this word conjured up for her, brooded over her favourite, deciding to mitigate the disappointments of this peculiar profession for her. Meydieu remarked, with a silly glitter in his eyes:

"Sarah Bernhardt? I don't see that name on the play bills. There are too many 'a's' in it. Now, if one called her Rosine Bernard, that would be much better, and she could play light comedy parts."

"Why not silent parts?" retorted Judith, snappishly.

Régis, Dumas and General Polhes all thoroughly approved of the idea; Félix Faure, who was to end up as a Carthusian monk, dreaded for his niece the promiscuity of the theatre. As for Judith Bernhardt herself, she instinctively disapproved of Morny's "little idea". The frivolous, middle-class Dutchwoman would have preferred a less indiscreet career, but, on the other hand, she liked the idea of getting Sarah's future settled; the awkward child would be working all day and would, in the evening, enjoy in her home, with her sisters, the family life which would do her the greatest good. So, definitely, Morny was right.

. . . . . .

"Monsieur de Morny is right!" cried Sarah too, some days later. "But I can't improve my way of pronouncing words, or change the shape of my mouth, or that of my chin. You're only wasting your time, Monsieur Dumas. God-father Régis and Monsieur Meydieu also try every day to make me pronounce my 't's' and my 'd's', telling me that I don't open my mouth wide enough; and they try to teach me to say idiotic catch-phrases and are surprised when I can't say them properly."

"My dear child, I only want you to work on classics. It is quite enough that your delivery should be right. The rest can look after itself."

"Oh, thank you! I can learn anything with you!"

Dumas's powerful frame overflowed the wicker chair in which he sat. And when the famous author walked up and down the green room he looked like a fat fish imprisoned in an aquarium.

"You must learn the part of Aricie in *Phèdre*. Today I'll give you the rough idea. Then you must study your lines, keeping well in mind the fact that Aricie is a gentle, shy, well-brought-up young woman, in love with Hippolyte."

And so it was that Alexandre Dumas gave little Sarah her first lesson,

31

himself playing all the other parts: Hippolyte, Théramène, Phèdre, and even Œnone. Engrossed in his business, he gesticulated, thumped the table and raised his voice, while "the sad Aricie" took the cues in such a melodiously modulated voice that Dumas could not help comparing it with a fresh-water spring.

A spring! Yes, a spring hurrying and bubbling over golden pebbles. "Careful not to be monotonous, my dear. Don't drop your voice at the ends of the lines. Keep to the rhythm, learn to breathe correctly, especially when you see that the end of the passage is still a long way off; conserve your breath so as not to 'die' on the last word of a sentence, like an asthmatic. Now let's start again."

Patient, tractable and attentive, Sarah began all over again. And at the moment when Dumas was declaiming a particularly thunderous passage, the door opened and Judith Bernhardt peered short-sightedly at these strange actors.

"What is happening? I didn't know you were here, my dear."

"I am making Sarah work."

"Oh, thank you! I'm always forgetting that my daughter is about to become an actress. No doubt I'll get used to the idea in time. Sarah! Just look at you! Tidy your hair and come into the drawing-room. Monsieur Berentz wants to see you. Thank you, my dear, for taking so much trouble with Sarah, but you ought to teach her to recite fables. It would make so much less noise. Won't you come too? Come and have a glass of malaga."

A dark-haired and dark-complexioned man stood in the drawing-room. His arms were too short, his beard was too long, but his eyes were extremely kind. Sarah had seen Monsieur Berentz three or four times since her return from the convent, and she would have fled at his approach had his eyes not been so sad.

As the girl held out a timid hand to the visitor, the Teutonic maid came in with a letter on a tray.

"Ah!" said Judith. "A letter from Morny. Excuse me. Oh, how nice! Look, Dumas, it is a letter of introduction to Auber, the Director of the Conservatoire. The entrance examination takes place in a month's time. With an introduction from the Duc de Morny, my child, you are sure of being admitted."

"Not at all!" interrupted Dumas. "Auber has nothing to say about the admission of candidates. It's for the jury alone to decide, and that consists of a small bunch of actors and professors."

"Oh, mama, how lovely that is!"

With Sarah, too, Morny's "little idea" had borne fruit; in that word "actress" there was something strange which delighted her. The idea of the theatre attracted and terrified her, in the same way as the idea of the public did. She wanted to give herself wholly to it, but at the thought of appearing on the stage a terrible shyness made her resolution waver, while in the depths of her heart there lay, not yet in bloom but fresh as an orchid, that longing for the Beloved Monster.

During the reading of Morny's letter the bearded man had been forgotten; but the turbulent entry of little Jeanne and the capers she cut behind Monsieur Berentz's back roused Sarah from her reverie and threw her into agonies of suppressed laughter.

32

THÉATRE ▬▬▬ DE L'ODÉON

SECOND THEATRE FRANÇAIS

———

Engagement

Entre nous soussignés, CHARLES-MARIE DE CHILLY, directeur du *Théâtre* ▬▬ *de l'Odéon*, domicilié à Paris, rue des Marais-Saint-Martin, n° 46,

et M*elle Sarah Bernhardt* d'une part,

se déclarant libre de contracter tout engagement et faisant élection de domicile, pour l'exécution du présent, à Paris,

d'autre part ;

Il est convenu ce qui suit :

M. DE CHILLY engage M *elle Sarah Bernhardt* pour remplir dans la troupe du *Théâtre* ▬▬ *de l'Odéon*, en tout temps, en tout lieu, en province, même à l'étranger, sans exiger aucune allocation ni dédommagement autres que les frais de voiture et de transport de ses effets, à toutes heures et dans plusieurs théâtres le même jour si le cas le requérait, en chef, double, partage et remplacement au besoin, tous les rôles, quelle que soit leur importance, qui lui seront désignés dans tous les genres, sans exception aucune, sans que, dans aucun cas, il puisse résulter pour le directeur l'obligation de faire jouer M   lorsque l'administration ne le jugera pas convenable ; de plus, M   devra paraître dans toutes les pièces.

M*elle S. Bernhardt* s'oblige à se conformer à tous les usages qui régissent le théâtre, à tous les règlements dont   déclare avoir une entière connaissance ; à se soumettre aux amendes fixées par l'administration, ainsi qu'aux lois et actes de l'autorité régissant les théâtres en général et celui du *Théâtre* ▬▬ *de l'Odéon* en particulier ;

2° A apprendre trente-cinq vers ou lignes de cinquante-cinq lettres par jour ;

Sarah's Contract with the Odéon, 1871

Moyennant l'exécution fidèle des clauses ci-dessus, il sera alloué à

M *elle Sarah Bernhardt* la somme de

Sept cents francs ~~francs pendant la première année~~;

par mois jusqu'au 31 ~~francs pendant la deuxième année~~;

Mai 1872 ~~francs pendant la troisième année.~~

Lesdits appointéments seront payés ~~par~~ et de

mois en mois, ~~à partir du premier~~ *le trois de chaque* ~~18~~*mois*, et

M *elle S. Bernhardt* devra être à la disposition du Directeur

pour les répétitions, le , sans pouvoir

exiger aucune espèce d'appointements jusqu'au jour de l'ouverture.

Il sera loisible à l'administration, si elle le juge convenable, de payer

la moitié seulement des appointements pendant les mois de juin,

juillet, août, — et, dans ce cas, cette moitié serait reversible sur les

mois de décembre, janvier, février.

M ne pourra faire usage de ses talents

pendant les mois de juin et juillet qu'en province ou à l'étranger, et

dans le cas seulement où M. DE CHILLY n'userait point du droit qu'il se

réserve, par le présent, de prolonger cet engagement, même par frag-

ments de mois, pendant la saison d'été.

L'administration se réserve le droit de rompre l'engagement de l'Ar-

tiste ~~en le prévenant~~ *trois* mois avant l'expiration de la première année.

Le présent engagement devra être exécuté de bonne foi, toutes les

clauses étant de rigueur, et ce à peine d'un dédit fixé à la somme de

~~Vingt cinq mille francs~~ payable comptant, et dont la valeur ne

~~pourra être diminuée~~ à quelque époque que ce soit, pas même dans les

derniers jours du présent engagement. Afin d'éviter les difficultés qui

pourraient survenir à la fin du présent traité, à l'occasion de son

expiration, les parties déclarent renoncer respectivement aux droits

qu'elles pourraient invoquer, au sujet de *la tacite reconduction*; en

conséquence, la date de l'expiration du présent dégagera immédiate-

ment les deux parties contractantes, et si, par un événement quel-

conque, M jouait dans un ou plusieurs

spectacles après l'engagement expiré, l'administration, non plus que

l'Artiste, ne pourraient exciper de cette circonstance pour prolonger

l'engagement d'une année.

Fait double, à Paris, le *Vingt Cinq septembre*
Mil huit cent soixante onze.

Approuvé

de Chilly

Left margin handwritten:

Huit cent cinquante francs, par mois, de quinze août 1872 au trente un mai 1873, et Mille francs par mois de quinze août 1873 au trente un mai 1874.
S. B.

Du premier Juin de chaque année au quinze Août suivant, il est accordé un congé à M elle S. Bernhardt pendant lequel elle n'a droit à aucun traitement.
S. B.

quinze mille francs
de Chilly

Raye Vingt Quatre Mots nuls.
S. B.

Sarah's Contract with the Odéon, 1871

"Jeanne, darling, go to your room."

And, in confusion, Madame Bernhardt turned towards Monsieur Berentz.

"Yes, my dear friend, I had thought of putting Sarah on the stage. But there is no hurry. Indeed, I would be very glad to have your opinion on the question, and to discuss it quietly with you."

Dumas looked furtively at Sarah. What did this sudden change of attitude mean? All that he understood was that he was in the way and that Judy regretted having momentarily forgotten the presence of the cave-man. Sarah did not understand either, but the problem did not interest her and she accompanied Dumas into the hall.

"You'll come tomorrow, Monsieur Dumas? I want you to teach me to recite one of my dear La Fontaine's fables. We'll make less noise and mama will prefer that."

"Just as you wish, dear. But that won't help you in the Conservatoire examination. Besides, I cannot come tomorrow. I've a long article to write about old Mademoiselle Georges. Tell me, who is that gentleman with your mother?"

"A friend of hers, a silk merchant. He's a Dutchman and very rich. I met him here one day during the holidays, before I left the convent; he had brought us two lengths of silk, one blue and one black. And as he was passing his hand over it to draw attention to its quality, mama exclaimed: 'Oh! Please stop, monsieur! Your fingernails are rough and I cannot bear the sound they make on the silk.' I was very embarrassed. You know my blue dress? Yes, the one I wore at the theatre. Well, that was made out of Monsieur Berentz's silk."

"Tell me, Sarah, are you really determined to go on the stage?"

"Oh, Monsieur Dumas! You're not going to desert me?"

And she began to recite from *Phèdre* in her most musical voice.

"You little rascal! There! *Au revoir*, my little star!"

And this time Sarah heard him and answered roguishly:

"*Au revoir*, my big sun!"

.   .   .   .   .

("And now, Lysiane, I must try to remember the day on which I entered the Conservatoire. Each time my mother tried to get me ready some annoying incident would occur to make me ridiculous. I was always having to struggle with the mischievous imps that lived, according to mama—and I believe she was right—in my hair, my pins, my ribbons, my collars, my skirts, my gestures and my scarves. Even now I still have to deplore that state of affairs. If I put my pencil down for one moment it vanishes. It is no use looking for it, it has been taken by some evil spirit.

"In short, let me admit it: I felt that I was ugly and, besides, my dress was scorched.")

.   .   .   .   .

Judy had decided to have her daughter's Conservatoire dress made out of the mysterious Monsieur Berentz's other length of silk. The black material made Sarah look even paler and thinner than she was. Her hair was plastered down with oil and had been pulled back, thus uncovering her ears, which were large and flat.

"She certainly isn't pretty," cried Régis, who had come that morning to exercise his rights as a god-father, "but at any rate she looks interesting!"

"Keep your opinions to yourself," retorted Judy. "My daughter not pretty? With those eyes, that hair, that skin? Now then, Sarah, it's time you got ready. You might at least try to get accepted. Madame Guérard is coming to fetch you in a cab. For heaven's sake try to behave sensibly. The stuff your dress is made of is scorched and Mademoiselle Clémentine had a fearful job to sew it. And your scarf. Let me arrange it for you; it looks like a dishcloth. Kneel down carefully in front of me."

"There's Madame Guérard!" cried Sarah, jumping up suddenly.

Crack! Monsieur Berentz's scorched silk could not stand up to such impetuosity and split loudly at the shoulder. Thoroughly mortified, Sarah looked at her mother, who looked at Madame Guérard, who, in her turn, looked enquiringly at god-father Régis.

"What *are* we to do?" muttered Sarah. And two tears came into her eyes.

"Anything, so long as you don't cry," exclaimed Régis hastily. "To go with red eyes would be the last straw."

By dint of rummaging in boxes full of old lace lying between Harlem newspapers sprinkled with pepper, they finally found a piece of Brussels lace which they put round the young girl's shoulders.

"Now then, get along with you, all three, otherwise Sarah's hair will begin to frizz up again. And don't waste time eating cakes at Véjà's after the examination, as I shall be waiting for you. I am too tired to go with Sarah myself. In any case my heart cannot stand excitement, and I hate the atmosphere of crowds."

Sarah, who could hardly keep still, embraced her mother and took her chaperons away.

"To the Conservatoire, 15 Faubourg Poissonnière!" she told the coachman.

.   .   .   .   .

Sarah found herself with the other candidates in the Conservatoire waiting-room. Madame Bernhardt's daughter had a delicate constitution. Let us not forget that when she was nineteen the medical profession gave her two years to live (she was actually seventy-nine when she died). And the time that elapsed between her arrival and her name being called threw her into a state of morbid agitation. Poor child! She was not at her best at that moment. With her hair drawn back from her rather ugly ears, her scorched black silk dress, her lace collar which aged her considerably, and her extreme pallor, she kept apart from the others. Her atrocious shyness weighed heavily upon her.

Around her, everything was in a state of turmoil. The candidates, each surrounded by his or her family, talked in loud voices, some in order to cover their nervousness and others just to show off. Here a mother smoothed her daughter's dress; there a curly-haired young man, his face to the wall, monotonously rehearsed a poem. A few overdressed women, already playing the part of "actress's mother", were summing each other up and wondering which of their offspring would be the first to blossom out.

Léautaud, who was charged by the Conservatoire with inscribing the candidates' names and introducing them, went up to the little Bernhardt girl.

"What are you going to recite, mademoiselle?"

"Aricie, monsieur, in *Phèdre*, Act II, Scene 2."

"And who is going to give you your cues?"

"Cues?" and Sarah paled. "Of course, Monsieur Dumas warned me, and I forgot all about it."

"Would you like me to ask that young man over there?"

"That young man? Oh no. He has been leering at me and I don't know him. No, I don't want to. I'll do something else. I'll recite a fable. Put down, please: *The Two Pigeons*."

Léautaud found it hard to conceal a smile; Madame Guérard, realizing that the child was almost at the end of her tether, advanced no argument against *The Two Pigeons*. As for Régis . . . Where the devil was Régis? Heavens! There he was, over there, tugging at his moustaches, which fell below his chin, and strutting up and down in front of a pink-and-white blonde.

"Sarah, I am going to pat you with eau-de-Cologne," said Madame Guérard. "It's so close in here."

The door leading to the stage fascinated the girl; none of the candidates returning through it seemed to be happy; red in the face, their foreheads beaded with perspiration, their eyes unnaturally bright, they all seemed to be thoroughly dissatisfied with themselves.

"I'm sure I'm going to faint," thought Sarah. "It must be like hell beyond that door. The stage is surrounded by flames. Only Monsieur Auber, the Director of the Conservatoire, sits on a marble throne, like Pluto, and——"

"Mademoiselle Sarah Bernhardt!" cried Léautaud in a loud voice.

"Don't be frightened, darling. Everything will be all right," said Madame Guérard when Sarah, rising like an automaton, followed the stage-manager and passed through the dreaded door.

Although the flames she had visualized were absent, in the girl's imagination Monsieur Auber, seated behind a table, was surrounded by snarling, sneering devils; there was even a she-devil among them: Augustine Brohan, with her lorgnette and her sharp voice.

Sarah climbed on to the little platform, followed by five pairs of eyes: those of Auber, Samson, Beauvallet, Provost and Augustine Brohan. She made a deep curtsey, listening for the scorched dress to split; then, raising her head and with a faraway look in her eyes, she began, in a slightly unsteady voice:

"*Two pigeons loved each other dearly.*"

At the end of the line her voice rose by a semi-tone on the word "dearly" and immediately the devils began to titter: their fingers drummed on the table, and whispered remarks began to reach her.

"She thinks she's still at school!" cried Beauvallet. "Fancy reciting a fable to us!"

"Oh well! It will be shorter to listen to!" replied Augustine Brohan, letting her lorgnette drop.

"Come, mademoiselle, go on with your piece," said Provost, not unkindly.

"*Two pigeons loved each other dearly.*"

"Louder!" cried Samson.

"My dear man," broke in Augustine Brohan, "if you keep on making her start again, it will be as long as a whole scene in a play!"

And all the devils laughed! Sarah was put completely out of countenance. What did they mean by jeering at her? Couldn't they see that she was beside herself with terror? That she was only a poor trembling child? How cruel they all were! And she began to rebel. No, she would not let it go at that. Were they laughing at her? All right! She would show them. She would jump down from the platform and hurl herself on that woman who thought she could do just as she liked. For the space of a couple of seconds Sarah stared at the jury and the jury stared at her. But where was the public? Where was the Beloved Monster? She loathed those faces turned towards her which seemed to be making a sort of game of torture; she no longer wanted to see them; she forgot Augustine Brohan's lorgnette and Samson's kindly eyes; she did not even hear Provost say to her, sympathetically:

"We're listening, my dear."

She imagined herself at the Comédie Française, like the other evening; two hundred, three hundred, four hundred people were gazing at her. She must rivet their attention. And from the little platform of the Conservatoire, Sarah started to recite *The Two Pigeons* again in a clear, well-pitched voice.

When she had finished she bowed; she bowed in deep silence which the jury respected, charmed, no doubt, by the music of her voice; then she stepped down from the platform, without looking at the devils, and walked towards the door. All that she wanted to do now was to escape from that hell.

"Very good, mademoiselle! Very good!"

Auber caught her dress as she passed. By a miracle the material held.

"Monsieur Beauvallet and Monsieur Provost each wants you in his own class."

Sarah turned towards Provost with his soft silver hair and looked at him from the depths of her clear almond eyes.

"Monsieur," she said, "I would like to go to yours."

.   .   .   .   .

"Mama! Mama! I've been accepted! I've been accepted!"

With her scorched dress split all down the back, half her hair over her left ear and her lace collar all crumpled on one shoulder, Sarah threw herself into her mother's arms.

Back in the Rue Saint-Honoré were gathered Meydieu, Dumas, Aunt Rosine and Jeanne, who, seized with sudden affection for her sister, completed the work of making rags of the mysterious Monsieur Berentz's silk; even baby Regina was there, seated in a deep armchair looking fretful and obstinate.

Judy kissed her daughter. She was flattered at being the mother of "the girl who had been accepted". Madame Guérard, who had been in a highly emotional state for four consecutive hours, blew her nose and powdered it alternately. A bottle of malaga was fetched out and Sarah, bubbling over with happiness and importance, regaled the company with the details of that memorable afternoon. They listened to her patiently, smiled at her fancies, sympathized with her fears, and congratulated her generally.

"Recite your fable again, dear," said Dumas kindly.

"Oh yes!" chirped Sarah, delighted, and, taking the centre of the room, she dropped a low curtsey and began:

"*Two pigeons loved each other dearly* . . ."

But at that moment the hitherto silent baby Regina scrambled down from her big armchair, planted herself in front of her sister and, lisping and beating herself on the stomach, began to perform a nondescript dance learned from her Nannie and then, falling into silence again, ran off to hide herself in her nursery.

"Come, it's your turn now, little star," said Alexandre Dumas, crying with laughter.

"*Two pigeons loved each other dearly*," began Sarah, for the fifth time that day.

CHAPTER VI

THE SUITOR

SARAH had been industriously following her classes at the Conservatoire for a year; because she had, luckily for her, disobeyed her teacher, Monsieur Provost, in a scene from *Zaïre*, by saying, "Hit me; I say I love him," in a gentle, affectionate voice, she was awarded second prize for tragedy. Yet Provost and his pupil got on extremely well together. When Provost fell ill, Sarah joined Samson's class. But Samson was rather dictatorial, and his methods of teaching, though in many ways excellent, often clashed with Sarah's stubbornness.

"The second important competitions are taking place in two months' time, mademoiselle. I am counting upon you to score a real success. The texts I have chosen for you are: for Comedy, *L'Ecole des Vieillards*, by Casimir Delavigne, and for Tragedy, *La Fille du Cid*."

Sarah made a face. She did not like either of these pieces, as she did not feel that they suited her.

"Could I not do something else, monsieur?"

Samson shook his head with its short curly hair and tapped his desk with an ivory paper-knife.

"I think they are excellent pieces for you."

"Well, I think they're abominable."

And she flounced out of the room in a temper.

Was it her fault if she had no "feeling" for Delavigne's style? If she found it both sterile and ludicrous? Yet Sarah worked hard, one might almost say fervently. She never missed a class and her reports were excellent; she conscientiously followed courses of deportment and dancing and fencing lessons and everything that might make her gestures less awkward and more natural and increase her freedom of movement; she learned to sit down by bending from the knees and not from the waist. In short, she learned all the things which she would eventually improve upon or alter, so that they became part of herself.

Sarah possessed the divine spark, but, from the day on which she recited *The Two Pigeons* until the day of her death, she worked hard at her art; sixty-five years! She learned her trade loyally, beginning by the puerile exercises of god-father Régis, until she reached that *furioso* or *amoroso* inflexion whose gamut she always studied so carefully. There was about her something of the virtuoso, who interprets with the heart and the body and hammers away, so to speak, at exacting and laborious daily exercises.

People who knew her used to say, "What a marvellous woman Sarah is!" And they ought to have added, "And how marvellously conscientious."

.   .   .   .   .

One day the Rue Saint-Honoré was very animated. A wayward, blustery, April day, elbowing its way through the trees which were still in bud; passersby gazed into the shop-windows, while others made their way further to the pleasures of the Boulevard des Italiens, with its Tortoni's restaurant, its newspaper kiosks, its pavements occupied by women pushing their crinolines before them or arranging them round their chairs; horsemen and carriages passed up and down the roadway, while cumbersome omnibuses, democratic and simple, threaded their homely way through the dandies, the ladies of fashion and the women of the town.

Two women came out of the Rue Saint-Roch into the Rue Saint-Honoré. One was about twenty-eight years of age, while the other seemed hardly more than sixteen. The younger one wore a large dark brown straw hat, tied beneath her chin with two capucine velvet ribbons, and a cockroach-coloured woollen dress; her light brown shoes were laced beneath her long pantalettes.

Madame Guérard and Sarah were returning from the Conservatoire.

Samson was so pleased with his pupil, in spite of her dislike of Casimir Delavigne, that he had given her a little note of praise which she was proudly bearing back to her mother. When they reached Number 265, Madame Guérard and her young friend hurried in and ran up the stairs four at a time.

"I'll go in first," giggled Madame Guérard, "and I'll say to Judith: 'My dear, I'm heartbroken! Sarah has been expelled from the Conservatoire!' "

"That's right," cried Sarah. "Then I'll come in with the letter on a tray, and say, 'A letter for you, Madame Bernhardt, from the Emperor!' " And she pulled the beaded bell-rope so hard that she nearly brought the bell down on their heads. The Teutonic parlourmaid opened the door and put her finger to her lips with an air of mystery.

"Madame has a visitor. She wants mademoiselle to go to the drawing-room at once and Madame Guérard to wait for madame in madame's room."

"Oh!" pouted Sarah. "What about my letter? Who has mama got with her?"

"Monsieur Berentz," replied the maid.

The girl made a grimace and opened the drawing-room door.

"Do you want me, mama?"

"Yes, Sarah; Monsieur Berentz has something to say to you. I'm going to leave you alone with him for five minutes."

For the first time, perhaps, Sarah sought her mother's fine, short-sighted eyes in vain. But they seemed to avoid hers and to rest on the bearded man or on Sarah's frock or anywhere else. Judy had left her famous yellow sofa and was standing awkwardly by a little imitation buhl table on which stood the inevitable decanter of malaga together with some anchovies on brown bread and some wretched little dried-up cakes.

"Well, I'll leave you."

Judy reached the door, came back again, and kissed her daughter on the forehead.

"Be calm and sensible," she whispered, and went out.

"You want to speak to me, monsieur?"

The mysterious Monsieur Berentz, who had been standing by the fireplace, took a step forward. "How hairy he is!" thought Sarah, as she studied his face.

His cheeks were hidden behind a mass of black hair which thinned out beneath the eyes into a fine down; this beard was carefully dressed and scented, but how often had Sarah and the unbearable Jeanne played at "Monsieur Berentz"! The game consisted of Sarah fastening a piece of black cloth round the lower part of her face and her younger sister tearing it off, and crying, "I've got your beard." And it was this man who stood before her, awkward and hairy, with his beautiful amethyst waistcoat crossed by a heavy gold watch-chain.

His deep-set, sensitive eyes, the beauty of which was wasted upon Sarah, were fixed on her with such adoration that she felt as though they were boring right through her.

"Would you like a biscuit, monsieur?"

The mysterious Berentz bit the dry cake and the crumbs fell into his beard. These he brushed away with an amethyst-silk handkerchief which matched his waistcoat, and Sarah was afraid that she was going to giggle.

"Mademoiselle. . . . Have you ever thought of getting married?"

It was out! He had spoken his piece very quietly while fidgeting with his pocket-book and nervously shifting from one foot to the other.

"Getting married?"

Sarah was dumbfounded. Surely this gentleman who was too old, too dark and too hairy was never going to ask her to marry him?

"No, monsieur," she replied politely. "I don't want to get married."

"Mademoiselle! You must marry me. I will make your life very happy; I am rich, very rich. You will never have to work again. I will give you a dowry of three hundred thousand francs. Five hundred thousand," he amended, after a short hesitation. "But don't refuse me at once. It would hurt me too much."

What kind eyes Monsieur Berentz had! Sarah would liked to have pleased him, in spite of his hair and his scorched silks.

"Monsieur," she told him, in her musical voice, "I am very fond of you, but I do not want to be married, either to you or to anyone else."

"I would be able to wait," he said forlornly.

"Unlike his scorched silks," thought Sarah, backing towards the door, which she opened suddenly.

"Oh no, monsieur! Don't wait. I am going to find mama. But thank you, thank you very much, all the same."

Madame Bernhardt and Madame Guérard were listening outside the door.

"You ought to have warned me, mama," protested Sarah, brushing past her mother.

Judy shrugged her shoulders.

"You're being foolish, my dear."

"Surely, mama," implored Sarah when the mysterious Monsieur Berentz had left the house, miserable, perhaps, but also very indignant, "surely you can't want me to marry him? He is horrible! And what about my stage career?"

"Your stage career, my poor child! That's not serious. I don't suppose you think you're going to be a Déjazet or a Rachel? Here is a rich man who loves you. How selfish you are! You never think of your family."

"But I hope to earn money and to give it to you. Didn't you get Monsieur Samson's letter?"

"That letter!" scoffed Judith. "Just an encouragement, that's all! Indeed, you might, one day, even manage to get a prize to encourage you."

"Judith," cried Madame Guérard, "you're unjust, yes, unjust! I prefer to go away!"

And, for once, that docile young woman slammed the door behind her.

"I promise you, mama, that in a month's time I'll get first prize for Tragedy and first prize for Comedy; then I'll get a part——"

"It's in this house that the comedy is being played. And it will soon turn to tragedy. Two years ago you wanted to become a nun; now you want to be an actress."

"Yes, I want it with all my heart! I want to be a great, a very great actress. I love my art and I love the public."

Could she explain to her mother what the Beloved Monster meant to her? No, it would be utterly useless.

"I shall be wedded to my public."

Judy stared at her daughter and shrugged her shoulders.

"Sometimes you terrify me. Your youngest sister has more sense in her head than you, for all your sixteen years."

"Would you have married Monsieur Berentz, mama?"

In spite of herself, Madame Bernhardt flinched slightly: but she got out of an awkward situation in the way that selfish mothers usually do.

"You are impertinent, my dear! Go and rest in your room. Monsieur Rossini is coming to dine with us."

"Are you angry with me?"

"Of course not," replied Judith quickly, fearing further, even more searching, questions. "You know that you are my darling little daughter, and that I love you better than anything in the world."

"After Jeanne," added Sarah to herself, and without the least bitterness.

Then she kissed her mother tenderly. She already belonged in some measure to that other, the Public.

. . . . .

Véjà's, the cake and ice shop in the Rue du Faubourg Poissonnière, a stone's throw from the Conservatoire, was full of high-spirited young people; the pupils ate, argued, speculated upon their chances, and returned to work. The boys, their collars limp with perspiration and their hair ruffled, glanced at themselves in the mirror before going back to confront the jury. Those who had passed with success, and were therefore pleased with themselves, held forth and stood their friends ices.

The final results of the examinations were not out yet. For the moment, they were all enjoying the breathing-space between the Tragedy and the Comedy competitions.

"Two praliné ices, please, Madame Véjà!"

"Leave the door open, Anatoline, so that these ladies and gentlemen haven't to keep opening it all the time."

Laughing, dark-haired Anatoline, nicknamed Ismène by the pupils of the Elocution School, wedged the door open and brought the praliné ices.

41

"Parfouru won't get the first prize for Tragedy," declared one who was Bonaparte's double.

Then the competitors returned to the Conservatoire. The streets were still full of excited pupils clinging to their parents' arms, of girls in tears, of anxious young men. The Comedy competition was beginning.

After an hour of comparative calm, which Anatoline employed in wiping the iron tables with a view to future assaults, a tall and beautiful girl, named Marie Lloyd,[1] swept into Véjà's, and said:

"Madame Véjà, give me a cordial quickly. 'The little Bernhardt' has fainted at her Comedy examination."

What had happened was this: shocked by the ordeal to which her mother had subjected her, Sarah, after heavily overworking herself, had, that very morning, given a very poor rendering of *La Fille du Cid*, and later had to face the jury once more for the Comedy competition. Forcing back her disappointment, and rallying all her fighting spirit, she was absolutely determined to get the first prize, in spite of Casimir Delavigne's text, and she gave the best of herself. Charming, deliciously moderate, gay, witty, she surpassed herself in *L'Ecole des Vieillards*. The jury applauded her enthusiastically, but, on leaving the stage, a mist came before her eyes, she swayed, clung to the arm of another competitor, and fell into a dead faint.

The first thing she saw on recovering consciousness was her mother's anxious face.

"Oh, my child, my child! I came along to see your triumph. First you gave us a comic display of tragedy and now you are giving us a tragic scene of comedy. Pull yourself together, dear. Your friend, Marie Lloyd, has brought you this. Drink it."

But Sarah hid her face in her mother's heliotrope-scented bodice.

"Nevertheless, I will get the first prize for Comedy."

"I think so too, Sarah. You must get up now, they are about to award the prizes. I hope I'll get some good news to console me for all the trouble you cause me."

. . . . .

"Second prize for Comedy!" repeated Sarah that same evening, lying in her peony room, while her temples throbbed with a splitting headache. Besides, the first prize had been awarded to Marie Lloyd! Beautiful she might be, but she had no talent, thought the little Bernhardt girl, but without any hard feeling or jealousy.

Her competitions only brought half-success to Sarah, in spite of all the heart she had put into them for two months, and in spite of her ceaseless application to her work. Second prize for Comedy? And how had her mother taken the news? She had said nothing, or next to nothing: she did not even seem very astonished, merely rather sardonic.

"You might have got nothing at all."

Strangely enough, Sarah was not discouraged. If anyone had told her, the day before, that she would have received only the second prize to crown

---

[1] This Marie Lloyd was a French actress, not to be confused with the famous English music-hall actress of the same name. [Translator.]

her efforts, she would have wept. Anyway, she always cried too much, and that made one ugly and coarsened one's voice.

Something gave Provost's and Samson's pupil a great feeling of confidence in spite of her disappointment, her headache and her mother's selfishness: and that was the way in which she had pulled herself together between the two competitions and had recovered her powers and her hold over her audience.

"I did what I wanted to do. Despite all!"

Madame Bernhardt entered her daughter's room on tip-toe. She leaned over the bed. Through her eyelashes Sarah saw her mother's eyes, filled with concern, studying her.

"You know, my dear, you need have no fear for the future. If you like, I can still write to Monsieur Berentz."

"I'll think about it."

She was lying. Her mind was irrevocably made up. She would be an actress. But thenceforward she would act a comedy to her mother too, in order to have peace and not to be hoarse with tears all her life.

CHAPTER VII

"DESPITE ALL"

At last, as a reward for so much labour, a letter bearing the seal of the Comédie Française arrived one day at the Rue Saint-Honoré; Auber had secured for Sarah an engagement at the greatest of all Parisian theatres. This engagement arrived almost immediately after the unfortunate June examinations when Sarah, who had failed in the Tragedy competition, got the second prize for Comedy.

The jury had been delighted with the way in which "the little Bernhardt" interpreted *L'Ecole des Vieillards,* but they also remembered that she had won the second prize for Tragedy in the previous year and were quite aware of the excellent annual reports she had received. And no doubt other elements influenced the Conservatoire judges: the little flame that danced round Sarah, in her eyes and in her hair; the extraordinary music of her voice; and that talent which, though still immature, marked her out, among all the others, to work a miracle, even though her teachers were still ignorant of how these real qualities could be amalgamated with her no less real defects. "The girl will one day be either sublime or execrable." This remark was attributed to Samson.

So, one September morning, three girls stood before the posters outside the Comédie Française. On them, in bold letters, was printed, "First appearance of Mlle Sarah Bernhardt in *Iphigénie.*"

"Are you excited at seeing your name in print?" asked Marie Lloyd, squeezing Sarah's arm.

"Oh yes!" she admitted shyly.

"I would like to see mine, too," added the third girl, who answered to the name of Léontine. "Papa would be so pleased."

"It will come," said Sarah kindly. "You must never lose courage."

Leaning on Marie Lloyd, Judy's daughter turned to look pensively at the people strolling up and down that part of the Avenue de l'Opéra which was still under process of being built. "The little Bernhardt" had changed, and changed to her advantage; the adolescent had developed into a tall girl of eighteen, a little too thin, but with a graceful figure and a good presence. Sarah had lovely legs and fine hands and feet; she carried her head high and her hair, swept back and neatly brushed, was soft and glossy, one fair lock falling across her intelligent forehead. Her eyes were very striking, not so much for their colour, which went from flax-blue to mauve-blue, and their long almond shape, as for the intensity of their open, romantic expression. Her mouth was still large and a little straight, but she had fine teeth and her face was given a strange beauty by her nose, which was straight and clean-cut, with aristocratically wide nostrils—such a nose as is still seen among a certain type of Jew which is becoming more and more rare.

On September 1, 1862, when the curtain of the Comédie Française rose on the second act of Racine's drama, a young beginner stood among the sceneshifters, trembling and pale beneath her rouge and grease-paint. Encouraged and supported by her two teachers clad in black, Sarah waited for her cue while running over her part in her mind. Her legs felt so heavy that they seemed as though they were paralysed.

"Has stage-fright ever prevented an actor from going on the stage?"

"No, never," replied Provost in a whisper. "Some unknown force always pushes him before the public at the last moment. Look out, there's your cue. Get on the stage."

Sarah did not budge an inch. Provost felt his pupil trembling against him, and the "unknown force" which propelled young Sarah Bernhardt on to the stage that evening was, actually, Samson.

Agamemnon, looking for Iphigénie, was already glancing desperately towards the wings when a strange, wild-looking creature flung herself upon him, clung to his tunic and began reeling off her lines at breakneck speed. Then Clytemnestra came on in her turn and Sarah turned her attention to that tragic mother, imploring and mumbling at the same time, while Samson, leaning against the wall in the wings, wiped his streaming forehead. On hearing Racine's beautiful language so butchered, the gentle Provost wrung his hands.

"She'll never get through it."

But, having recovered her wits, Sarah now turned to Achilles and addressed him, at the same time flinging out her long thin arms towards him.

Her reply did not come from Olympus, nor from the Son of Thetis and Peleas: but it did come from the Gods, hurtling down from the gallery, where a hooligan, in a loud hoarse voice, cried to the furious Achilles:

"Mind the kid's toothpicks!"

And the Beloved Monster roared with laughter.

. . . . .

They carried a poor white and crumpled little object back into the over-heated dressing-room where the only bouquet, sent by Provost and Samson, was wilting. Judith Bernhardt remained in the auditorium, yawning in her box.

"Leave me alone with Sarah," Provost told Madame Guérard.

"Why?" he asked the girl simply. "Why?"

Sarah looked at her teacher and her eyes filled with tears.

"Please forgive me! Stage-fright, nervousness. But that's all past now. Now I'm going to play properly. Forget that last act, Monsieur Provost, I beg of you."

"I will gladly forget it, and so will Samson, and so, even, will the public. But Racine must be very angry," he added with a smile.

Left to herself, Sarah gazed in her mirror at her strained features and at the wild look in her eyes. She felt terribly weak and tired, but she would act and all the forces of hell would not prevent her from going through with the task she had set herself. She picked up a stick of greasepaint and blotted out the

45

reflection of her face with its dark-ringed eyes from the mirror. She blotted it out with the words "Despite all."

Sarah interpreted the remainder of the piece in a more rational frame of mind; but the critics almost entirely ignored Mademoiselle Sarah Bernhardt's first public appearance.

"Everyone thought you looked very pretty!" said Dumas, to hide his disappointment.

. . . . .

"Overwork, delicate health, lack of fresh air, madame. Your daughter is far more ill than you suppose. I have sounded her and find that her lungs are weak and that her bronchial tubes are highly congested. Besides, she is so thin and delicate."

"I am quite aware that my daughters are not large-boned," said Judith indignantly. "Anyway, Doctor, what do you advise?"

The conclave at the Rue Saint-Honoré had met again; some of those who had attended the family council three years before were today listening to the words of young Dr. Leger, one of the fashionable doctors of the moment.

"Country air, more country air, and still more country air, if we are to avoid galloping consumption."

He took his leave of Judy, who was horror-stricken by this news, while Morny, who had got him to come to the Rue Saint-Honoré, accompanied him as far as the hall.

"If she does not take great care of herself, that young woman will never see her twenty-first birthday."

Hardly had he shut the front door than Sarah softly opened her own.

"Monsieur de Morny!"

"I thought you were in bed, Sarah."

"I got up, but don't tell mama. Monsieur de Morny, you asked me what I would like as a souvenir of my first stage appearance. I would like a box of notepaper."

"Right," said Morny with a smile. "And what colour?"

"I don't care, so long as my motto is engraved on it." And she handed him a piece of paper folded into four.

"Despite All!" read the Emperor's friend. "Many people might use that. All right, Sarah. At least you will write to me on that paper?"

"Yes, Monsieur de Morny. And in a year's time I'll send a sheet to Dr. Leger to thank him and to tell him that *despite all* I am still here."

CHAPTER VIII

THE SLAP

As *Iphigénie* and *Valérie* and in *Les Femmes Savantes* "the little Bernhardt" made, as it were, three first appearances which left her in the shade. Francisque Sarcey, who in later years was one of the tragedienne's most ardent admirers, devotes a few lines in his diary to her: "She holds herself well and enunciates her words with perfect clarity. For the moment that is all that can be said of her."

Sarah was in the same state of mind as that of a traveller setting out on a pleasant journey who finds that the first part of it lies through a dark tunnel. She knew that the sun was shining at the other end and yet she could not reach it; its brightness seemed constantly to recede as, weary and discouraged, she stumbled along in the darkness.

In September 1862 Sarah had a long tunnel to travel through; in her eagerness for life she made a breach in the roof of the tunnel, climbed on to the top of it, lost her balance, nearly killed herself and one fine day found herself free again, a grown woman and famous at last. But that was not until 1868, so that it took six years for Sarah Bernhardt's name to be, in the ears of her family, of her friends and of the Beloved Monster, anything but that of an unbalanced, obstinate and rather insolent young woman. Six years for her eccentricity to be accepted by those who loved her, as an inherent part of her vitality; for her obstinacy to be accepted as the result of that "Despite All!" attitude which brushed aside all obstacles in her path; and for her insolence to be transformed into a feeling of human dignity capable of accentuating qualities which were yet to develop. Six years, in spite of that first love which was soon to change her whole life, for her to become really enamoured of the other love, the Public, to which she dedicated her life.

But to return to a day in 1862.

That day the Comédie Française was full of excitement. The Molière festival brought the whole personnel of the theatre on to the stage. The public, called upon to join in the glorification of Jean-Baptiste Poquelin,[1] author, actor and producer, was waiting for the curtain to rise on this elegant production. Sceneshifters were bustling about putting finishing touches on the *décor*. On a pedestal draped with crimson velvet stood a white marble bust of the great French comedy-writer, and Monsieur Thierry, the manager of the Comédie Française, was hesitating, with wreaths in his hands, between crowning the head of the great Master with laurel or with roses. It was finally decided that Beauvallet, after reciting a sonnet by Théophile Gautier and a poem by Auguste Barbier, should place on Molière's brow a wreath of laurel brought on by two young attendants: one Dorine, played by Madeleine Pata, and the other Georgette, played by Sarah Bernhardt.

Sarah, filled with pleasant emotions at the thought of the ceremony, foolishly succumbed to the pleadings of Regina, now aged about six, to take

---

[1] Molière's real name.

SARAH BERNHARDT

her to the theatre, on condition that she promised to keep quiet and to stay with Madame Guérard and not to fidget.

"And you are not to sing either."

Because from that little mouth, so small in her seraphic face, strange, not to say vulgar, songs and remarks were in the habit of issuing at the most unexpected moments.

At first everything went well. Regina, seated in the wings on Madame Guérard's knees, amused herself by watching people passing to and fro with their painted faces and their velvet and brocade costumes. And when Sarah had put on her peasant costume, she went and kissed Regina and said:

"You're a very good little girl."

But the child began to cry:

"I don't know you, and you smell funny."

"Really!" said Madame Guérard. "Don't you recognize Sarah?"

And the angel stopped crying, yelled with laughter and, slapping her legs, observed:

"What a funny face you've got!"

"Regina, you promised you'd be good," whispered Sarah, looking round her in alarm.

"Yes, but please, Sarah, take me on the stage before the curtain goes up!"

Placing her little hand in her sister's, Regina slid to the floor and Sarah led her up to the bust of Molière. The little girl jumped up and down with delight and plied Sarah with questions.

"Why are you going to put a crown on him?"

"Because Molière was a great man, and great men sometimes get crowned."

"Nannie tells me that where she comes from they crown fat pigs before killing them. Do you think it's to console them for being fat, Sarah?"

Sarah gently hushed her. Just then a stout matron draped in a bright blue velvet dress with a long train passed before the bust. She eyed the little girl ironically and said:

"Your little sister, Mademoiselle Bernhardt?"

"Yes, Madame Nathalie. Say 'how-do-you-do', Regina."

One of the actors had come up to adjust a detail and Nathalie did not see the little girl's dive forward nor did she hear the unexpected clicking sound with which she accompanied her little curtsey.

"Now," said Sarah, "go back to your seat. The show is going to begin."

Yes, but in order to reach the exit it would have been necessary to disturb Madame Nathalie again, as she stood between two flats talking with Augustine Brohan. In order not to walk in front of her, Sarah stopped, glad that Regina was now quiet again. Nathalie started off again; but she suddenly gave a piercing scream: a piece of the beautiful blue velvet dress had remained beneath Regina's feet. Regina raised terrified eyes to her sister.

"I didn't mean to do it," she said.

But a strong hand tore the little girl's hand from her sister's and flung the child into the wings, where she fell, striking, in her path, a stucco column which cut open her forehead.

Immediate pandemonium broke out. Regina, her little face smeared with blood, screamed "Bitch! Bitch!" at Nathalie. And Sarah, wild with rage,

48

Sarah Bernhardt in 1870

Sarah and her old friend Mme. Guérard

Sarah Bernhardt in 1875

Sarah Bernhardt and her son Maurice, c. 1872

threw herself on Nathalie and gave her a resounding slap. Completely bewildered, the outraged Nathalie emerged from this ridiculous situation by collapsing into the arms of one of the actors, who, fortunately, happened to be endowed with strong biceps.

The younger members of the cast crowded round Sarah: some of them commiserated with her, others admired her, and some even congratulated her in whispers; she had avenged them for the pinpricks which they had to suffer daily from Madame Nathalie, a cantankerous old actress, full of her own importance. Rose Baretta, who was very fond of Sarah, warned her that this act would mean the termination of her engagement. But Sarah declared that she did not care a fig and, as the members of the audience were beginning to show their impatience by stamping their feet, Monsieur Thierry, who had been sent for, appeared among his company like a policeman in the middle of a scrimmage.

"To your places! Please! To your places!"

He gave Sarah a crafty smile, scratched his well-coloured nose and muttered between his teeth:

"We must think out a reprimand for tomorrow."

A sentence which Rose translated by the less elegant words, "You're going to get the sack."

.   .   .   .   .

What a time that tunnel took to get through! After leaving the Comédie Française company, Sarah got engagements in one or two theatres where no one took any notice of her. She seemed to be under a spell which prevented her talent, her charm, and her temperament from manifesting themselves. She did not show up particularly badly in either the *Maison des Enfants* or the *Démon au Jeu*, in which she appeared at the Gymnase. She was just negligible.

"Nothing seems to go right," she explained to Dumas, who was disappointed in his "little star", but was always infinitely kind and patient with her.

"Sarah," he told her, "talent is a fickle lord who rides about in a beautiful carriage. He does not always stop when he is hailed, like a cab plying for hire."

"Then how can one attract his attention?"

"An act, a part, a word, a shout, a gesture; and one fine day talent notices you, stops, holds out his hand and helps you into the carriage and you are off!"

"There cannot be much room in that carriage of yours, Monsieur Dumas. So many people have talent nowadays."

"This lord possesses a vast livery stable. I suspect him, in years of great plenty, of even hiring omnibuses. But genius has a much more restricted retinue."

"I wouldn't mind a place even in the omnibus," said Sarah sadly.

"You have a delightful voice, good delivery, plenty of passion. You must try— how shall I put it?—to cut a little piece of yourself off for the Public. Yes, a piece of your heart, of your flesh, of your muscles. The public is rather like Shylock. When it pays, it demands its share of nerves, of tears, of blood and of sweat."

This conversation took place in the house in the Rue Saint-Honoré, some months after the slapping episode at the Comédie Française. Monsieur Thierry

D

had demanded that Sarah should apologize publicly to Madame Nathalie, who was a Sociétaire, or full member, of the Comédie; but Sarah, thinking that the old actress had been entirely in the wrong in ill-treating a child, had refused to do so. Whereupon her engagement was terminated and she was dismissed.

"Mama says I was wrong, Monsieur de Morny says I was wrong, and my aunts say I was wrong. They keep on repeating 'You cannot leave the Comédie Française.' Even you, Monsieur Dumas, will not support me. And yet, how could I apologize to that fat vixen?"

"Nathalie is an old Sociétaire and you are only a newcomer. The matter might have been patched up. Anyway, what's done is done. What are your plans now?"

"To play in Raymond Deslandes' new play at the Gymnase."

"*Un Mari qui lance sa Femme?*"

"Yes, I owe it to Monsieur Meydieu to have been given a part in spite of my reputation of being a mediocre actress with a hasty temper."

Sarah began to cry and the big man kissed her forehead with its fringe of golden curls.

"Don't forget, Sarah. The carriage, the shout, the gesture that will call attention to you."

"Alas! the producer, Montigny, has cast me for an absurd part: that of a mad, idiotic Russian Princess. I feel so uncomfortable in it that at each rehearsal I want to throw it up. I daren't do so, on account of mama, who hardly speaks to me since the Nathalie episode."

"I'll be at your first night, Sarah. And, dear, I am nursing a slight hope that if you work very hard you may be able to play the part of Anna Damby in my play *Kean*."

"Oh," cried Sarah, throwing her arms round his neck, "to act in a play by you! When? When?"

"When you've become sensible," replied Alexandre Dumas, quickly shutting the door of the Rue Saint-Honoré apartment behind him.

·   ·   ·   ·   ·

Though *Un Mari qui lance sa Femme* received a very questionable reception, nevertheless the play marked a date in the intimate life of Sarah Bernhardt. Not only was she ridiculous in the part of the intolerable Princess Dunchinka, but no one really noticed her at all.

On the first night, raising her eyes casually to the first-tier boxes, she saw her mother looking at her with sadness and disapproval; her expression did not change; only the shortsighted eyes gazed at the poor, badly dressed child, prancing about on the stage, embarrassed by her part which she played with the courage of desperation. Behind Judy, the imposing figure of Alexandre Dumas was outlined in the shadows.

Sarah faltered and went through the rest of the play in a dream; and when her mother came to fetch her after the performance she realized that something had broken between them. Not a word was spoken on the way home. In the hall Judith kissed her daughter.

50

"Anyway, I hope you are not too tired?"

"No, thank you, mama."

"Anyway, try to get some sleep."

"Yes, mama. Good night."

Sleep! How could she? Her world was tumbling about her ears. The engagement at the Gymnase on which she had pinned such hopes ended in this grotesque part. Without any doubt, her mother thought her incompetent. Dumas only spoke to her out of affection, and the person who was responsible for all this, that Morny who, having nothing better to do one fine day, had put ideas into the heads of these very ordinary people with the words, "Why not send Sarah to the Conservatoire?"—("Yes," Sarah used to say, "just as he would give his horse a lump of sugar")—now seldom visited the Rue Saint-Honoré. Sarah's aunts, with the exception of frivolous and scatterbrained Aunt Rosine, were always speaking about her behind her back. Madame Guérard alone remained sympathetic.

"I must get some sleep."

But, two hours later, huddled between the sheets, beneath the green and pink counterpane, Sarah was still awake.

"Sleep, or I shall go mad!"

Should she go to her mother's room to get a sleeping-draught? No! But she remembered that in a little room leading off the drawing-room there was a medicine-cupboard and that in it there was some laudanum. "Not to be touched", Judith had written on the bottle, which she used sometimes for compresses to relieve pain.

"I'm going to kill myself," the girl decided suddenly, with a feeling of exhilaration. "If I die, I shall be playing a real part, a part in which I shall be excellent. I shall never be ridiculous again. I shall be able to sleep at last. Tomorrow I shall be found dead, and mama, and even Jeanne and Regina, will be sorry."

She got out of bed, lit her lamp and examined her reflection in the mirror. She was very pale. "Naturally; like a corpse," she whispered, smiling to herself. Then she hesitated a moment; was laudanum painful? No, she would take enough for death to do its work quickly. She put on her dressing-gown and softly opened the door.

And at that moment she heard a faint sound of knocking coming from the hall.

CHAPTER IX

THE OTHER JOURNEY

WHEN the curtain fell on the last scene of *Un Mari qui lance sa Femme,* Alexandre Dumas, without commenting upon Sarah's performance, offered to drive Judy and her daughter back to the Rue Saint-Honoré. But Madame Bernhardt, who was not feeling well, declined her friend's offer. And they parted rather coldly.

Dumas had arranged to meet a young woman and Monsieur Viel-Castel. While eating his supper and paying the pretty girl a thousand compliments and describing in his wittiest manner the play he had just seen, he suddenly stopped short.

"I wonder if that confounded wench will do anything silly," he said.

"Whom are you talking about?"

"About a young actress, the daughter of a friend of mine. She seemed so distressed this evening. My dear, look after mademoiselle for me. I must drop in to . . . Anyway, it is only just round the corner."

History does not relate how the lady felt about this desertion. As for Alexandre Dumas, he dived into a passing cab.

"Judy is too severe," he muttered to himself. "At this very moment, perhaps, a drama may be unfolding itself in that awful Dutch apartment."

The novelist had great difficulty in persuading the *concierge* in the Rue Saint-Honoré to open the house door, and when he reached the second floor he paused and listened intently. Not a sound came from the apartment. He had been imagining things. No doubt Judy, Sarah and the children were all sound asleep. And yet? Suppose that his young friend needed help? Dumas rapped gently on the door with his signet ring, and, after a few moments, an unsteady voice asked, "Who's there?"

"Me, Dumas. Is that you, Sarah? Open the door. I've got something to say to you."

     .   .   .   .   .

("You have told me, grandmother, that even without the intervention of Alexandre Dumas something would have restrained you, at the last moment, from swallowing the poison?"

"This gesture, Lysiane, which seemed to me to be so brave in a moment of childish exaltation, would have seemed an error of taste at the moment of making it. You know how I despise suicide.")

     .   .   .   .   .

The door opened and the novelist's bulky form rolled into the hall without a word. Dumas took Sarah's hand and led her back to her room.

"Can't you get to sleep? How pale you look!"

She stood in front of him, trembling and as though in a trance, and Dumas could think of nothing better to bring her back to reality than to give her a good shaking, half in anger and half in affection.

"You're hurting me, Monsieur Dumas!"

"All the better, because it's time we put an end to a misunderstanding. There's something very wrong here. You are fighting shadows and I myself loathe shadows. I like romance, but with people who struggle and shout, who eat and fly into rages to the accompaniment of clashing swords. I have no use for neuropathy, which is a disease of the idle, which certain rich people parade as they might a piece of vulgar jewellery."

"But, monsieur——"

"Don't interrupt me, my dear. I am half responsible for all this business. I encouraged you to become an actress; I may have been wrong, I may have been right. Anyway, for the moment you are on the wrong road. You must turn off it and go and rest for a while. Go away!"

"What?" cried Sarah in amazement. "But where to? No, monsieur, I cannot desert either my post or my mother."

"Haven't you got an understudy? Well, then, don't worry about your part. I'll arrange all that with Montigny. And I'll fix it with your mother too. Haven't you become emancipated since you got into the Comédie Française?"

"Of course. When ought I to go?"

"At once."

"How? Without saying good-bye to mama?"

"Do you want to stay here and eat your heart out? And do you take me for a fool? Swear to me that you did not intend to do anything foolish tonight. Swear it!"

"No, Monsieur Dumas, I will not swear it. I intended to kill myself."

"Sarah! Do you trust me? Yes? Then let me help you because, at the moment, you are your own worst enemy, far worse than theatre managers and your detractors."

There was so much power, so much persuasive charm, in this big man. Sarah raised fascinated eyes to his.

"What am I to do?"

"*Take a chair, Sarah, and observe to the letter the law which I lay down for you on everything.*"

"*I will obey you, my lord,*" replied the girl, with a sad smile.

In ten minutes Dumas had fastened wings on the little Bernhardt, awakening in her the desire for travel which is innate in every child of the Jewish race, and had persuaded her to leave behind her the awkward encumbrances of her childhood. To go away! These words held a strange fascination for Sarah. They fluttered like a bird with striped plumage, beating against the blue-green room. To go away! What music there was in those words, and what promise!

"Oh yes!" she cried suddenly, jumping up and down at the risk of waking her mother. "Let's go! go! go!"

Then her spirits sank. She looked at Dumas and said:

"But I've got no money."

"That will be provided. For the moment, don't talk any more; pack your bag and come with me. There is a train for Brussels tomorrow morning. That is where you are going. I have great friends there: the Bruces, and Bolfans, the manager of the Théâtre du Parc."

All this had taken only half an hour; the excitement of the unknown had transformed the despairing little person into a young girl eagerly looking forward to her first journey, as she bustled about the room choosing things to pack.

"I can't ask you back with me tonight. That wouldn't be . . . well . . . Madame Guérard will look after you until tomorrow morning."

"Yes!" replied Sarah, beside herself with joy. "And my Little Lady will go with me: she would never let me go to strangers alone."

When Dumas went to the Rue Saint-Honoré he had not given a thought to any of these details, but the story was now developing itself logically and clearly. Judy's daughter was in a morass. It was no good giving her a helping hand here for her to sink again three steps further on. The child had to be lifted right out on to dry land. Afterwards they would see.

"How am I going to break the news to mama? She's got a weak heart."

"What time does your mother get up?"

"At nine o'clock."

"All right," said Dumas with a sigh. "I'll be here at a quarter to nine. I can explain better in words than in a letter."

CHAPTER X

THE MASKED BALL

IN Brussels, after leaving their luggage at the Hôtel de Hainaut et de Flandres, recommended by Dumas, the thought uppermost in the minds of the two women was to explore the charming old town. They crossed the Place Royale, reached the Groot Market and, after admiring the Town Hall and its tracery, entered a little restaurant in the Rue au Beurre; there they had a light meal, though Madame Guérard thought it rather improper for unaccompanied women to dine outside their hotel.

It was decided that Madame Guérard should remain in Brussels another day before taking the train back to Paris. Then Sarah would stand on her own feet, dividing her time between Dumas's friends and the managers of the Brussels theatres; she would probably soon get an engagement. So it was with a calm and happy heart that Sarah, on the first night of her escapade, slid between the coarse sheets of the Hôtel de Hainaut et de Flandres. Madame Guérard, for her part, was a good deal more perturbed as she fell asleep, thinking of the storms in the Rue Saint-Honoré which she would have to face forty-eight hours later.

. . . . .

Two days later Sarah, proud of being left to her own devices in a foreign town, received a letter from Dumas. The scene between Madame Bernhardt and himself, though pretty violent, had ended happily owing to "certain details" which the novelist saw fit to add to his story. Sarah smiled. Alexandre Dumas, by giving Madame Bernhardt a highly coloured account of Sarah's attempted suicide, had managed to get round her. He advised Sarah to send her mother an affectionate and respectful letter.

Just as Sarah was beginning to write on her beautiful notepaper there was a knock on the door, and a red-cheeked servant girl came in and handed her an envelope, containing an invitation to a masked ball to be given in four days' time by the Bruces. Dumas's friend added, *I will call on you at midday today with my daughter Lisbeth, to take you out to luncheon.*

For a moment Sarah was vexed. Why could not people leave her alone to enjoy her liberty for a little while? She would accept the invitation to luncheon, but not the one to the ball, which would certainly bore her to death; she hated crowds.

. . . . .

(Crowds, yes. You did not hate them, grandmother, but they frightened you. The presence of five people in a room made you feel awkward, though this merely gave your face additional charm. But solitude? If the events which I am about to record had not occurred, I doubt whether you would have been able to bear two days of that loneliness in Brussels or anywhere else. You hated being alone. If you were left alone for five minutes you always called for your companion, your secretary, your maid, or one of us, and you would complain, "No one thinks of me any more!")

．　　　．　　　．　　　．　　　．

"I won't go to the ball!"

Sarah's misanthropic reflections were interrupted by another knock on the door. The maid handed her a card which bore the inscription: "BIENFÉ, costumier, wig-maker, purveyor of cosmetics. Fancy dress for hire. By special appointment to His Majesty King Leopold I." And in Jean Bruce's handwriting were added the words, *For you to choose a costume for our ball.*

Sarah was about to send a curt refusal when a personage appeared before her, bent almost double in a deep bow. He was a man of about fifty, clad in light-brown check trousers, a moss-green waistcoat and a puce jacket. A little negro boy, dressed in a red corduroy velvet suit and a white satin turban, stood behind him, with one foot resting on two large cardboard band-boxes. The apparition spoke.

"Monsieur Bienfé, to submit to Mademoiselle Bernhardt a selection of costumes and fancy dresses for the forthcoming ball which 'we' are giving at the Bruces. Coal-Dust," he went on, addressing the little negro, "please show mademoiselle, the interpreter of the parts of Aricie, Iphigénie and of other noble rôles, what is contained in those unworthy boxes."

The maid roared with laughter, rocking on her fat legs. As for Sarah, she was thoroughly amused by the absurdity of the fellow, disarmed by his prattle and flattered that her reputation as an actress should already have reached Brussels. So her reception of him became quite gracious.

"I doubt whether I am going to the ball, but I would love to look at your dresses, Monsieur Bienfé. You are Flemish?"

"Quite possibly. My mother, who was the widow of a Belgian distiller, took as her second husband a shipowner from Marseilles; I have never known whether my father was the distiller or the shipowner."

"But . . . your mother?"

"A devout woman, and the soul of discretion! She never told me."

"Well, is your name that of your Belgian father or of your French father?" asked Sarah, laughing.

"Neither one nor the other, because neither of them would have anything to do with me. The name Bienfé is that of my mother's third husband, whose son I certainly am not, but who acknowledged me as such."

In the meantime, Coal-Dust had unpacked the cardboard boxes and spread costumes of various periods over the bed, on the table and on the chairs. Sarah, assisted by the giggling maid, tried each of them on, becoming more and more enchanted by the Venetian dresses, the Louis XV panniers, and the flowing mediaeval robes.

"All right! I'll take this one."

"Queen Elizabeth of England. A great queen, but a criminal queen. Her hands were full of poems and yet her fingers were stained with blood. But, mademoiselle, do not let that deter you!"

56

The Elizabethan dress suited Sarah. It filled her out, concealing her rather lean arms and emphasizing the slimness of her waist; the dark red velvet material enhanced her delicate colouring and the romance of her deep blue eyes.

"I will dress your hair myself, mademoiselle," added Monsieur Bienfé.

"Hm?" thought Sarah, who hated anyone to touch her hair.

When Monsieur Bruce was announced at the Hôtel de Hainaut et de Flandres, Sarah had just finished her "affectionate and respectful letter" to Judith Bernhardt.

Sarah immediately took to Jean Bruce, who was a man of about sixty. In spite of his baldness and of a birthmark which disfigured part of his forehead, his bold, finely cut features gave him a very noble appearance. His daughter, Lisbeth, was pretty without any particular charm, and rather stupid. That, at any rate, was how she struck Sarah. They drove through the Porte de Namur as far as the Château de la Malibran, just before reaching the Luxemburg road.

Dumas's friend was a man of intelligence. Having abandoned a diplomatic career which promised extremely well, he had preserved all his contacts with the Royal Palace and the aged King. The luncheon was most pleasant. The other guests were Lisbeth's companion, a cross-grained Englishwoman who looked like an old grenadier; a handsome, pretentious youth, engaged to Lisbeth; a chubby red-faced doctor, rather too hearty, whose flow of words hardly stopped long enough to let the excellent fare through his lips, so encumbered were they with chatter and laughter.

Sarah was happy. In order that she should feel more at her ease, Jean Bruce had not asked many people to meet her. But then, of course, besides the letter of introduction which the girl had presented to him, he had received from Dumas a very detailed letter about Sarah's past life, her gifts and her disappointments, her strange character, her turbulence and her contemplated suicide.

It was not for nothing that Jean Bruce had been called "the super-diplomat" by his friends. He, too, tamed Sarah. For the next few days he showed her the beauties of Flemish art, made her eat at all the best restaurants, and took her to visit all the more picturesque corners of the Belgian capital.

.   .   .   .   .

It was a warm June night. Low clouds floated through the sky, with every now and then a rift through which the last quarter of the moon appeared, hanging like a golden brooch between two clouds.

At eleven o'clock all the streets leading to Jean Bruce's mansion were filled with carriages; coachmen with their cockaded hats stood in groups, smoking malodorous cigars. In spite of the mildness of the weather, grooms had covered some of the horses with linen rugs. The horses themselves waited there patiently, while the Brussels sparrows stood hopefully by.

The ball had begun. The blare of the orchestra floated through the open windows in Strauss waltzes, quadrilles and polkas. The Brussels populace strained their eyes to catch a glimpse of the dancers between the trees round the house. A few fellows, bolder than the rest, had climbed up the iron entrance gates, under the noses of the flunkeys in satin knickerbockers and gilt garters who scrutinized the invitations.

Inside the mansion the Bruces' three immense reception-rooms glittered in the light of their lustres and chandeliers. The orchestra, installed in a loggia, could be heard all over the house, even in the dining-room and the smoking-room, where some sixty waiters were busying themselves. The main attraction of the evening centred round the words engraved at the bottom of the invitation card, *Masks are essential*. Save for the host, his daughter and his future son-in-law, the guests in their fancy dress and their masks spent their time in trying to identify one another, as often as not being completely at fault. Eyes seem to shine more brightly and lips to smile more sweetly in faces thus half concealed. Young Sarah-Elizabeth enjoyed herself thoroughly; she never missed a dance and her ivory dance-programme was covered with Christian names: First waltz Jean, polka Roland, etc., as, for the moment at any rate, the dancers were very careful not to reveal their identities.

.   .   .   .   .

(How romantic your dance-programme is, grandmother! It is here in my room among other souvenirs and speaks to me of you when I stroke its yellow ivory!)

.   .   .   .   .

Sarah's head-dress, fitting closely to her head, was one of Bienfé's master-pieces. Her dark red velvet dress, with its embroidered bodice, enclosed her slim tapered waist and attracted many an admiring glance through masks, themselves of velvet. On several occasions a fair young man dressed as Hamlet, not very tall, but well proportioned, had attempted to approach her. But, whether by mischance, or perhaps out of mischief, she always managed to slip away on the arm of another partner and to start dancing, laughing and care-free. On the other hand, this Hamlet had no lack of women or girls to dance with him. Indeed, it was amazing to see how many of them seemed to make a set at the young man. And when, in an interval, he made his way to the bar, a phalanx of Venetian ladies, of marchionesses, of *merveilleuses*, of Josephines de Beauharnais, and of Dutch girls, crowded round him. He smiled brightly at them behind his mask, affable, witty, charming, unknown. Unknown at least to Sarah, who was sitting up at the bar hesitating to drink the glass of champagne (a wine of which she was completely ignorant) which was being forced on her by an importunate Florentine page with bow legs, who had danced attendance upon her from the very beginning of the ball. Conscious of the Hamlet's eyes fixed upon her and thinking that the young man was smiling rather cynically at her, Sarah raised her glass and finished it at a draught. Tears came into her eyes and a merry glow began to pervade her. The orchestra embarked on a polka.

"This time, I hope, you will grant me a dance," said Hamlet softly, bowing to Elizabeth.

"Sir," replied Sarah, "I am torn between you and another glass of champagne!"

58

Hamlet frowned, tapped his foot on the floor and then, without more ado, masterfully led Sarah to the dance floor. The other women scattered, laughing half-heartedly. The Hamlet-Elizabeth combination, on the other hand, whirled through the three dance-rooms, until the young man steered his partner with considerable skill to a bow-shaped balcony overlooking the gardens. At that distance the music and the chatter of the guests seemed to rise and fall in two distinct but confused notes. The crescent moon appeared between two clouds.

"Madame! Mademoiselle! Won't you take off your mask?"

"Why should I, monsieur?"

"To please me."

"Why should I want to please you—"

She never finished her sentence. Hamlet took a quick step towards her, held her close to him and tried to kiss her lips. But Sarah's left hand reached his cheek first.

"Ah, Monsieur Hamlet," she cried, "it isn't as though I had come as Ophelia that you should dare to take such a liberty!"

Completely taken aback, the young man was about to reproach her for her petulance when, in a mirror in the room opposite the balcony, he suddenly saw the reflection of Hamlet and of Elizabeth of England quarrelling with each other. The absurdity of the situation changed his irritation into hearty laughter. He kissed Sarah's hand, made his respectful apologies and added, playfully, pointing to the mirror:

"The Prince of Denmark beseeches Her Majesty of England to pardon his error of taste: *To forgive or not to forgive?*"

"*To forgive,*" replied Sarah, smiling.

How attractive he was, this young man in his black doublet, with his fair hair and his lean face half covered by a mask above the clear cut lips curled back from his brilliant white teeth!

They danced again and mingled with the crowd. Hamlet held Elizabeth close to him and breathed the violet scent with which Bienfé had sprayed her hair. Again he asked her name, but she refused to tell him; nor did she ask him his.

.   .   .   .   .

Four o'clock in the morning. After dancing again and again with the bow-legged page, with Jean Bruce and with Hamlet, Sarah felt exhausted. She was so tired that she longed to be back in Paris in her blue-green room, under her mother's short-sighted eyes and within reach of Regina's soft cheeks which were so nice to kiss.

She was tired of dancing and talking and flirting. The Bruces' carriage was there to take her back to her hotel, so she sent for it. Suddenly a shadow detached itself from the garden and leaped on to the steps leading down to the drive.

"So, Madame Elizabeth, you were going without taking leave of me?"

Hamlet smiled and Sarah gave him her hand. Then he handed Sarah a beautiful scented rose round whose long stalk was wrapped a handkerchief.

"This rose, Mademoiselle Bernhardt," he said, "is like your own character, bristling with cruel thorns; so I have made the thorns harmless. Since I know

59

your name but not your face, and since I am determined to see you again, will you please deign to wear this rose when you drive out tomorrow morning, so that I may find you more quickly. You owe that, at least, to the unhappy Prince of Denmark."

The carriage halted before the steps; the unknown dancer opened the door and helped the girl to get in. Then he removed his mask and waved it in a gesture of farewell. But the moon chose that moment to disappear behind a cloud and Sarah, turning round, could distinguish only Hamlet's silhouette and his bright smile.

When she got back to her room, Sarah removed the handkerchief from the rose. In one corner of the fine linen she discovered a closed crown with a small "L" embroidered inside it.

CHAPTER XI

THE PRINCE

THE next day Sarah got up late and did not leave the hotel until nearly half past twelve, when she ordered an open hackney carriage.

"I want you to take me to the most fashionable promenade. And please drive slowly; I am in no hurry."

Her appointment with Belfans, manager of the Théâtre du Parc, was not until two o'clock. The sky had cleared; a few clouds lingered round the horizon, but the sun threw brilliant patches on the streets. Sarah, weary from lack of sleep, longed to get into the shade of the Boulevard de Waterloo and the Boulevard de la Toison d'Or. Her eyes were shining and there was something very flower-like, that summer morning, about her pale face, faintly flushed by the heat of the day. Monsieur Dumas had really done her a great service. How happy she felt, and how well! Sarah had dressed herself with fastidious care. She wore a yellow silk dress (not scorched this time!), the gift of Monsieur Berentz, who perhaps still nursed a faint hope, and over the dress a mantle of *broderie-anglaise*; a large Winterhalter hat, trimmed with ears of corn, made a pretty frame for her face, and *the* rose was pinned on her bosom.

At length her carriage reached a wide street where carriages followed each other closely at a walking pace. To the right ran a pavement filled with little boys in white and little girls in thin dresses over nainsook drawers, and ladies in bright colours; to the left, on a sanded ride, horsemen and horsewomen pranced and greeted one another. When Sarah reached the end of the avenue her coachman turned his horse to repeat the promenade in the opposite direction. As the carriage passed beside the track reserved for riders, a fair, slim and elegant young man, mounted on a magnificent thoroughbred, looked intently at Sarah, his gaze being fixed upon the rose on her bosom. He bowed gallantly and said:

"Ah! Madame Elizabeth!"

"Hamlet," replied Sarah, colouring.

Leaning over his horse's withers, her last night's dancing partner looked at her tenderly.

"How lovely you are! Exactly as I expected you to be. I knew about your mouth, your hair and your blue eyes, but I did not know about the sweet look in your eyes, or about the roguishness of your smile. Won't you get out? I will take you home in my own carriage."

Before Sarah had time to answer yes or no, he called his groom and dismounted.

"Jim," he said, "take my horse back, pay off mademoiselle's carriage and call my tilbury."

This amazing young man seemed to be able to give orders to everyone, and Sarah gladly obeyed his imperative instructions, which she would have resented in anyone else. So she left the old hackney carriage and climbed on to the tilbury, while the young man took over the reins and the mettlesome young cob set off at a smart trot. Sarah covertly studied her companion, taking in his fine profile and his wavy hair, which, at the sides, overflowed the rim of his high silk hat. She wanted to say something, but felt too embarrassed. And it was he who broke the silence.

"Will you dine with me tomorrow evening, mademoiselle? I would like to introduce myself to you, but I cannot do so properly at the moment, with the reins in one hand and the other hand on my heart. Will you come? Or do you consider my invitation impertinent? Are you afraid of going to a man's house alone? Should I have invited Bruce, his daughter and his future son-in-law? Talk to me. Anyway, I have so much to say to you that one evening will not be nearly enough."

"Do you imagine, monsieur, that, when I do not even know your name, I would accept such an invitation?" replied Sarah, blushing to the roots of her hair.

She lied brazenly, though she knew nothing of this young man save his title, his initial, and that he fascinated her.

"So you will come?"

"And why should I not come?" retorted the girl. "I'm not afraid of anything! Until tomorrow, monsieur. Here we are at my hotel."

.   .   .   .   .

"His Highness awaits you in the library."

This grandiose phrase greeted Sarah at the Prince's mansion on the Boulevard Toison d'Or on the following evening. She hoped she did not look as excited as she felt. The day had dragged out interminably. At five o'clock she had put on a coral-coloured dress and the amethyst ear-rings Aunt Bruck had given her, and placed a rose (without a thorn) in her beautiful hair. When Prince de Ligne's carriage stopped outside Sarah's hotel she had already been looking out for it through the curtains in her room for half an hour.

And now she followed the footman along a vast marble corridor where ancestral portraits alternated with suits of armour and panoplies.

"Brrr!" she thought. "It's not very jolly here."

At last the servant opened a door carved in pure Flemish style and announced:

"Mademoiselle Sarah Bernhardt."

"It is so nice of you to have come," said the Prince softly, untying her hat-ribbon for her. He was wearing a black suit with a satin waistcoat; his cravat was tied with consummate art.

The library struck Sarah as being comfortable and friendly. White bearskin, ocelot and panther rugs sprawled on the thick pile carpets. Bookshelves lined the room, while the furniture was a mixture of English and Flemish eighteenth-century styles. Two superb collies were stretched on the bearskin at the foot of the Prince's writing-desk.

"Let me introduce Florimond and Gusta. And allow me to introduce myself."

"That is unnecessary," replied Sarah, rather primly. "I know your name already, monsieur." Actually she had heard it a short while before from the red-cheeked servant-girl, when she announced the Prince's carriage.

62

The young man did not pursue the subject. He showed Sarah round the beautiful home of the Lignes, a veritable museum of painting and armour. As they passed before the solemn ancestral portraits, the Prince reeled off their names: de Croy, de Barbançon, d'Epinoy. . . . "This is my great-grandfather, the friend of Voltaire."

On the tables stood tall vases filled with lilies and roses, and the delicacy of these flowers contrasted oddly with the coats of mail, tilting-lances, harness and cuirasses, and the panoplies of halberds, scimitars, rapiers and sabres.

On their return to the library, the Prince placed two large armchairs facing each other; inviting Sarah to sit down, he took her hand and gazed into her eyes.

"Your face is a poem which I want to learn by heart. What are your thoughts? What are your ambitions? What is going to happen to you? I want to share all your thoughts and all your hopes. I have never met anyone like you. Talk to me, Sarah; tell me about your life."

He slid to his knees at Sarah's feet and she, still on the defensive, rather alarmed, deeply moved, placed her hands along the arms of her chair, like a well-brought-up little girl on her best behaviour. She fixed her eyes on the curls at the nape of the Prince's neck and began to talk. She told him all about herself and lost her reserve and her defensiveness. Her hands left the chair-arms and played with the young man's hair. She offered her short past life to the Prince as though it were a bouquet of flowers, and, as she went on, so she unconsciously approached the exit of the tunnel through which she had been still groping her way. On the horizon the weather was fine and bright. Soon she would be running about in these lush meadows which she could already see in the distance. And even if this was still only scenery made of paper, what did it matter? She would tear her way through it and any more like it until she reached the real country where she could live, love and work.

Ah! How sweet it was to choke with happiness.

For the Prince was kissing her and holding her close to him, and Sarah could hardly breathe; but she felt so light, so flexible in his arms. Her whole being rested on the bosom of that man scented with vanilla and mild tobacco.

.   .   .   .   .

Brussels, June 1863.

. . . *So, my dear Dumas, your young friend, Sarah Bernhardt, has taken Brussels by storm. At our ball she made a conquest of Prince de Ligne. I think they have met since. Are you angry with me for having given this young lady too much to distract her mind, or are you going to congratulate me for having helped an actress to shed her prejudices? Everything depends upon the point of view from which you look at your protégée: from the respectability of her present or from the greatness of her future. Ever yours, J. Bruce.*

P.S. I have just returned from the Hôtel de Hainaut et de Flandres. Sarah has not put in an appearance there for a week. She is said to be travelling "with friends". I am rather afraid that these friends, reduced to a single person, have limited the extent of her travels to the Boulevard de la Toison d'Or. That is what happens when one lets a dragon-fly loose with a butterfly. You have been warned. Like Pontius Pilate I salve my conscience with the sentence in your letter: "It is time this child spread her wings. Her vocation is entirely out of tune with the careful maxims with which her mother loads her. I would rather see her do something foolish than just fritter away her life."

I believe, my friend, that your prayers have been answered. J. B.

.   .   .   .   .

That very morning, Sarah returned to the Hôtel de Hainaut et de Flandres and got her letters from the hall porter.

She walked slowly upstairs to her room, putting off opening them. For a week she had been living in a dream; and now she had a presentiment that one of these letters might jerk her roughly back to reality. Was her love to be destroyed already like a poor wounded bird?

With a sigh, Sarah opened the first envelope: it contained a letter from the Mother Superior of Grand-Champs, who, having heard of her decision to leave home, was anxious about her and sent her blessing. Another envelope contained a line from Dumas: *Everything was all right at the Gymnase.* And, finally, the third letter was from Madame Guérard. Come! That was not so bad, and she would soon be able to rejoin her beloved Prince. And Sarah closed her eyes the better to see the young man's face, the face that could be so gentle, so cruel or so passionate.

But, as she read the first words written by Madame Guérard, the colour left her face and she quickly looked for the date on which the letter was written. It was already five days old. Her mother, said Madame Guérard, had had a severe heart attack. She was in grave danger and was asking for Sarah.

"When does the train leave for Paris?" she asked the hotel manager, in a panic.

"In an hour's time, mademoiselle. But it is a slow train and you would have to change."

"My mother is very ill and I must catch that train. Please have my bill made out."

She hurriedly fastened her trunks and had them taken downstairs. There were still ten minutes before she had to leave for the station. Sarah would have liked to have run all the way to the Boulevard de la Toison d'Or, to tell the Prince; but she dared not do so, as the young man was entertaining his family at luncheon that day, and her unexpected appearance would no doubt have embarrassed him. So she scribbled a note, tore it up, and wrote another.

My mother is dangerously ill, and I must go to her at once. Perhaps it is as well that I should leave you in this way. Our lives follow different paths. You have told me that you would do everything in your power to bind me to you, but that perhaps this would be beyond your strength. I know you love me. You will not forget me. I will wait for you.

Was that certainty on her part a form of pride? A way of expressing her sorrow? Or a form of self-deception? Sarah, in her sorrow and anguish, knew that, when she left Brussels that day, "the little Bernhardt" no longer existed; but that it was a woman, a woman in love, a woman resolved to fight, who was returning to Paris.

64

The Elder Dumas

Victor Hugo

The duc de Morny

Victorien Sardou

CHAPTER XII

DESTINY

"I THOUGHT your mother was going to die, but this morning the doctor pronounced her to be out of danger. I have told her you are here."

"Is mama still angry with me?"

"Since her illness, she seems to have forgiven you."

The taffeta curtains in Judy's room were drawn, allowing a shaft of pale blue daylight to filter between them. Judith Bernhardt lay back, her handsome face buried in a cloud of lace; her hands, clasped upon her chest as though in prayer, impressed Sarah.

"Mama! I'm here."

"You nearly came too late, my dear. But you could always have visited my grave."

"Madame Guérard's letter reached me very late."

"Evidently! Perhaps you had left the address you gave us?"

Sarah became crimson, and blessed the hand that had dimmed the light in the room.

"Anyway, we have a lot to discuss. This escapade of yours is a deplorable example for your sisters. But I am glad you have come back, Sarah. In spite of everything, you are my beloved little daughter, aren't you?" insisted the sick woman.

It would be nice to cry on that soft warm shoulder, to hug that mother to her, to tell her the whole amazing story, to describe the beloved features and to make her understand the marvellous passionate love which thenceforward would beat in the heart of her child; Sarah bent down to kiss her mother.

"Listen, mama!"

But Judith pushed her daughter gently away and her fine, short-sighted eyes sought Sarah's with more curiosity than tenderness.

"How strongly your hair smells of tobacco, child!"

.   .   .   .   .

"There, my Little Lady! Now you know everything. For the past five days I have been dashing all over the place to try to distract my mind from its obsession. For five days I have been waiting for news from Brussels. I tremble every time a bell rings. When I come in I question the maid. I don't say, 'Has a letter come for me?' but 'Give me my letter!' and she looks at me in surprise. I need scarcely tell you that I have bought her goodwill."

"And your mother?"

"She has not spoken to me yet. But I have decided upon one thing, which is that I am going to leave the Rue Saint-Honoré and take a small apartment in the Rue Auber. I have already signed the lease. Oh, don't scold me! I'm suffocating here. Mama is quite happy with Jeanne and Regina. Personally,

I have done with docility. I am devoted to mama but, as you know quite well, she suffers me to exist but she does not allow me to live."

"I quite understand," replied Madame Guérard sadly. "Besides, you are of full legal age, very much in love, and fundamentally an artist: three good reasons for wanting your liberty."

Sarah was chatting with her friend in the blue-green room. Absently, in order to put away a book, she opened the door of the cupboard which she used as a library.

"Hullo!" she said. "Jeanne's schoolbooks and toys! No doubt mama has already promised her my room."

This was no more nor less than the truth, and Madame Guérard began to cry.

"Very well, then!" went on Sarah in a hard voice. "As soon as mama is well I shall go to my new home."

"How do you propose to live?"

"I've still got a little money. As for the future, I am a fatalist, with that happy complete fatalism one can only have at the age of nineteen."

The Teutonic maid knocked on the door and handed Sarah two letters.

"If madame found out that I gave mademoiselle her letters direct, I should get the sack," she grumbled.

"There's one from him!" whispered Sarah. And her hands trembled with happiness, emotion and anxiety. But as she took in the contents of the letter the expression on her face changed to one of bitter disappointment. When she had finished she handed it to Madame Guérard, who read it through in her turn.

"Your matrimonial projects seem to be meeting with difficulties," she observed, "but don't be too depressed about it, Sarah. Your Prince loves you. His whole letter is filled with the ardour of that love. He implores you to have patience and especially to come back to him as soon as possible."

"His love is not strong enough to fight against his family. I was afraid of that. It is not only his living relatives who stand against me. There are those others, the ancestors; the dead, even more irreconcilable than the living. Their memory, their patrimony, their names all weight the scales heavily against me. How can I swing the balance in my favour with nothing but myself and my poor heart?"

"This young man has responsibilities towards you?"

"No, none at all!" replied Sarah quickly. "What I have done I have done of my own free will. Do you think I ought to go back to him?"

"What is in the other letter?" said Madame Guérard suddenly. "Where is it? What have you done with it?"

And the two women searched the room. The letter seemed to have vanished.

"The elementals have probably taken it," declared Sarah quietly. "Let's wait until they bring it back."

"Here it is!" cried Madame Guérard, grovelling beneath the bed. "It's from the Théâtre de l'Odéon."

"From the Odéon?" cried Sarah in excitement.

Slitting open the envelope, she ran quickly through the letter and suddenly she caught hold of her friend and began to dance and sing.

"Chilly has sent for me! Chilly himself! He is re-forming his company and wants to see me! Ah, my Little Lady! The Odéon! The young people's theatre where I have always dreamed of working!"

"Yes! But . . . the other summons? The other appointment?" stammered Madame Guérard. "The Prince?"

"I'll go and see him tomorrow in Brussels. No, I can't do that: my appointment with Chilly is for the day after tomorrow. What am I to do? Give me a coin quickly. As I am a fatalist I will follow the dictates of destiny, whatever they may be: heads I go to Brussels; tails I go to the Odéon."

"Heads! So you'll go to Brussels!" cried Madame Guérard.

Seated on the pink and green counterpane, Sarah held the Prince's letter in one hand and Chilly's letter in the other.

"What will Judy say?" said Madame Guérard disappointedly. "Besides, you mustn't let this young man think that you cannot live without him. Men are so vain! You ought to wait a few days."

"Don't alarm yourself," replied Sarah firmly. "I shan't go to Brussels."

"But won't you be sorry? And what about destiny?"

"Destiny often needs a little help from outside. I will go to the Odéon, and we'll see what happens afterwards."

And Sarah's eyes were full of tears.

CHAPTER XIII

"MADEMOISELLE SARAH BERNHARDT"

DURING her first months at the Odéon, Sarah was picked out for notice in several of her parts. Her personality was slowly making itself felt.

If the Beloved Monster was still being rather reserved, it was beginning to flirt with the young actress. It paid her compliments and added a few shouts of enthusiasm to its applause, and this by the intermediary of its most joyous and most daring representatives, the Paris students.

"Come and have supper with me this evening. My son wants to meet you."

Having just refused an invitation from the Prince, Sarah capriciously accepted one from Dumas, who had recently returned from Italy. The Prince de Ligne had come to France after his letter had remained unanswered for a week. "When you are by my side, I have more strength to fight," he said. He renewed his battle with his family to win this girl whom he loved. But, back in Brussels, the ancestors in the great hall refused to admit a little actress into their ranks.

The young people had not given up hope. They made their plans, light as card-houses, in the streets, in the wings of the theatre, amid the laughter of Montmartre and the scenery in the old quarters of the town, and in fashionable restaurants. And the Flower of Love refused to wither.

They were full of confidence in themselves, and a little mad.

· · · · ·

After a dull start, the month of July at last succeeded in keeping the sun in its sky. The real Parisians considered the choice of a seaside resort at which to spend their holidays. Some of them, suddenly discovering a taste for travel, chose the country which should have alarmed them most, namely Germany. The dandies were all either dead or decrepit, and those who remained in Paris venerated the country of Bismarck, applauded Offenbach, paid compliments to Winterhalter and bowed their heads reverently when they met German notabilities. Prussian blue was the fashionable colour.

Startled by the Americans, Parisian ladies smoked, and deserted the boudoir for the Champs-Élysées and the sofa for the victoria. Alone, the Empress chose neutral colours for her dresses. The Imperial French Eagle lived in the gilded cage of the Tuileries. The German Eagle sharpened its beak in silence.

The fashionable restaurant of the day, more than the Café Riche or the Café Hardy, was the Café de Paris; its clientele carried on the great French tradition of gastronomy combined with wit, which our ancestors have bequeathed to us with their arthritis. Round the tables were gathered Parisian and foreign notabilities and the dandies of the Second Empire, while the first democrats of the Third Republic were fussing about the Boulevard des Italiens in their carefully studied untidiness, their eyes shining with enthusiasm and their mouths full of trite maxims.

68

"What will you take, Sarah?"

"A fillet of sole. I'm not at all hungry. Tell me, Monsieur Dumas, who is the man who looks like a young Franz-Joseph of Austria at Madame Adelina Patti's table?"

"That Franz-Joseph," replied the younger Dumas, twirling his moustache, "is named Arthur Meyer. He is a good journalist and a good fellow. I will introduce him to you, and he will become one of your admirers."

"I would prefer him to be a friend."

A man of about thirty had just entered the Café de Paris; he looked around him rather awkwardly, then made rapidly for a table at which a diner sat alone. The two men exchanged a few words in an undertone and left the restaurant together.

"It is my turn to tell you now," said Sarah, smiling at the younger Dumas. "The man with the cropped hair is——"

"Henri de Rochefort," interrupted Dumas. "He is earnest, dangerous, but of superior intelligence."

"The other one was introduced to me yesterday at the Odéon. His name is Grambetta or Gambetta——"

"Léon Gambetta," corrected the elder Dumas. "He is a provincial lawyer and a Parisian politician. What do you think, Alexandre, of all the eyes riveted on Sarah? I'm getting jealous!"

"I am thinking of Madame Doche and of Marie Duplessis, the Lady of the Camélias!"

"You are the only man to whom Marie Duplessis, or, rather, Marguerite Gautier, has ever brought any money," observed the elder Dumas.

He laughed a little bitterly, thinking of the very moderate success of his last works.

"Head waiter!" he cried. "Can't you ask the orchestra to alternate its czardas with a few French pieces? If it searches long enough it may be able to find some."

Preceded by the Marquis de Massa, the young Comtesse de S—— made a sensational entry in a dress of precious white lace; she was flanked by Madame de Bartholony in a blue dress, and by another woman in red. A murmur of admiration ran through the room as they appeared.

"It's a living picture," remarked Dumas.

"More like a living flag," said someone.

Men in evening clothes accompanied this graceful trio. The last to enter was a fair, slim young man. Sarah blushed deeply.

"Look! There is the Prince de Ligne," she muttered carelessly.

The elder Dumas stole a glance at her and ordered more champagne. The younger Dumas went off to fetch Arthur Meyer, whom he wanted to introduce to Sarah Bernhardt.

When the Prince noticed her, he bowed with a sardonic smile which gave his face infinite charm. He timed his arrival at the Dumases' table to coincide with that of Arthur Meyer, so that, in a sort of general confusion, everyone was introduced to everyone else.

"Will you take a glass of champagne?" said Alexandre Dumas.

"With pleasure," replied the Prince. "We are rather like your Three

Musketeers, monsieur, and, like them, we are four, to defend Mademoiselle Bernhardt against the curiosity of the other diners."

There was some truth in this sally. Several people had recognized the Odéon actress and were pointing her out openly, which pleased the Dumases very much but irritated the Prince.

"I thought you were tired, my dear?"

"I was. But I no longer am."

"Why did you refuse to dine with me?" asked the young man in a low voice. "I have something to say to you."

"So have I," replied Sarah.

In a loud voice which rose above the music, the elder Dumas had launched into a story about Naples as interesting as it was remarkable, and from which the neighbouring tables also benefited. Under cover of this monologue and of the wild gypsy music of the orchestra, Sarah and the Prince held a private conversation of their own. They had parted that afternoon; the Prince looked at Sarah with sad solemnity.

"You've had news from Brussels?" she asked. "And not good news either?"

"Exactly. But I shall not give up the struggle. And you? What do you want to say to me?"

Sarah grew very pale and stammered something inaudibly.

"What?" said the Prince.

"Nothing. It's nothing of importance. You must go now. If you stay at this table any longer your friends will be annoyed with you."

Taking advantage of the fact that Dumas was pausing for breath and drinking a glass of champagne at the same time, the Prince took his leave of him and rejoined his guests.

"Monsieur Meyer, come and sit beside me. I want to talk to you."

The girl was visibly upset, but the journalist pretended to notice nothing, and congratulated her politely on her most recent performances.

"I thank you, monsieur, but I am conscious of the fact that the Lord of the Carriage has not yet noticed me."

"Anyway," put in the younger Dumas, "there's a young man over there looking for you. He doesn't look as if he had come from a carriage, but one can never tell."

"Heavens! My *concierge's* son! What on earth is he doing here?" And Sarah hurriedly crossed to the restaurant foyer where the porter was holding back a boy of thirteen or fourteen, who was gesticulating and pointing to the Dumases' table.

"Mademoiselle! My mother has sent me to tell you that your house is on fire."

"What! My apartment!"

"It's burning! You must hurry!"

Accompanied by the elder Dumas and Arthur Meyer, who asked to be allowed to come with them, Sarah left the Café de Paris in a whirl without a glance at her beloved Prince, who was dining with the women in the tricolour dresses.

Sarah was not particularly attached to her furniture, but this fire would leave her poor and homeless, and the thought of that distressed her so much

70

that she burst into tears. Sitting in the carriage, now leaning on Dumas's shoulder, now drying her eyes on Arthur Meyer's handkerchief, she felt rather sick; and the Prince's words kept coming back to her: "I will not abandon the struggle. The news is bad. What do you want to tell me?"

Fortunately, she had held her tongue.

.   .   .   .   .

A small crowd of night prowlers had gathered before Number 16 Rue Auber to get a good view of the fire; nor were they disappointed; long tongues of flame issued from Sarah's apartment and licked the outside walls.

"What a lovely fire!" someone exclaimed. Sarah could have killed him.

On learning that the young woman was the occupant of the doomed premises, the police allowed her carriage to draw up at a short distance from the fire, while the firemen went about their business, directing columns of water on the fierce flames. At the end of an hour the fire was under control, but from the first floor up the house was merely a black shell. Nothing was saved, and the cause of the disaster was never discovered.

"I know of one insurance company which will be pleased tomorrow," said Arthur Meyer.

"Yes. But I am afraid I am not insured."

"Not insured? But you're crazy!"

"I had meant to sign the proposal form, but I kept putting it off and now this has happened and I have lost everything!"

In despair, Sarah began to sob.

"Mademoiselle, please control yourself, I beg of you," gently insisted Arthur. "We will organize a benefit for you. Leave it to me."

But these words of comfort fell upon deaf ears, for Sarah suddenly fell forward unconscious in the carriage, crumpled up in her frilled dress of flowered muslin.

"Poor child! She's fainted. I'll take her back to her mother's house. Will you come too, Meyer?"

"Alas! I've still got my article for tomorrow to write."

Sarah did not recover consciousness until she reached the Rue Saint-Honoré. Cold perspiration lay upon her forehead. She was so weak that Dumas had to help her upstairs. Was Judith proud of this girl whose name was beginning to be heard on all sides like an echo reverberating in the mountains? Anyway, contrary to what the novelist feared, Judy made no objection or criticism, and did not embark on a lecture.

"Don't be distressed, darling, and go back to the blue-green room for as long as you like. Jeanne will sleep with the baby. I will send Madame Guérard to you. She is comforting Regina, who woke up and cried for you."

"One thing puzzles me," said Madame Guérard, bringing Sarah a cup of orange-flower infusion, "and that is that you should have fainted. Such sentimental weakness is so unlike you. Yes, I know . . . the insurance! And you will have to pay for the damage; but you've told me so often that your house only represented one more set of scenery to you."

"What are you trying to say?"

"You're hiding something from me. Your maid told me that you weren't feeling well this morning; you're ill and you won't admit it. Have you been spitting blood again?"

Sarah, in her long nightgown, looked like a Nordic fairy with eyes like deep pools and silken hair. She leaned towards Madame Guérard, who was seated on the bed, and took her friend's soft face between her hands. She muttered something which Madame Guérard did not catch.

"What did you say, Sarah?"

Then Sarah put her lips close to her friend's ear, and Madame Guérard went through a series of emotions. At first she was terrified, then delighted, then she wept.

"Heavens! What are you going to do?"

"Work! Work! Live for my art, and for the little child that is soon to be born. Oh no! Don't be sorry for me. I am happy! Happy!"

CHAPTER XIV

AT LAST!

FOUR years passed. Sarah scored no sensational success at the Odéon, but the little star was rising to the firmament in different parts: *Le Marquis de Villemer, François le Champi,* etc.

Sarah now lived in the Rue de Rome with her son Maurice, nearly four years old, her maid, Félicie, and Madame Guérard. Judith Bernhardt had put on weight and tired very easily: she seldom left home but continued to receive her friends; apart from Dumas and Régis, the Rue Saint-Honoré coterie had changed; there one could meet a Marshal of France with long hair, François-Certain Canrobert; a young politician, formerly a Havre tanner, of the same name as Sarah's uncle: Félix Faure. Meydieu and Rossini were dead, and so also was Charles de Morny, the delightful friend and grand seigneur, of whom Sarah often thought, "Put her in the Conservatoire."

Jeanne the Favourite still possessed her pretty face and her odious character. Regina rarely spoke save to talk to her sister in a broken voice and to say loving things to her, interspersed with vulgarity.

One day in January 1869, Sarah was sitting with her little boy while he ate his luncheon; her love for him was fierce and selfish. As she was unable to devote the whole day to this fat, pink, boisterous child, she had given him into the charge of a young nurse; but as soon as her son was out of her sight, hearing and reach Sarah worried about him. When the child was only a few months old his nurse had orders to wheel him only between the first and the twelfth tree in the Champs-Élysées, and when Judith laughed at her alarms, Sarah replied: "I am always afraid someone will substitute another little boy for Maurice."

When she heard that her daughter was about to become a mother Madame Bernhardt was no more shocked than she had been when the apartment in the Rue Auber burned without being insured. The really important happenings in life left Judy indifferent, for she believed that they were all predestined. In her love of order and with her middle-class mind, she felt it was unfortunate that there was no father present at Maurice's baptism. But at the same time Madame Bernhardt was a woman to the tips of her tapering fingers, and she was touched that her daughter, an actress, could, in the atmosphere of "the horrible theatre" and of cardboard scenery and painted people, of those wings which were never properly scrubbed down, preserve the weaknesses and the feelings of a woman, and an impressionable heart, and that all this should have resulted for Sarah in this radiant motherhood, utterly indifferent to what people might say and only thinking of the joy of kissing this pretty little boy and of his fragrant smell of youth, eau-de-Cologne and milk.

Lunch was over. The nurse was patiently listening to her mistress's instructions, while Maurice, with a spade on his shoulder, was toddling about among the dining-room chairs.

The front-door bell rang violently and, as Félicie was out, Madame Guérard answered it. And as soon as the door opened the apartment was filled with clatter, footsteps and laughter.

"Sarah, I've got some news for you!" cried Dumas. "Not ordinary, not everyday news."

"Is it good news?"

"Good for me: and I hope good for you too. Your friend, Arthur Meyer, is the only one who knows."

(Arthur Meyer had kept his word: some days after the fire in the Rue Auber he organized a benefit performance with the help of Adelina Patti, Marquise de Caux; it was a huge success, and the "Great-hearted Nightingale", as Sarah called her, sang to a packed audience.)

"Well, what is it?"

Dumas was so excited that he struck the sideboard with the handle of his walking-stick and knocked off a plate.

"That's lucky," said Sarah, laughing, "but don't break them all."

"You are going to act in *Kean*, my dear. I've arranged it with Chilly. Rehearsals start in ten days."

"The part of Anna Damby? Oh, how lovely! Anyway, you promised me that part, master, 'When you become sensible,' you told me. Have I become sensible?"

"Certainly not!" exclaimed the novelist, impetuously. "But you've become a good actress."

. . . . .

(In relating Sarah Bernhardt's life, I must sometimes allude to certain political or historical facts about which she spoke to me. Her life as an artist, her personality, her ardent patriotism, which worked itself up into a perpetual "National Defence", as it were, were too often mixed up with them.

I cannot, in order to simplify my task, just slur over the background of the fresco she painted for me in telling me of her long life of work, struggles, sorrows and victories. So I apologize now for all these reminiscences.)

. . . . .

In February 1868, Victor Hugo was in exile. But his formidable work grew, like a beautifully designed granite monument. To some people Hugo was the symbol of democracy; to others he was the author of eight dramas in verse; to others again an outlaw whose plays must be acted during his exile; but for all of them he was Hugo, the great Hugo, peer of France and academician.

Feelings were running high in Paris. On the night of the revival of *Kean* the audience was a seething, growling mob, laughing at all the wrong places. Chilly was at his wits' end and the nerves of the actors were strung to breaking point. The Beloved Monster in the velvet-upholstered stalls was unsheathing its claws, and was employing its lungs to shout and its lips to whistle.

The matter was further complicated for Dumas by a sentimental story of which no one understood very much, except that the novelist intended to be present at this revival with a lady who was not popular with the public. When his imposing bulk appeared in a box beside this lady they were both well and truly booed. The lady left in confusion and Dumas was then applauded.

Sarah saw all this through the spy-hole in the curtain. She was happy and

74

yet uneasy: happy in her part, but uneasy about the audience; uneasy also about her dress, which had been rather boldly designed by the costumier with the connivance of the management.

"Keep your chins up, my children," said Chilly, before the curtain went up. "Do your very best. Even if the public shouts too loud."

"Hugo! Hugo! Hugo!" cried the Monster. "We want *Ruy Blas*! *Ruy Blas*!"

The curtain rose in the middle of this shouting. Dumas, seated in his box, drummed his fingers nervously on the back of a chair, muttering imprecations which must have surpassed in precision and vehemence those of the audience. The entry of the actor Berton failed to calm the over-excited audience, and when Sarah Bernhardt made her appearance dressed as an eccentric English-woman she provoked such a cascade of laughter and catcalls that she stopped in bewilderment. Her heart was racing, her hands were icy cold. However, a few students, aware of her distress, applauded her loudly, to the accompaniment of "Sh's" and angry exclamations on the part of their neighbours.

"Despite all, I will speak. I *will* speak."

And when it came to her turn to deliver her long tirade, the one in which she confesses her love for Kean, Sarah faced the audience and addressed herself directly to it in a loud, clear voice, which she toned down as she proceeded. The music of her voice left the young woman's lips, passed over the footlights and distributed its charm like a philtre, and the scene ended in complete silence: no one either spoke, or coughed, or moved. Then from the height of this temple rolled out the thunder of the applause. It rolled out in the gallery and broke out afresh in the stalls. Sarah had won the day. The curtain was raised five times as she took her calls.

After the last act, Chilly congratulated his pupil.

"You were amazing. I owe you more than I can say, and so does Dumas."

"Why has the master not come to see me?" asked Sarah. "I would like to have hugged him. Have you seen Maurice, Félicie? Was he asleep?"

"Sleeping like an angel."

"Are you sure he wasn't flushed?"

"Oh no, mademoiselle. Not at all."

"But he wasn't too pale, I hope?"

Félicie reassured Sarah as, seated before the mirror in her dressing-room, she removed the greasepaint from her face with large dabs of cold cream.

"I wonder what would become of us if young Maurice were to catch a cold," murmured Chilly, with affectionate irony. "We would have to make a public announcement about it."

There was a knock on the door and the stage-manager whispered something in Chilly's ear. Chilly's face lit up with a smile.

"What's the matter?"

"Nothing; but if you will allow me, I will see you to your carriage. Have you one of your own?"

"I've got Aunt Rosine's. She always lends it to me when she goes away. Where is Madame Guérard?"

"She has gone off with Madame Bernhardt, who was exhausted, but delighted with mademoiselle's success," replied Félicie brightly, picking up the little bunches of violets thrown by the students.

"Give me those flowers!"

Sarah pinned them on to her toque, her mantle and her muff.

"They will keep my heart warm."

"Are you coming?" asked Chilly, impatiently.

They descended the steps leading from the dressing-rooms to the stage-door. Sarah, who was chattering gaily, suddenly stopped and clutched her manager's arm.

"What is that noise outside! Can you hear it? It sounds like a riot of some sort."

"Yes!" said Chilly, laughing. "A nice little riot. Open that door," he said to the stage-door keeper, who, with his eye glued to the peep-hole, seemed prodigiously interested by something in the street.

"You go first. I'm afraid of being hit."

The young woman stared indignantly at Chilly, but, in the meantime, the door was opened and Sarah found herself on the threshold, lit up by the gas-bracket on the stairs. In the cold night air, one cry only, uttered by a hundred voices, greeted the actress: "Bravo!" And while she hesitated, not realizing yet what was happening, and while Chilly, behind her, was quietly laughing and Rosine's coachman, standing on his box, was beckoning to her with his whip, her name was being repeated over and over again by the deep ranks of the crowd which she could not distinguish between her and the carriage.

"Long live Sarah Bernhardt! Bravo, Sarah! Long live Sarah!"

And Sarah clung to Chilly's arm for support. She was overcome. Thus, after six years, the Beloved Monster turned its face towards her, looked for her, recognized her, wanted her! Falteringly, as though going to her first love-tryst, she advanced towards it and her smile was like a flower on her lips.

When she reached the carriage Sarah turned to greet this swaying crowd of people and to thank them. Then a man's hand, issuing from the interior of the carriage, helped her to get in.

"I wanted to kiss you. . . . This evening, for the first time, the carriage awaits you at the theatre door: you have conquered talent."

And old Dumas, leaving by the far door, disappeared into the night.

A swarm of young people crowded round the actress's carriage.

"Don't be afraid, Sarah! Here are some more violets, mademoiselle! Bravo! Bravo! You are our fairy! Slow there with the horses. Coachman, get down and lead them. They may get frightened. Michard, undo the traces. Come on, you others, take the shafts! And the rest of you, push behind!"

Having taken the horses from the shafts, the students gaily pulled the carriage and, as they went along, the people in the streets entered into the spirit of the party and followed them, swelling the cortège. Yes! The carriage for which she had waited so long was now, indeed, rolling down the street, accompanied by laughter and song! And Sarah, like every woman whose nerves have been strung to breaking point and who does not know what to do with her heart and her emotions and her actions, began to cry softly to herself.

At the Boulevard Saint-Germain the police stopped Aunt Rosine's carriage. But they could not stop the carriage which, thenceforward, carried the young woman on a marvellous journey throughout the world.

PART TWO

CHAPTER XV

THAT 19TH OF JULY, 1870

BEFORE ringing at the apartment in the Rue de Rome, the younger Dumas wiped his forehead.

The warmth of the day was not the only reason for this unwelcome perspiration. On his way down the Boulevards, Dumas had passed rows of soldiers and mobs of young men singing the *Marseillaise*, blocking the street with their bodies, while other men were furiously shouting: "To Berlin! To Berlin!"

The famous telegram of July 13, 1870, arranged by Bismarck, had precipitated events. Diplomacy was unable to patch up what Diplomacy had shattered. Germany had injected the microbe and France felt the fever mounting in her veins.

"It is a disgrace! The Empire will fall in ruins!" cried the Empress Eugénie.

Sarah did not believe that the conflict was imminent. With her straightforward, hasty, but loyal character, how could she disentangle the skein of international politics, weaving all its plots in the dark, like some monstrous spider?

On that 19th of July, Sarah had just finished her toilette. Her little boy was playing beside her, as she had refused to let him go out with his nurse into the hot, crowded streets. The apartment in the Rue de Rome was a picturesque jumble. It already contained many of those heterogeneous objects which grew in volume during her turbulent life: objects given to her by various people, or bought by Sarah in all the four quarters of the globe. Sarah was more interested in the shape or the colour of a curio than its origin, its antiquity or its value, and, although some of these souvenirs were precious or rare, others were frankly hideous. Sarah Bernhardt had an intense dislike of period style in furnishing a room. In 1870 her apartment contained Dutch sixteenth-century furniture, copper bowls and particularly vases, for which she always showed a great predilection. "If they are ugly," she would say, "one can always fill them with flowers. If they are beautiful one can sell them!" Bright-coloured silks were draped over the backs of the chairs; she had inherited from her mother a taste for striped materials, acquired in colonial bazaars or from the great silk merchants of Paris or Amsterdam, or from those itinerant merchants who wander about the world.

She also conformed to the taste of the period. A queer taste, tending to confusion. She hated bare walls, and uncovered floors "like skeletons showing their bones". So the floors were covered with pile carpets, oriental rugs and furs on which lived and frolicked Sarah's "familiars". Dogs, cats and pumas, with charming fantastic names. Birds chirped in their cages, and on perches magpies, cockatoos and grey parrots chattered, screeched and chuckled, all of them behaving fairly reasonably among the hangings and the flowers which bloomed

77

and faded in the bowls which even stood on the carpets. The drawing-room and the other rooms were not only scented with the perfume of this mass of flowers, but they were also impregnated with strong, clinging essences, with their amber and jasmine bases, which Sarah sprayed all over them, emptying her scent-bottles even on the cushions and the curtains.

When the younger Dumas was announced, Sarah hastened away to put on a dress. Maurice, now six years old, was wearing a policeman's helmet made for him by Félicie, and was giving his own version of the shouts which came from the street:

"To Berlin! Hoop-la! On my little grey horse!"

"Be quiet, darling! Félicie, tell Monsieur Dumas that I will be with him in five minutes. Maurice is not to go out without Monsieur Régis."

The five minutes became ten and then lengthened into fifteen. In the drawing-room Dumas curiously examined a canvas on which Sarah was working, representing a girl dressed in grey against a grey background. He smiled.

"So like her to seek out such difficulties!" Grey on grey. Actually he did not know that the young actress had a taste for painting. And it was not so bad. Some rather childish mistakes in composition, but a sense of colour and probably a rather good likeness; the drawing was, however, a little weak.

A slight noise made him turn his head: his straw hat, which he had left on an armchair, was being slowly dragged beneath it by a large velvety paw with alarming-looking claws. Dumas took a step forward to save his headgear but the "tiger" (which is how the animal appeared to him) suddenly revealed himself, forestalling Dumas and crossing his fore-paws over the hat. And he slowly devoured it, relishing it straw by straw, every now and then casting a steady look at the novelist from his beautiful black-ringed green eyes. Dumas was furious, yet he dared neither call for help nor stretch his hand out towards the bell-pull. At the slightest movement this stupid catamount showed his teeth: and what teeth!

"A good idea of mine to come here this morning. She must be mad to live with a puma!"

Fortunately, someone in the courtyard called out and the animal left the armchair and bounded out of the room through the door hangings.

"You're an idiot, sir! You're an idiot, sir!"

Dumas started and felt a light weight on his shoulder; with great care a grey parrot was removing his cravat and tugging at his collar while carrying on his monologue. "You're an idiot, sir! Pretty Polly! Pretty Polly!"

"Go away, you nasty beast!"

But the bird gave the visitor a peck on the cheek which kept him quiet. The parrot now turned its attention to his waistcoat buttons, and one was already off when a couple of collies bounded into the room, barking and jostling each other. This frightened the parrot, which released Dumas from its remarks and its beak and fluttered clumsily to the top of the easel emitting feminine shrieks.

"I must get out of here!" thought the author; but as he reached for the manuscript he had brought with him one of the collies seized it and held it in his mouth.

"Don't you dare touch that book!" the faithful hound seemed to be growling, while the other dog, which was more hospitable, placed its great paws so roughly on Dumas's shoulders that he lost his balance and fell back on the sofa, dragging with him in his fall a large cauldron full of water and peonies.

"God Almighty!" he roared. "What a madhouse!"

A cool laugh answered him. Sarah stood, fair and diaphanous in a white dress, at the top of the three steps leading down to the drawing-room; the sunlight was caught in her hair. She was about to apologize, but when she saw Dumas with his trousers soaking, his collar torn, his cravat missing, his waistcoat undone and a wild look in his eye, she was seized with such a fit of laughter that she collapsed on the bearskin.

"No doubt it's all very funny," said the visitor, rising abruptly from the sofa, "but personally I think the joke is in the worst possible taste."

"Oh, I'm so sorry!" stuttered Sarah. "The *concierge* usually looks after my animals, but he has been so agitated by all that's going on that he forgot to shut the cage-doors. I really am mortified. My pumas are never allowed in the drawing-room except when I am there myself, and then they always behave beautifully."

"Really? And what about the parrot which pulls off buttons? And the dogs which devour manuscripts?"

"They all got loose by mistake," said Sarah, sincerely contrite. "I beg you not to be angry. Have you any news of your father? We're not going to war, are we?"

"I am afraid so," replied the author, slightly mollified. "I came to give a manuscript into your keeping, but that idiotic dog ran away with it."

"Ahasuerus!" cried Sarah to the dog skulking beneath the piano. "Bring it here. Bring it here at once!"

The dog left his hiding-place and came and meekly licked his mistress's hand.

"Where is the note-book, Ahasuerus? Are you sure, my friend, that it was Ahasuerus who took your manuscript? I think it is more likely to have been Esther; she is incorrigible."

"What do I care whether the dog is called Ahasuerus, Esther, or even Mordecai?" cried Dumas, suddenly losing his temper. "All I know is that my hat has been devoured, my manuscript has disappeared, my trousers are soaking wet and my waistcoat buttons have been torn off. If I am ever mad enough to give you a part, madame, I will beg you to meet me at the theatre and not in a zoological garden."

"Mama!" said Maurice, jumping down the three steps. "Here's a book I found in Esther's mouth. I thought it was one of your parts."

And the charming little curly-haired boy solemnly handed his mother the famous manuscript, of which only the title-page was missing.

"Thank heaven not much harm has been done. This is my son, Maurice. I apologize again, and now, monsieur, you have my leave to go," Sarah concluded coldly, because Dumas's bad temper was beginning to get on her nerves.

Mortified, Alexandre Dumas bowed, took his manuscript, and made a dignified exit. But as he reached the street he collided violently with a newspaper boy who was tearing down the street crying "War declared!" and who ran straight into him. Without hesitation, Dumas climbed the stairs back to Sarah's apartment four steps at a time. She opened the door herself.

"War, madame! War is declared!"

She stared at him uncomprehendingly.

"War? War? How awful!"

"Yes. And I wanted to tell you . . . I'm sorry for my bad temper. Take this manuscript. Read it. Oh, you know it by heart, but, just the same, study the part. You would be perfect in it. Good-bye!"

Sarah shook hands with him.

.   .   .   .   .

War! Sarah put away Dumas's manuscript without even having the curiosity to open it. War! No doubt the theatres would close. What was to become of her? France in a state of war. The Emperor's eyes, those light eyes fringed with long lashes, haunted her. Was it true that Eugénie de Montijo had forced the country into this conflict which she called "her war"? Sarah could not believe it. She recalled the reception given at the Tuileries when she and Agar went there to play François Coppée's *Le Passant*, during the triumphal run of that little masterpiece at the Odéon. The Empress had been charming, with admirable eyes, tiny feet, but an ugly voice. No! Fate, against which man had no defence, was what led to wars: that was the real truth! The Emperor did not want this catastrophe and only submitted to it against his will, so that France should not be humiliated in his own person. "Brutes! Yes! To Berlin!" Sarah found herself thinking, though she hated that word "war".

.   .   .   .   .

But was everything irremediably lost? A miracle might occur at the last moment. In which case the Odéon would continue its performances of *Jean-Marie*, in which Sarah and Porel (the Parfouru of the Conservatoire) scored a nightly success. Ever since *Le Passant*, Sarah's little star shone more and more brightly and became more firmly fixed in the sky. What, actually, was this play that Dumas had handed her, and why had he not gone to Chilly in the first place? A revival? Oh, this war!

The memory of a face with fair hair and a cynical youthful smile brought a melancholy softness into Sarah's eyes. What would he say, what would he do, when he learned that France was going to fight? France in which his son, their son, was growing up as a Frenchman.

She decided to find out immediately what the manuscript was that Alexandre Dumas had brought her. That same afternoon, when she went out driving with Maurice and Madame Guérard—if one was still able to go for a drive—she would take the author back his manuscript, with a polite note. Sarah lay down on her bed. In the next room Maurice went on playing soldiers with Madame Guérard, who had just arrived.

"I wonder why my Little Lady goes to see my son first? She thinks I don't notice. Ah, of course, the title of this play is now reposing in Esther's stomach!"

Sarah glanced through the list of characters: Marguerite Gautier, Armand

Sarah's studio in the Rue Fortuny

Sarah Bernhardt and her son Maurice in the Rue Fortuny

Duval, Georges Duval, Nichette. She got up a little flushed, and smiled. *"La Dame aux Camélias,"* she thought. "Yes, I could play that part. The play is conventional, but very moving." Into what depths of despair must that woman have been driven for her to renounce not only her lover, but that purity which she had suddenly assumed like a white robe among the dresses of her harlotry?

Sarah read the first act, then the second act. Confused sounds rose from the street. People stood in a knot beneath her window, arguing. The weather was amazingly fine, as it always is when disaster is impending.

"Leave me alone," she told Madame Guérard, who came to the door. "Don't interrupt me. Tell Félicie to serve luncheon in ten minutes' time. Go and entertain mama and Porel. And see that Maurice's hair is brushed and that his nails are clean."

The third act: Marguerite was going to die and Sarah was quite carried away and reached for her handkerchief. She had forgotten the war. The light pouring through the window was so comforting. How could men dream of fighting one another when God gave them the sun, which did not belong to any country, flowers blooming in every soil, and Art, always ready to fill people's minds with different emotions? Down below the *Marseillaise* broke out. First the music, no doubt from the band of a passing regiment, then the words sung by hundreds of voices—young, ardent voices, among older, more serious voices. Sarah, her eyes reddened by her reading, dropped the manuscript and ran to the window. The Rue de Rome was black with people, and a huge crowd followed the soldiers marching along in their red trousers.

People shouted to them and threw them flowers. Rude's *Le Départ* appeared before Sarah's eyes with its inexorable face and its wide-open mouth. *"Aux armes, citoyens!"* sang Sarah with the crowd.

Tears of sadness welled into her eyes to join those of Marguerite Gautier.

CHAPTER XVI

THE WAR OF 1870

AFTER the armistice of November 11, 1918, when the question arose of a theatrical tour in reconquered Alsace, my grandmother spoke to me of the other war, and of "that province torn from France which would always leave a raw wound in the country".

"Lysiane," she said, "I promised you some notes about 1870. Call Pitou."

Pitou, who was then my grandmother's secretary, was an intelligent youth with monastic features and an inborn love of music; he deplored the fact that Sarah Bernhardt was a great tragedienne rather than a great singer. He put a great deal of imagination into his work and I remember several disputes between my grandmother and him which ended in drama or in comedy. He exasperated her, arguing with her over the most unimportant matters. "You're a miserable wretch!" Sarah Bernhardt would tell him, in a rage. "You're trying to make me kill you, but I won't do it!"

Instead of letting the storm pass, Pitou, using a screen or a door as a shield, would continue his explanations and his peevish gesticulations until some projectile, aimed with a sure hand, crashed against the door or the screen. That was the drama.

The comedy consisted in the repartees of this eccentric secretary. My grandmother often reproached him for his slovenly appearance.

"Really, my poor Pitou, your jacket is disgusting. With all the money I give you, you can at least be clean."

"Which you give me, madame?" Pitou replied, in a pleading voice. "You mean which you promise me!"

One day she gave him a letter to be handed personally to a high official at Aix-la-Chapelle, and before his departure she gave him minute instructions as to how to deliver it. However, when he reached Germany he found that the addressee was not at home when he first called, so he posted the letter in the Aix post-office and quietly returned to Paris by train. On another occasion towards, I think, 1920, I entered my grandmother's boudoir in the Boulevard Pereire; she was seated in her cretonne-covered armchair and was studying a part; I was about to withdraw, when she raised her head.

"Hear my part for me, Lyseron."

Then I observed, in amazement, that my grandmother's ears were stuffed with cotton-wool.

"I don't want to listen to Pitou's idiotic remarks any more," she explained.

For a fortnight they communicated with each other through the medium of a little note-book.

"I'm going to the post-office, madame," wrote Pitou.

"No, don't go to the post-office, Pitou," replied Sarah Bernhardt.

And Pitou, to annoy my grandmother, went to the post-office.

However, on that day in November 1918, my grandmother asked her secretary to look in her archives for certain papers relating to the previous war.

A bright fire burned in the grate and my grandmother, whose leg had been amputated since 1916, was resting and chatting with me. When I shut my eyes I can see every detail of that boudoir dressing-room: to the left a large marble washstand, with two taps in the shape of swans' necks; before the window a dressing-table surmounted by a mirror and covered with scent bottles and cosmetics; on the right there were several large cupboards; one of these was kept locked and contained "letters which should not be left about". Another, which held Sarah Bernhardt's clothes, also concealed a small safe of which everyone in the Boulevard Pereire knew the combination. In this safe were kept copper cylinders bearing Sarah's motto, in which she kept her gold, as she always insisted upon part of her salary being paid in gold coins. To complete the picture, add two or three dogs snoring or yapping, and masses of flowers.

But to return to our papers.

"What notes do you mean?" asked Pitou.

"My personal notes relating to my ambulance at the Odéon, my journey to Hamburg, etc."

"I'm afraid," said Pitou, waving his arms and hopping from one foot to the other, "that I don't remember quite where I put those papers."

"My poor boy, I bought you a filing cabinet which cost four thousand francs and you don't know where to find my papers? Look under G. Yes, G for Guerre."

"I would only find documents relating to the 1914 war."

"Well, then. Look under A for Ambulance."

A quarter of an hour later, still hopping about and gesticulating, Pitou returned.

"Madame, you must have used those notes for your *Memoirs*; I can't find them anywhere."

The situation was becoming alarming, and I envisaged the moment when Sarah, by her own unaided efforts, simply by holding on to pieces of furniture (I had already once seen her perform this difficult feat), would go to the library, "Pitou's lair", and throw everything into confusion.

"I am surrounded by traitors!" scolded my grandmother. "All my things get lost or stolen!"

I myself searched through the four-thousand-franc filing-cabinet; O for Odéon, R for Rome, B for bombardments. And suddenly Pitou rushed joyfully into the boudoir.

"Here they are, madame! Here are your papers!"

"And where did you find them, my poor friend?"

"Under M, madame."

"Why M?"

"M," explained Pitou, triumphantly, "for Misfortune. When I filed the papers I put into one pigeon-hole all the misfortunes of your life. Yes, madame; see how easy it is. Under M you will find your notes relating to the 1870 war, the fire in the Rue Auber, the death of Madame Bernhardt and of your sisters and of your husband Monsieur Damala, your operation——"

He did not finish. A flower-vase, flung straight at him, missed Pitou's obstinate head by inches and smashed against the marble washstand. I quickly shut the door on the secretary.

Sarah then handed me a school copybook, torn and yellow with age. It was full of pencilled notes in that firm, illegible handwriting in which each word ended in a straight line. When my father protested that he could not always decipher her letters, she replied, "How can I find time to finish my words?"

"July 28, at Metz, the Emperor takes command of our army; and this set me thinking of that evening at the Tuileries when I walked on his arm. On August 1, three divisions attacked Saarbruck under the eyes of the Prince Imperial, a charming youth with rather a sad smile."

"I was tormented by that war. Each of these events affected my health, Lysiane. One morning I started spitting blood again. I went off to Eaux-Bonnes with Maurice and Madame Guérard. At first the war news was not alarming. Every day I sent Félicie to read the despatches pinned up in the Casino. My friend Canrobert's heroic defence; Gravelotte; September 1: Sedan! I only gathered the details of that disaster bit by bit: the Germans turning the French Army at Bazeilles and Donchéry, the heroic charge of Galliffet's cavalry, the Emperor having the white flag hoisted over Sedan. When Félicie returned from the Casino for perhaps the fifth time that day I was tired to death. Did Maurice, your father, seated beside me, understand the gravity of the hour? He, who was usually so restless, was looking at a picture-book and humming softly to himself, being unable, in spite of everything, to prevent himself from being a happy, healthy little boy. From Félicie's expression and her pallor, I knew that some great misfortune must have occurred. She held a piece of paper in her hand.

" 'Give it to me quickly,' I said, like a condemned man impatient to swallow his poison. And I read, 'The Emperor Napoleon III has surrendered his sword to the King of Prussia.' I hardly had time to send Maurice away. A bitter taste rose into my mouth, and the wounds of France sank into my own lungs. I fainted in a hæmorrhage.

"But if Death disregards you, you can recover from anything, from a hæmorrhage or even from a disaster. I returned to Paris, where my mother told me that Maurice must not remain there under any pretext whatever. Capitulation did not imply immediate peace. I submitted willingly to my mother's reasoning. She adored my son and would know how to look after him and how to protect him. And on the following morning three assorted vehicles drawn by three old screws went from the Rue Saint-Honoré to the station, bearing my mother, my sisters, my little boy, Aunt Rosine and Aunt Annette."

"Aunt Annette? Where does she come in? You have never mentioned her to me before."

"I must have forgotten her. The stations were attacked, so to speak, by maddened crowds, and trains were taken by assault. But my mother had her own way of dealing with crowds: she had herself preceded by two or three energetic friends who, with their elbows out, walked along crying, "Make way there!" And if anyone crowded my mother or jostled a child, she would pinch the offender's arm or would dig him in the stomach with her fist or her elbow.

"In the booking-office the crowd was terrifying. 'You are cowards, yes, cowards and idiots!' cried my mother, furiously. But in the end, my dear ones got on board the train somehow or other. One after the other I kissed these creatures of my own blood, whom I would perhaps never see again. When I

84

finally decided to leave their compartment the train was already moving, and I ran beside the carriage to have a last word with my adored little boy, who wept and held his arms out to me. As the rattle of the train died away, so the tumult in my heart became more imperative. Why had I remained in Paris? The crowd pulled and pushed me to the station entrance; exhausted, I had lost my hat, my bodice was torn and my morale was in shreds."

"But, grandmother, do you remember September 1914? The departure platforms of the Quai d'Orsay? The closed gates?"

"Yes, it was once more war in the East! But this time, my child, you do not need me to tell you about it. Look. Among the papers which Pitou has unearthed, here is the poster about my ambulance at the Odéon and here, edited by Madame Chesneau, an account of the journey we undertook after the armistice, thanks to the kindness of Monsieur Thiers, to go and fetch Maurice from Hamburg. Because your great-grandmother thought it would be a subtle move to go and live in Germany at the end of hostilities. While I thought my son was living quietly in Havre, I received a short note telling me that 'they were all safe and sound at Hamburg-les-Bains!' Mama explained to me later that, in view of the gravity of events, she had thought it better to be 'already' in Germany."

"And your ambulance?"

"I have already described this tragedy in four acts in my *Memoirs*: the war, the siege of Paris, the bombardment, the Commune. And the unfortunate wounded who died because there was no room in the hospitals. And that January night when they brought me more wounded than my rooms could hold, and the poignant appeal of the stretcher-bearers in the street crying: 'Ambulance! Ambulance!'

"Look, Lysiane, take all these papers away and let me rest. This delving into those years of war has made me tired, so tired, just as though I really was seventy-eight years old.")

.   .   .   .   .

(Extracts taken at random from Sarah Bernhardt's note-book.)

"December 5th, 1870. Death of my poor friend Alexandre Dumas the elder, at Puys.

"January 9th, 1871. The bombardment increases in vigour. The following places suffered: the Louis-le-Grand school, the churches of Sainte-Barbe, the Home for Sick Children, the Salpêtrière, the Luxembourg, the Val-de-Grace Military Hospital. The hospitals seem to be the main targets of the besiegers. Ominous whistlings and people take refuge in their cellars. In the Rue Blomet a shell fell in the middle of a crowd of people waiting for their wood vouchers; bombardment of Southern Paris. The bombardment usually starts at 10 at night and goes on until the morning."

Those, in their bitter brevity, are a few lines from Sarah Bernhardt's notes on the 1870 war.

Although reunited with her family, Sarah was still unable to live in Paris.

The Franco-Prussian War was over, but the fratricidal war was beginning. Sarah Bernhardt's devotion, her courage under the bombardment, her strength of character, her daily struggle to save the wounded, her skirmishes with the authorities to obtain food and medical supplies for her ambulance, were all so many efforts which she now felt had been wasted. United with all Frenchmen against the common enemy, Germany, could she now approve of one political party more than another? Gambetta was her friend, and Henri de Rochefort, and Paul de Rémusat, and Émile Zola and Georges Clémenceau, with whom she quarrelled and made it up several times, and many others of different cliques. Sarah loved the Third Republic, as people loved it under the Empire; but she also loved Napoleon III, "over-confident and very unhappy"; why should people insult the captive? The Emperor's detractors, who supported their speeches with the word "fraternity", were sadly lacking in logic. And, lastly, the revolutionary power set up in Paris after the raising of the siege revolted her as something hideous. What did these "rebels against everything", fostered by German propaganda, want?

For Sarah Bernhardt the street-fighting was much more terrible than the battles of the war; her friends were shooting her friends. Before the posters pasted on the walls of public buildings, soldiers and others stood and allowed themselves to be caught by these political snares, like flies on a flypaper.

Sarah fled to Saint-Germain with Madame Guérard and Maurice; there she entertained an occasional friend, rode in the forest, studied and painted.

One evening, on the terrace with its orderly trees, the wind brought a swirl of blackened paper; a smell of smoke reached the pleasant town. Paris was in flames.

. . . . .

At the end of May 1871 "that horrid little Thiers with his perverse, middle-class mind", as Sarah described him in her *Memoirs*, had the last word. The Commune was dead; the Republic, bruised but full of courage, rose from among the débris. She shook out her apron, adjusted her cap of liberty, counted her dead, and paid her debts, £200,000,000! Sarah had but one thought: her beloved Odéon Theatre, scarred by shell-fire. She hired a carriage and left Saint-Germain; the travellers passed the Neuilly barrier, went down the Champs-Élysées and reached the centre of the city. Alas! War and Revolution had left their marks on the fair face of Paris; here and there gaped burned-down houses; the streets had caved in and in certain houses, whose front walls were missing, pink or blue wallpaper, looking ludicrously new, could still be seen. The streets were disgustingly dirty, the house doors were begrimed and the houses themselves bespattered with bullet-holes and filth. A smell of burning hung in the air. The people in the street seemed to have nowhere to go; squalid children begged outside the shops and played in the sewers.

. . . . .

But the chestnut and plane trees on the avenues and boulevards were putting out their fresh, clean new foliage. Sun and sap, indifferent to ruins and human misery, were accomplishing their mission. Sarah, who had been chattering gaily with her friend when they left Saint-Germain, was silent now.

She held Maurice close to her for the comfort of feeling that her child was alive, warm and young.

What had happened to her dear Paris? It appeared to her like a neglected convalescent who still reeks of his illness and his medicaments. She thought of the mothers, the wives, the sweethearts of the dead, some of whom died to defend the "sweet land of France" and others because someone howled at them that these defenders, their brothers in arms of yesterday, were traitors. The inconsistency of humanity, its stupidity, its presumption, filled Sarah with almost intolerable grief, and she began to cry quietly, her face buried in the hair of her strong, brave, loving son, who would himself one day become a man.

    .   .   .   .   .

On their return to the Rue de Rome, Sarah began to tidy up her house. This, too, reeked of smoke. She sprayed the cushions and the curtains with scent and sent Maurice out with Madame Guérard to buy fresh stocks of toys and books.

When they had gone, each tugging at the other, Sarah closed the shutters, drew the curtains and lay down on her divan. The only dog she had managed to keep during the hostilities, I think it was Ahasuerus, paid her a formal call. "The war is over, mistress. The weather is fine! Let's go out and have a romp."

What a miserable homecoming it was! Sarah had hoped to find a letter telling her that the Odéon had reopened. But there was nothing! Yes, a few flowers which she had not had the heart to put into water. What good did such tributes of friendship do? Was the Beloved Monster also offended because no one tried to amuse it these days? And Sarah fell asleep, possessing the admirable faculty of being able to drop off whenever she felt like it.

The continuous ringing of the front-door bell awoke her. Félicie was out shopping, so Sarah opened the door herself.

"You, Chilly!"

"I heard that you had come back."

"Oh, Chilly! Chilly! How nice of you to come!"

"But your place is in complete darkness. Why do you shut yourself up in such beautiful weather?"

"Chilly! I am so unhappy I could die. I've been living too much on my nerves and now I'm suffering for it. Besides," she added in a lower voice, "there is something which is slowly poisoning me: the German victory! I cannot get it out of my mind. It is here!" and she struck herself on the chest. "I was so longing to see Paris again, and this first contact with it has broken me. I am going away, Chilly, with my son."

"You're going to desert? You?"

"Yes, I. In the first place, I'm ill. I look awful. I am terrifyingly thin and I've been spitting blood again. And nothing seems to interest me any more."

"That's a pity," replied Chilly, "as I came to put an interesting proposition to you."

"Pooh! By the time the theatres are in a fit state to give performances I shall be either insane or dead, with cobwebs in my hair."

"We are opening in a month's time, with *Jeane-Marie*," said the manager of the Odéon, glancing at his old pupil to see what reaction this announcement

87

produced on her. "Porel is returning to his part and I thought of you. Don't interrupt! Afterwards, we are giving *Ruy Blas*, by a certain Victor Hugo, and again I thought of you for the part of the Queen of Spain. But, as you prefer to rest, I'll try to find someone else for the parts. Good-bye!"

He was already mounting the three steps that led from the drawing-room when his name, uttered in a strident voice, pulled him up short. Sarah rose with a bound and seized him by the jacket.

"Do you swear all that is true?"

"But, of course," said Chilly, freeing himself. "Come to my office tomorrow and we'll discuss details."

And he went away, laughing to himself.

"Madame Guérard! Maurice!" screamed Sarah. "Where are they? Félicie! Ah! You're back! Pull back the curtains, open the windows and the shutters, put the flowers in water, buy the best you can for dinner. Run, as fast as you can, or I'll turn your kitchen upside down."

"Here is Master Maurice!" cried Félicie.

Sarah picked the child up: her loves had returned to her; she wanted to live at top speed with this little fellow who belonged to her, and to return to her nightly trysts with the Beloved Monster.

Without the Beloved Monster, life was very dreary.

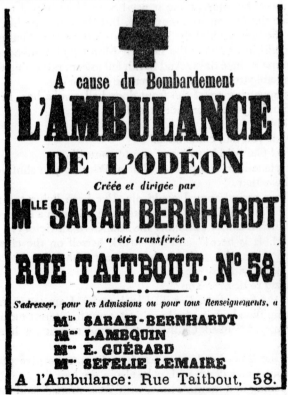

Sarah Bernhardt's Ambulance Poster during the Franco-Prussian War

CHAPTER XVII

VICTOR HUGO

THE great Victor Hugo's note was rapidly passed round Sarah Bernhardt's friends gathered about her that day. She had formed the habit, towards five o'clock in the afternoon, of inviting a few of what she called her "Little Court" and occasionally asking fresh people to meet them. These receptions had begun soon after the 1870 war, owing to the assiduity of two or three of her friends, whose number gradually increased until now about fifteen or twenty appeared every day.

"We look as if we're playing hunt-the-slipper," said the hostess, impatiently. "Not one of you seems able to give me any advice. Shall I go to Victor Hugo, as he asks me, to read through *Ruy Blas*, or shan't I? If only my poor Dumas were here he would solve the problem for me!"

"You ought not to put yourself out. You must not break with tradition like that. The right place for a play to be read is in the theatre," put in a young playwright with bitten nails and long hair.

There was a moment's embarrassment, as everyone knew quite well that this stickler for etiquette had never had a play performed, whence his silly contempt for Victor Hugo.

"Let's hear what Croizette has to say," said Sarah to Arthur Meyer. "She represents the Comédie Française and she will give me good advice."

"My advice," said Croizette with a disarming smile, "is for you to do what the great poet asks."

Then they all started talking at once and offering different advice. Some of them, the flatterers, declared that Sarah, in view of her "exceptional position", could not possibly accept an ultimatum from this Monsieur Hugo, who had only recently returned from exile. Why should she take orders from him? But Sarah felt that it would be absurd for her to answer "No" to the author of *Ruy Blas* for a mere question of pride and of custom; she sought in vain for a solution which would reconcile her pride with her best interests and her conscience.

Lying on her divan, in a white dress trimmed with grebe feathers, and her borzoi standing guard over her, this is how Sarah Bernhardt appears to us in the portrait by Georges Clairin, painted in 1876 and now at the Petit-Palais in Paris; with a black satin slipper dangling from the tip of her toe, Sarah is at the same time real and ethereal; her hair was not really so fair; she was a pretty woman of twenty-eight, slim, spirited and unconventional, free from constraint.

These five o'clock receptions constituted a break in the actress's busy existence, a delightful haven into which friendship and love had free right of entry. The young woman was already attracting round her people who, all their lives, would give her proofs of their affection. I have seldom seen a woman whom so many people loved keep so many friendships.

Questioned as to what answer to give Victor Hugo, Clairin refused to commit himself. The younger Dumas pulled his moustache and said nothing, and old Régis, seeing this, tugged at his own Viking moustache and said:

"All these striplings would show their intelligence better by working a little harder and talking a little less."

The situation was growing more and more tense when Félicie, who had now another maid to help her, suddenly appeared at the top of the three steps and announced, "Marshal Canrobert."

Silence fell immediately. The hero of the Crimea and of Saint-Privas kissed Sarah's hand and she quickly explained the situation to him.

"Well," said Canrobert, smiling, "let's vote upon it. Isn't that the up-to-date way of deciding matters? Those who think that Victor Hugo should not be obeyed will hold up their hands, those who consider that his orders should be respected will remain still."

And three-quarters of the people present held up their hands.

"That is how power is overthrown!" observed the Marshal.

"In any case," retorted Sarah reproachfully, "that exonerates you from giving your own personal opinion."

"Not at all! This is what I suggest, my dear friend. Don't go to the Master, but make some good excuse for not doing so—a sore throat, for instance. You must not forget that Victor Hugo is a genius."

And the look in the Marshal's face, as he gazed round all the friends and toadies of the Little Court, indicated clearly enough what he thought of the whole business. The incident was closed.

So Sarah wrote the following note which received the approval of her friends, of her flatterers and of the Marshal of France.

Monsieur, the Queen has caught a cold. And her chief lady-in-waiting forbids her to go out. And you, better than anyone else, know the etiquette of the Spanish Court. Pity your Queen, Monsieur.

S. B.

And Victor Hugo replied:

I am your servant, Madame. V. H.

.　　　.　　　.　　　.　　　.

"When I really got to know Victor Hugo, I nearly wept, Lysiane, for having followed my friends' advice. I ought to have rushed to see him. Who was I by comparison with that brilliant brain, that prodigious poet, who was also so kind and so generous? The first time I crossed the threshold of his house, one morning about ten o'clock, to ask him about something, I was almost shocked to find him drinking a glass of red wine accompanied by a crust of bread. At the theatre, during rehearsals, he intimidated me and, because of this, I did all sorts of silly things when I was not actually working, such as whistling, laughing or talking in a loud voice. But he must have been satisfied with my work, because he merely looked at me and listened to my nonsense with ironic tolerance. One day when I was behaving more foolishly than usual, seated on a table and swinging my legs, he made up the following couplet:

Une reine d'Espagne, honnête et respectable
Ne devrait pas ainsi s'asseoir sur une table.

" 'Sit down, mademoiselle, please,' he said that morning on which I first met him. He talked to me about my work, the theatre, art, life, France; I was confused, ashamed of my presumption, furious with the Little Court, and lost in admiration for this man and for his mind.

"I wanted to throw myself at his feet, to confide in him. But he probably understood that this nervous young actress was not quite so stupid and vain as she usually seemed to be as, when I left, he held my hand in his and looked at me with such kindness that I whispered:

" 'Please forgive me, Master!'

" 'We are friends, great friends,' he replied, smiling.

"And I tripped downstairs with joy in my heart, resolved never again to set myself upon a pedestal."

.   .   .   .   .

On January 26, 1882, the whole of fashionable Paris attended the first night of *Ruy Blas* at the Odéon.

Surrounded by her fellow-actors (Geoffroy, Lafontaine, Tallien), Sarah scored a remarkable and very impressive personal success. She was no longer "the charming artist with considerable talent": *Ruy Blas* brought her fame in a fanfare of trumpets! Sarah's face, her hair, her figure, her gestures, her marvellous diction, her voice, her lyricism, her presentation of the amorous queen, all left the public amazed, and charmed in every sense in which the word can be used for fascination. The Beloved Monster recognized in Sarah one of its elect, a being apart, such as is only given to the world once in a generation.

Among the many admirers of both sexes who, on this first night, crowded into Mademoiselle Sarah Bernhardt's overheated and flower-laden dressing-room, there were not only French celebrities but diplomats, musicians, authors and Russian princesses.

"Make way there, please!" cried a young Englishman. "His Royal Highness the Prince of Wales wishes to congratulate Mademoiselle Sarah Bernhardt."

And the Prince of Wales bowed over the hand of Doña Maria. He wore a white carnation in the lapel of his coat; he was gracious, simple and elegant. Sarah searched for English words in which to express her gratitude, and all she could think of was: "Very much. Very much."

Which was, after all, fair enough. But suddenly the Prince whispered to her, "Look, mademoiselle, here he comes!"

Everyone stopped talking and fell back slightly to each side, leaving a narrow passage through which an elderly man came slowly towards Sarah. As he advanced, he stroked his short white beard and kept his eyes fixed on the young actress who stood alone at the end of the room.

"Victor Hugo," said the future Edward VII in a tone of respect.

There was a moment's impressive silence, while men and women stood on tip-toe to get a better view, and the great poet halted before Sarah and said but two words:

"Thank you!"

CHAPTER XVIII

RETURN TO THE COMÉDIE FRANÇAISE

SARAH loved the Odéon. She loved it not only because she had won celebrity there with *Kean*, and glory with *Ruy Blas*, but also because she had a particular attachment to the building itself. She loved the atmosphere behind the scenes, its position in Paris, its shape, like that of an ancient temple, its arcades, its entrance, its foyer and the warm, sympathetic auditorium in which the Beloved Monster awaited her every evening. As soon as she arrived in her carriage, accompanied by the faithful Madame Guérard, and began to mount the steps leading to her dressing-room, she felt completely happy.

Her home life was calm and unruffled. She was young, admired and irradiated by a talent which asserted itself more and more with each of her successes. Her son filled the hours she spent in his company with delight; he was growing up at her side, loving, spirited, handsome and strong.

But, although the young woman was rich in love, affection, adulation and hope, the household was often short of money; she earned little in comparison with what she spent. Her contract with the Odéon Theatre, in which the word "Imperial" is run through with a thick stroke of the pen, tells us that Sarah was to receive a salary of seven hundred francs a month until May 1872, eight hundred from August 1872 to June 1873, and one thousand from June 1873 to May 1874. She never actually received the last amount. For one day a slight incident tore a hole in the web of these halcyon days and her happiness was reduced to dust.

It was really the most stupid thing in the world. Sarah's pumas had died during the war, and, in addition to her collie and her parrot, she had acquired a monkey named François and a Brussels griffon which she called Hamlet (no one ever discovered why). These animals remained quietly in the Rue de Rome under the supervision of Félicie and sometimes of Madame Guérard or of Maurice, who, on his return from school, would roll on the floor with the dogs and play at hide-and-seek with the monkey; indeed, one day Maurice and François were found both shut up in a cupboard and half suffocated. But the griffon, on account of his diminutive size, had the right and the honour of accompanying his mistress to the Odéon. It was an insufferable little beast, full of self-importance, never brushed, always yapping, and thoroughly bad-tempered, and whenever anyone came near Sarah it would stare balefully at him with its bulbous eyes half hidden in a tangle of tawny hair.

One evening, in the second act of *Ruy Blas*, the Queen of Spain, Doña Maria de Neuberg, made her entry followed by Hamlet the griffon, a tousled figure of fun. The public entered into the jest and the success the dog scored had certainly not been anticipated by either Victor Hugo, Sarah, Don Guritan or Chilly.

Luckily the creature, dazzled by the footlights, quickly scampered back into the wings and Sarah took up her cue amid the laughter of the Beloved Monster. The incident was duly reported to the managerial office, and Chilly was annoyed. He was wrong, of course, not to wait until the end of the performance to rebuke Sarah : for, holding the griffon up by the scruff of the neck, he brandished it before the Queen of Spain's nose as she left the stage after four curtain calls. Sarah was wrong, too; she took the incident very badly, and, snatching Hamlet from Chilly's hands, begged him, in no measured terms, not to ill-treat her dog. Upon which Chilly followed her into her dressing-room and threatened her with a fine.

"Pay me properly, my dear fellow, and I will engage a footman to look after Hamlet."

"I do pay you properly."

"If it were not for the Master, I would leave at once, and it would be a long time before you saw me again."

"What a horrible character you've got ! Is it my fault if your dog interrupts the performance and makes the public laugh? I must beg you to leave the mongrel at home in future."

"And I, Chilly, must implore you to behave yourself."

"You're going to be late," flung Lafontaine at her, putting his head into the dressing-room door. "Hurry up. The house is rather restive this evening."

Chilly turned on his heel and went away, deciding not to argue any more with Sarah, but to put a notice up at the stage door, "No animals of any kind are to be brought into the wings." If he did not do that, Sarah would be quite capable, either out of sheer perversity or merely to irritate him, of introducing a cat or even a monkey into the theatre.

As soon as the performance was over, Sarah, whose anger was still simmering, asked to see Chilly. He shrugged his shoulders.

"It's no good bickering, Sarah. You're in the wrong, your dog's in the wrong. I was wrong to abuse you. The incident is closed."

"Certainly," replied Sarah, truculently; "the incident is closed so far as Hamlet is concerned ; but I repeat, in spite of all you say, that you don't pay me properly. I have so many expenses——"

"Is it my fault that you keep horses and carriages, that you give receptions, and keep up a style of living beyond your means?"

"You would not have me live like a small shopkeeper's wife, would you?"

"That does not concern me. You signed your contract and I signed it, so let us respect it."

"Then you refuse to increase my salary?"

"Certainly. You actresses are all the same. The moment you have a little success you think you are geniuses !"

"Really?" said Sarah, rising. "Well then, my dear, you can find someone else for your next play. I'm leaving."

"You're leaving, are you? And where will you go? It would be interesting to know. For the moment I cannot think of any theatre capable of making use of your talents and your shortcomings and to do justice to your personality. The Ambigu? The Gymnase? The Vaudeville? The Gaité? You will spend your time either 'resting' or wearing yourself to a shadow trying to make both ends meet. Come, Sarah ! Let's make it up; in a few months, in the usual way, you will get a small rise."

Some devil must have possessed Sarah that day. She could not help herself; she felt that she was making a mistake, and yet her irritation got the better of her, and she could not help compromising her exceptional position at the Odéon and putting an end to that marvellous period in her young life.

"You are forgetting one theatre, Chilly, for which I would be perfectly fitted, a theatre which for some time now has made me attractive offers: the Comédie Française."

"The Comédie Française!" repeated the manager of the Odéon, slowly.

Then suddenly he burst out laughing, beat his desk with his hands and rocked backwards and forwards.

"The Comédie Française! But you're mad! They would never take you back with your wretched character. Come! I'm quite happy now. I'll see you tomorrow, Sarah!"

He held his hand out to her. But Sarah, placing the shivering Hamlet on the managerial desk, folded her arms and fixed her blazing eyes on Chilly. All their softness and poetic depth had disappeared and their normally pale irises were now dark with fury.

"You cad!" she said to him, simply, and she picked up her dog and swept out of the room, slamming the door behind her.

Sarah was not lying when she said that Perrin, the manager at that time of the Comédie Française, had been considering her return to that Company. Charging certain intermediaries to sound her on the subject, he had expected an affirmative answer, but Sarah always replied, gently but firmly:

"I love the Odéon."

It would be wrong to think that Sarah's Little Court influenced her to the point of enforcing their wishes upon her. No! She had very definite opinions on most things, but what she expected from her friends was complete approval of her acts and gestures, in order to strengthen her at the moment of making an important decision. In this case the real cause of her quarrel with Chilly was solely the question of salary. As I have said before, Sarah was short of money, and the sum left to her by her father, of which she had received only three-quarters, thanks to the surly vigilance of Maître Clément, was slipping daily through her fingers. Now, she knew from the emissaries of the Comédie Française that they would offer her fifteen thousand francs a year. Of course, Sarah can be reproached for having once again broken her contract, and this time for purely personal considerations; but it must not be forgotten that she was only twenty-eight at the time.

When, without breathing a word of her decision to anyone, she called on Perrin next day, he, anticipating a visit from her, had the papers all ready for her to sign. Perrin had no particular liking for Sarah, but he thought she would be in her right place at the Comédie Française, relying on her reputation as an excellent artiste and on the publicity which both her friends and her enemies would give her.

"Please read through this contract, mademoiselle, and sign it and the counterpart."

In signing the first copy, Sarah, no doubt agitated by her cool and courteous reception by Perrin, made a blot.

"I am very sorry, monsieur, but this is rather a bad pen."

And then she made another blot on the other copy.

"Will you do me a favour?" she said, leaning towards him with her head on one side. "Fold the paper over the blot, so that I may know whether I am being either very foolish or very clever."

"I beg your pardon?" said Perrin, puzzled.

"You are not superstitious, monsieur, but I am—terribly. I am quite certain that if that second blot turns into a butterfly it means that I was right to sign. If not—well, so much the worse."

Perrin smiled condescendingly: he folded both sheets and looked at them surreptitiously, while Sarah was studying the statutes of the theatre.

"Look, mademoiselle! It's a butterfly!"

And, indeed, the spreading ink had formed itself vaguely into the shape of a butterfly.

"Ah! Then that's all right," said Sarah with a sigh.

What she did not know was that the second sheet contained a wingless outline, and was now hidden in a drawer in Perrin's desk.

"How cold, pretentious and inhospitable this theatre is!" thought Sarah as she left the manager's office.

She passed several actors who greeted her politely, and perhaps a little ironically. The shade of Nathalie the Taboo seemed to be peering at her from behind the busts, and even though Monsieur Perrin seemed to be more frank than Monsieur Thierry, he was no more amenable.

"I've no reason to be proud of myself. By my conceit and my selfishness I have betrayed my friends and Madame Guérard."

Sarah already regretted her gesture, her dear Odéon, her comrades at the theatre, even Chilly and his meanness.

Once outside, she breathed freely again. She would have to announce her decision to her present director, to her Little Court and to her family. Chilly would probably sue her and once again she would have to pay damages for breach of contract. But something much more serious was worrying her: she thought of herself as a wild bird that had inadvertently got trapped in a cage.

"Drive back along the Champs Élysées," she told her coachman. "I want air."

CHAPTER XIX

THE INK BEGINS TO RUN

NOVEMBER 6, 1872, the date at which Sarah reappeared at the Comédie Française in *Mademoiselle de Belle-Isle*, was the beginning for her of a series of worries and misfortunes. First it was the health of her mother, who was now constantly having fainting fits; then it was the favouritism of Perrin, who, though always coolly courteous to her, gave Croizette all the best parts; then there was the jealousy of her comrades at each fresh production; that is, with the exception of Coquelin, Mounet-Sully, Worms, Laroche, Marie Lloyd, Sophie Croizette and Madeline Brohan. And yet, amidst all these difficulties, these fights, these exasperations, Sarah, from the time she played in *Ruy Blas*, was climbing the garlanded rungs of the ladder of success. The Monster was becoming enamoured of her; and, below, the zealous throng was swelling. And all the time Sarah climbed and climbed.

At the same time as the struggle was going on in the theatre, another battle was taking place in her dressing-room, in her home, even in her bedroom—the battle of scandal. Journalists, self-confessed or in disguise, produced it like confetti at a carnival. Sarah let people say what they liked. Was she right or wrong? On the rare occasions on which she joined in the scuffle, trying to plead for a little fair play, she was defeated. In the theatre, the Beloved Monster acclaimed her; outside the place of worship it tore her to ribbons. That was but human. Sarah was both the mistress and the victim of the Public which she loved. She loved it all her life, addicted to it as to a drug. And no one has ever pretended that the Public is kind or fair: those are not its functions. It pays its idols and raises them up to the pinnacle of glory and either keeps them there or lets them fall. It has the right to whistle, or to laugh, or to cough, or to talk or even not to come to the theatre at all: in which case the artiste just disappears; his or her name is blotted out, and their attraction withers like a diseased plant.

In 1872, public opinion gathered the daily facts concerning Sarah Bernhardt's life, hawked them about and altered their substance to make them amusing to the public. I think it better here to let Sarah Bernhardt herself speak, by reproducing, as faithfully as possible, the stories which she told me on many occasions.

• • • • •

"We comedy actresses are the slaves of the public and of journalism. The former gives us our artistic life, the latter preserves it for us. And yet, Lysiane, journalists did not spare me at that time; since then I have known some who were charming, sincere, just or severe, who have become my friends.

"I was at the Comédie Française; out of work hours I painted and did sculpture. I was modelling a group for the 1876 *salon* and, to be more comfortable, I used to change my street clothes for a white silk shirt and trousers.

"(The Press: 'Mademoiselle Sarah Bernhardt dresses in men's clothes. Does she want to play juvenile leads too?')

Sarah Bernhardt in London in 1886

Henry Irving, 1886

Sarah Bernhardt and her family

Left to right : Saryta, Jeanne Bernhardt's daughter ; Jacques Damala,
Sarah's husband ; Sarah. *Seated :* Terka and Maurice Bernhardt

"Also for this group—which, incidentally, received an honourable mention—I took up the study of anatomy. One day a doctor friend of mine brought me a life-size wax torso. My under-housemaid, coming into my studio, found the doctor and myself bending over the naked torso. She screamed and ran out. The following day . . .

"(The Press: 'We have it from an unimpeachable source that Mademoiselle Sarah Bernhardt, the sculptress, sometimes undresses her guests to study their anatomy. There's conscientiousness for you! What does Mademoiselle Sarah Bernhardt the actress think of all this?')

"In 1874 I had a small house built in the Rue Fortuny. The plans were drawn by Escalier, a talented architect who was already making a name for himself. Clairin, Stevens, Parrot and Abbéma were decorating it. And I, to surprise and encourage my friends, used to arrive there unexpectedly. We used to send for food from the nearest restaurant, and I assure you that those meals, in the midst of plaster and paint-pots, were far from being dull! One afternoon, while I was lunching with my young friends, dressed in their working blouses, Aunt Betsy came to see me. Two days later . . .

"(The Press: 'Mademoiselle Sarah Bernhardt, who loves the populace and needs its approval, is not proud. She lunches with her bricklayers and house-painters, and the hands of "Zaire" dispense cheap wine in generous measures.')

"I had bought another puma at the Zoological Gardens, but since the incident with the younger Dumas I kept him on a lead and only took him out in my courtyard. The story was . . .

"(The Press: 'Mademoiselle Sarah Bernhardt lives surrounded by her tigers. It is lucky for her that her neighbours do not bring their children into the Rue de Rome to see the menagerie and feed the wild animals.')

"I never had time to go for a walk. I would like to point out that I am seventy-eight years old and that fresh air has never worried me. The microbes in theatres, the dust of scenery, the refuse in the wings, over-heated dressing-rooms, carbonic acid gas from stoves are the things that suit me; I thrive under them. In short, the only exercise I ever took was horse-riding.

"(The Press: 'Mademoiselle Sarah Bernhardt was seen yesterday, near the Longchamps plain, riding without a saddle or stirrups. She was wearing a red habit and looked like a lion-tamer. "Have you been run away with?" asked someone. "Far from it," she replied. "I am training for the Grand Prix. Comedy and tragedy actress, sculptor, painter and even writer, I am now aspiring to become a jockey." ')

"My sister Regina had become seriously ill with a lung complaint, and as mother, between two fainting fits, had recovered her urge for travel, the poor child lodged with me.[1] I looked after her night and day. She slept in my bed, while I slept in my coffin. Yes! From the day on which, in the Rue Saint-Honoré, Dr. Leger had sentenced me to death, I begged mama to buy me a pretty coffin. She refused, naturally. But I did not want to be put on a bier in something ugly. So I bullied the Little Court until it bought me a mahogany coffin upholstered with white satin. Anyway, you know it.

"(The Press: 'Mademoiselle Sarah Bernhardt can only sleep in a coffin. This macabre jest merely caps her other eccentricities. There is a limit even

[1] Regina died a few months later.

G   97 to bad taste. Though it is true that this Comédie Française actress is so thin that the coffin already contains nothing but bones.')

"Yes, I was terrifyingly thin. Caricaturists, led by André Gill, Valloton, Bib, Forain, Sem, Capiello, Luque, Barrère, Rouveyre and Grimm, represented me at various times as a broomhandle or as a chimney-stack with a nest on the top of it. And the inscriptions beneath them were supposed to be witty.

" 'Mademoiselle Sarah Bernhardt left her cab, and immediately disappeared; in order to avoid reporters she had taken refuge between two paving-stones.'

" 'Mademoiselle Sarah Bernhardt spent yesterday alone with her dog. It is feared that the dog may have gnawed her in error.' "

.   .   .   .   .

Caricature is the small change of glory, and Sarah took it all in good part. She appreciated its originality but sometimes took umbrage at the baseness which it attributed to her. Then she would fly into a mad rage and brandish a whip and vow vengeance; but she would soon forget all about it. Sarah had a sweet character. Not merely on the surface but with a happy, generous sweetness. She loved life too much to allow any place in it for malice: only the present time mattered, warm and palpitating. Yesterday "already reeked of death".

In 1877 Gustave Nadaud reproached Sarah Bernhardt in a poem of cornering every profession.[1]

Nevertheless, among the serpents, the woodlice, the lions, the faithful hounds, the lady-killers, the celebrities and the failures who made up the Little Court and the acquaintanceship of Sarah Bernhardt between 1873 and 1880, the devotion of a few people touched her deeply, and a few great joys illuminated her path, as, for instance, the diamond which she wore on a chain around her neck: the diamond which, as bright as a tear-drop, was given to her by Victor Hugo in 1877 on the occasion of the revival of *Hernani*, with the following note:

Madame, you are great and you are charming: you have touched me, me the old stager, and, at one moment when the public, thrilled and enthralled by you, applauded your performance, I wept. This tear which you made me shed is yours. I lay myself at your feet.

V. Hugo.

So, too, were certain little bouquets of violets in the form of hearts, humble and pathetic, thrown on the stage by those who could not get into her presence. Such, also, were verses of obscure poets: *In Love with a Star*; such, too, was the admiration of those sensitive men who won her heart and aroused her love. And such the affection of Madame Guérard, the love she had for her mother, her friendships with women, and the constant presence of Maurice, whom she needed to make her laugh and live.

[1] Unfortunately, this poem is quite untranslatable. Good poetry can sometimes be interpreted in another language, but bad poetry cannot. [Translator.]

CHAPTER XX

THE UNIVERSAL EXHIBITION OF 1878

WHEN Sarah reached the age of thirty-four she bore lightly on her slim shoulders the creation or the interpretation of about thirty parts. She had also to bear the less pleasant burden of all the eccentricities attributed to her and the bickering with Perrin which was a constant mortification to her.

She still retained her passion for living at high speed and high pressure; no amount of fatigue or of discouragement could sap her vitality or, on the other hand, soften her character. Just as she had been as a little girl at Grand-Champs, showing her faults and her qualities in embryonic state, so she was twenty-five years later, with her strong character and personality, sometimes hard, but never hypocritical or disloyal.

She was now living in the Rue Fortuny with Madame Guérard and her son, now aged fourteen, and the peculiar style of the Rue de Rome manifested itself in even more magnificent fashion in her little home there.

The Universal Exhibition of 1878, in spite of its deficit of thirty-eight million francs, had attracted a large number of people to Paris. Whenever Sarah had a moment to spare, she would drive to the Champ-de-Mars or to the recently built Trocadero Palace, and would stroll through the beautiful gardens with their tinkling fountains; sometimes visitors would press around her, recognizing in this slim young woman, always dressed in white and followed by a host of admirers, the Dona Sol of the Comédie Française. And that Exhibition was to be for Sarah, as it were, the beginning of the end; the cause of her rupture with Perrin.

She usually devoted Thursday afternoons to Maurice. Besides going to the Exhibition, Sarah and her son used to wander about Paris, eating ices at Chiboust's, sauntering past the shops or, again, going to the Bois de Boulogne to eat biscuits and cakes. One day Maurice expressed a desire to see the captive balloon belonging to the aeronaut Giffard, which was tethered in one of the courts of the Tuileries. While he was enthusiastically admiring the silk fabric of the balloon, its cable and its nacelle, a man greeted Sarah.

"Oh, Godard, my dear," she said, giving him her hand to kiss, "I wish I could go for a trip in a balloon."

But, as her son was looking at her disapprovingly, she lowered her voice and said:

"Come and see me at the Rue Fortuny tomorrow."

Godard arrived punctually. He was announced while Sarah Bernhardt was talking to Maurice, who had returned from school with a rather mediocre report. She had been trying to think of some means of showing her displeasure without punishing herself at the same time. Godard was a member of the family of balloon fame, and was a friend of the celebrated Giffard. Sarah had made their acquaintance some days before through Georges Clairin, and she had expressed her wholehearted admiration of the inventor's recent discoveries. Giffard had not forgotten this.

"Giffard is already having a beautiful orange-coloured balloon made for you, in which you may go for a trip with your friend Clairin and your humble servant."

When Giffard told her that, Sarah was delighted, but she cautioned him.

"For the love of heaven don't tell anyone about it. I don't want to alarm my son or Madame Guérard, neither do I want to put the Press on my track."

Once more let us hear Sarah Bernhardt's own account of this amusing episode, which, however, had such serious consequences for her. Here is the passage from her book,[1] in which a chair is supposed to be narrating the flight of the three travellers.

"The crowd assembles: the balloon is fully inflated. I see Dona Sol among the crowd. Louis Godard comes to fetch me from my shed and I am placed in a little laundry basket. A passage opens in the crowd, and through it comes Dona Sol on the arm of Monsieur Tissandier, followed by the young painter, Georges Clairin. The two celebrated Godards look into the basket to see if I am steady and whether anything is worrying me.

"I was going to thank them for taking so much trouble when I was blinded by a cloud of lace.

"Dona Sol had sat on me.

"Georges Clairin and young Louis Godard jumped into the nacelle. It was half past five. The crowd pressed more closely round the balloon: raising of hats, handshakes, farewells, and the balloon shoots upwards in the midst of affectionate applause. And so into the void. The earth below, the sky above. And I hear Dona Sol murmur, 'I would like to live like this always.'

"But suddenly the scene changes: the clouds part and the balloon begins to descend over the Pont de la Concorde, a hundred yards from where it took off. The crowd, which is still assembled in the Tuileries, makes a dash towards the river bank. We ourselves seem to be heading straight for the Seine. Clairin turns enquiringly to the aeronaut.

" 'I am having a joke with them. Look!'

"And he empties a bag of ballast and up we shoot again."

Yes; but wait. That afternoon it so happened that Perrin unfortunately took it into his head to walk across the Pont des Saints-Pères, as he had a perfect right to do, and that there he met Robert de Montesquiou, who had just witnessed the departure of the intrepid trio. The young poet buttonholed the worthy director of the Comédie Française, and said:

"Have a bet with me! Do you know who is in that beautiful orange balloon? I insist upon two tickets for the next presentation at the Comédie Française if you cannot guess."

Perrin raised his eyes, hesitated a moment and then suddenly became very red.

"I hope for her sake," he said, "that it isn't her."

"Who do you mean by 'her'?"

"Sarah Bernhardt."

[1] *Impression d'une Chaise.* (J. Charpentier.)

100

"Oh," said our tactless friend, disappointed, "how did you guess that?"

"Whenever some particularly foolish escapade takes place, one is seldom far wrong in mentioning that name. You shall have your tickets, my boy, but it is she who will pay for them. Yes, she shall pay me for them . . . dearly."

The return from this celestial trip was much less joyful than the departure had been. When they arrived at the Rue Fortuny, Clairin and Sarah met with loud reproaches. The news of the ascent had travelled from mouth to mouth; Madame Guérard was in tears and some friends who were there criticized Georges Clairin for having countenanced this fresh prank of Sarah's.

"You had no right to risk an accident, Sarah! And Perrin is furious," said Louise Abbéma warningly.

And conflicting opinions flew backwards and forwards like tennis balls.

"That's enough!" cried Sarah loudly. "You all bore me. After all, my life is my own. I'm going to bed. I wish you all good night."

She swept out of the room in a fury, while her guests, like a lot of parrots let loose in an aviary, all began chattering together.

"Maurice, are you, too, angry with me?"

The boy was reading in bed. He looked sulkily at his mother.

"Why did you not take me too?"

"My dear boy, when I commit what people call a folly, I prefer to do so alone."

She kissed his beautiful fair hair and his blue eyes.

"Then," said Maurice, hugging his mother close to him, "since you yourself commit follies, how can you expect me to be good? You lied to me."

"I won't lie to you any more, darling. Besides, you know what you asked me for. Soon I may be able to give it to you. Have a little more patience."

"Mama!" cried Maurice, throwing off the bedclothes. "My horse! When shall I get it?"

Sarah put a finger to her lips.

"You must promise that you will work harder."

"Yes, mama! I'll work hard if you won't go up in balloons any more. How can you expect me to work when I am worried about you?" he concluded artfully.

For the past month, Maurice, who proved to be a perfect horseman, had been thinking of nothing but "his" horse. He had already got ready, in the yard of his mother's house, the stable which was to receive this welcome guest. Of course, Maurice loved the dogs and the parrot and the monkey and the puma, but what he really wanted was a pony of his own, spirited and tractable at the same time.

"Nacelle," he decided. "I'll call it Nacelle."

The boy had been horrified a short while before when he heard that his mother was floating about in the sky without him. It was a journalist, a pleasant, elderly man, who told him of her ascent. This gentleman pretended to have an appointment with Sarah Bernhardt, but Maurice knew this was not true; journalists always said they had appointments, in order to be able to get into the house in the Rue Fortuny and to poke their noses into everything.

"They've got noses that twitch like those of bloodhounds," thought Maurice. He did not like them; journalists offended his sense of modesty; they seemed always to be wanting to tear some article of clothing from his mother's back.

But this particular gentleman had been polite and in his presence Maurice did not dare show his anxiety for his mother's safety.

"I know. My mother told me she was going up in a balloon."

"And who is with Madame Sarah Bernhardt?"

"Monsieur Godard, no doubt."

"Didn't she take a friend with her? Perhaps you would be good enough to tell me the names of the people who come here most often. I could write a lovely article about your mother. And I'd put your name in too."

"Oh no! Mama hates anyone to talk about me, monsieur; but I can tell you the names of the people who live here," said Maurice seriously. "For instance, there's Monsieur Bovary . . ."

"And who is Monsieur Bovary?" asked the journalist eagerly, bringing out a note-book.

"A very fine gentleman who talks very well. He costs mama a great deal."

"In what way?" asked the old gentleman in astonishment.

"He has to have a special diet. Anyway, I will introduce you to him."

Two minutes later Maurice appeared with a magnificent cockatoo, crest erect, upon his shoulder.

"I am very sorry I can't introduce you to François the monkey. He's busy at the moment. Why? Aren't you going to wait for my mother?"

The journalist cleared his throat crossly, and said: "No; I must be off now. Thank you, young man."

Left alone, the young man in question went through a few dance steps; then his face became serious. He hurried upstairs to the room of his old friend Madame Guérard.

"Mama has gone up in a balloon! Did you know?"

"But that isn't dangerous, Maurice. You mustn't get excited."

"She lied to me. She said she was going to the Trocadero."

This lie hurt his feelings. Because, in any case, his mother was too much like a character out of Jules Verne for him to be very much surprised at her balloon escapade.

.   .   .   .   .

The following day, on her arrival at the Comédie Française, Sarah found a note from the management asking her to go immediately to see Monsieur Perrin. Sarah was not a patient woman; she was totally ignorant of the meaning of the word "phlegmatic", and thought it best to get the matter over and done with. Always correct in his behaviour, the Director drew up a chair for her, and then began.

"Mademoiselle, it is my duty to speak to you as follows . . ."

And for ten minutes (Sarah declared that she kept her eye fixed on the clock) he upbraided her for all her recent misdeeds.

"Your health is poor; instead of resting, you model all night, you write, it seems, and you paint. In fact, you are killing yourself, mademoiselle. As it is, you cannot undertake certain modern parts because you are so thin."

"Another two minutes and I'll pounce," thought Sarah.

"And now you go up in a balloon. It is unbelievable! Do you know, mademoiselle, that it is laid down in our statutes that no junior is allowed to travel without our authorization? I am sorry to have to fine you one thousand francs."

In the midst of the droning sound that came to her ears, this last sentence stood out clearly.

"It seems to me, Monsieur Perrin, that you are in very witty vein this beautiful May morning!"

"What do you mean?"

"Do you really think that my jaunt into the skies authorizes you to impose a fine upon me? You may, if you like, monsieur, address more or less justified and discourteous remarks to me on my way of life, but as for this fine, I refuse to pay it."

"That is for the Committee to decide, mademoiselle. You are, of course, aware that the Comédie Française is shortly visiting London; this balloon business must be settled before then. I believe I am giving you good advice in begging you to reconsider the matter."

"I *have* considered it, and I refuse to pay. And I will not go to England."

"You might, perhaps, return to the Odéon. Poor Chilly is no longer there to prevent you."[1]

"If Chilly had still been alive, I should have left here long ago."

"The woman isn't an actress, she's a shuttlecock," observed an actor named Lamoisan, to whom Perrin told the story.

We will not argue the rights and the wrongs of the case. The management decided that Sarah had, morally, overstepped her rights. A wild animal had got into that house in which order and discipline ruled; no doubt this wild animal attracted the public, but it had to be broken in, otherwise it would sow revolt and disturb the established order of things; Sarah would soon be making paper balls of the statutes, with which to amuse her dogs. Although the Director congratulated himself upon the box-office receipts, he was irritated by the successes of the most eccentric and the most unruly of his juniors.

As for Sarah, she had already left the theatre. What would she do now? Pooh! Other theatres would be delighted to offer her an engagement! Perhaps she was yielding to the sin of vanity, relying on the power of her name and on the love of the Beloved Monster.

Actually, when the English managers heard that the Comédie Française was coming to London without one of its stars, they gave a point-blank refusal to Perrin's proposal to substitute someone for Sarah Bernhardt. As the Gaiety Theatre had already been hired for the first three productions, the Director tore his hair. It meant either giving in or cancelling the tour. So he sent for the rebel once more, and, without a word, he handed her a letter from the London impresario. This was addressed directly to her and begged her to reflect and not to cause the breaking of a contract which, as much for closer intercourse between the two nations as for the reputation of the Comédie Française, was so very important.

Sarah looked at Perrin, and Perrin, his face working, looked at his junior.

"Right!" said Sarah lightly, to conceal her real feelings. "Let us forget

[1] Chilly died on June 4, 1872.

all about it. I am prepared to go," (Perrin smiled), "but," (Perrin shuddered), "I want to be made a full member of the Comédie Française. Go and call your Committee together quickly, monsieur."

And on the following day Sarah and her great friend, Sophie Croizette, were made members for the whole duration of their contracts.

. . . . .

The English tour from June 2 until July 12, 1879, was a great success. It brought in an average of 13,350 francs for the productions in which Sarah Bernhardt appeared.[1] The tragedienne immediately appealed to the English public. It loved her at once and was faithful to her all her life: and when she died it paid her tribute. She played in the second act of *Phèdre*, in *L'Étrangère*, in *Zaire*, in *Hernani*, and in other pieces as well. Having gone to conquer London, she carried all before her. As the elder Dumas had said, "she cut off a little piece of herself for the public".

When an Englishman abandons his reserve, he roars his admiration. One evening Sarah, exhausted and supported by Mounet-Sully, saw that all the audience was on their feet; hands and arms were stretched towards her. She seemed to be looking at a hawthorn hedge in blossom, swayed by a warm breeze. Cheers and bouquets soared over the footlights, and Sarah Bernhardt fainted in the wings from weariness, emotion and gratitude.

Although she was loaded with laurels, her return to Paris was a disillusion. Jealous comrades, merciless journalists and unsuccessful dramatists bore a grudge against Mounet-Sully, Croizette, Coquelin and Sarah for their success on the other side of the Channel. Especially against Sarah. It was Sarah, the most fêted, the most triumphant, the most splendid of them all, who suffered most from all the accumulated hatred and jealousies; the caterpillars and the green-fly attacked the rose-bush because it was too proud of its roses. The Press flew at her about everything and about nothing. At first Sarah tried to defend herself; she wanted to bite and to scratch, but to do that she would have needed real declared enemies, and she saw nothing around her but hypocritical smiles as she shook limp hands and received Judas kisses.

Matters went from bad to worse.

Having to play in *L'Aventurière*, and not feeling well, Sarah asked Perrin to postpone the date of the play. There was another quarrel.

"The reason that you are ill is that you tire yourself out unnecessarily."

So she played and was not a success. And on April 18, 1880, feverish and irritable, without consulting with anyone, she sent the Director her resignation. Her wings had been folded for too long and they were itching to spread again.

"Maurice, you are the first to know: I have sent in my resignation to the Comédie Française. Émile has just taken the letter round."

(Émile, who was then a young servant looking after Maurice, remained with Sarah Bernhardt for forty-five years and became her steward.)

"But, mama, what will Monsieur Perrin say?"

"He will attack me, darling, but we will defend ourselves. This evening, I shall tell my friends what I have done."

"Yes," replied Maurice, "you are dining at home. I've asked my cousins,

[1] *Memoirs*. (E. Fasquelle.)

the Ker-Bernhardts and Leopold Stevens to remain behind when the others have gone. Who else is coming?"

"Clairin, Parrot, Louise Abbéma and your grandmother."

"And Aunt Jeanne?"

"Aunt Jeanne too," replied Sarah, smiling, knowing that, subconsciously, the young man admired his young relative with her flaxen hair and her large grey eyes.

Jeanne, also, was on the stage; she got engagements at various Paris theatres for her pretty face and her name Bernhardt; she had no talent and lived in the orbit of her sister. Her character had in no way improved, and her private life was so involved that Judith Bernhardt had given up trying to keep pace with her favourite's love-affairs; and although she lived with Jeanne, Judy was drawn more and more towards Sarah, that "awful child" whom she had so misunderstood. Besides, in the Rue Fortuny lived her grandson Maurice, a handsome boy of fifteen, polite, affectionate, courageous, and not always very good, on whom she doted.

"Mama," continued Maurice in an undertone, "I want to show you something. Come with me."

The boy led his mother down to the little courtyard of the house. Beside the stable housing Sarah's chestnuts a stall painted white and with a green shutter drew Sarah's attention. Maurice opened the door: the empty whitewashed stall and the bed of fresh straw seemed to be awaiting their guest. On the top half of the door was painted the word *Nacelle*. Sarah turned to Maurice with tears in her eyes.

"Darling!"

"Oh, I'm in no hurry, mama," said the boy awkwardly. "I only wanted to tell you not to buy the horse, now that we are going to have worries."

"You shall have your horse, Maurice. You shall have it in a fortnight. Your last month's school report was excellent; I will keep my promise."

. . . . . .

That same evening, between six o'clock and eight, Sarah held her usual reception. Clad in a long dress of white pleated muslin, her waist encircled with a wide copper belt encrusted with turquoises, with her hair twisted in a bun at the back and in a curly fringe in front, she cast a last glance over the refreshments and the flowers in the drawing-room.

On her shoulder, François, her marmoset, was stroking her neck with his hand like that of a little old man. Everything was in order. They could come now.

Friends? Yes, a great many. Enemies? A few.

"Why do you let that woman come?" asked Clairin one day. "She spreads the most awful tales about you."

"I am always hoping to disarm her," replied Sarah.

She decided to wait until the last minute before informing the Little Court of her decision. Soon the drawing-room and dining-room began to fill with visitors. At the door young Émile (he was eighteen years old and about three brickbats high), in a blue livery with engraved buttons, announced the visitors as they arrived. The less important ones were the first to come; among them were hungry poets who, after greeting Sarah, made straight for the buffet, and the curtain which separated the dining-room from the drawing-room was kept drawn during the first hour of Sarah's receptions, so that these poor troubadours might be able to refresh themselves without embarrassment.

In a note-book which Émile gave me after my grandmother's death were jotted down the names of the people who came to these receptions in the Rue Fortuny in about 1890. From them I have picked out the names of Victor Hugo, the younger Dumas, Émile Zola, Jules Lemaître, Louis Pasteur, Jean Richepin, Edmond Haraucourt, Ernest Renan, Victorien Sardou, Émile de Girardin, Catulle-Mendès, Charles Gounod, Ferdinand de Lesseps, Léon Gambetta, Coquelin, Alfred Stevens, Georges Clairin, Henry Irving, Oscar Wilde (whom she had known in London and whom she always defended), Augusta Holmes, Croizette and Louise Abbéma.

The more celebrated among them took up their positions round Sarah, either on the divan or on the chairs, or on cushions on the floor. Conversation, serious or light, and isolated phrases kept the groups of guests connected, as though by gossamer scarves of different colours. But, on that particular day, Sarah was uncommunicative; Perrin knew now. Young Émile had delivered the letter to the Director of the Comédie Française in person.

"Is it good news?" asked Perrin, smiling.

"It is certainly news, monsieur," replied the lad, making himself scarce.

At about half past seven Sarah could contain herself no longer. The casual acquaintances had left, and only the Little Court remained. She rose and, a white figure against the dark hangings of the room, with her arms outstretched, she announced:

"My friends, my dear friends, listen to me. At this moment Perrin is fulminating in his office; for the second time I have resigned from the Comédie Française."

If she expected to create a sensation, she was not disappointed. Her words were received in complete silence.

"You ought not to have done that!" suddenly cried Coquelin.

"I swear to you . . . oh, I beg of you . . . My nerves are on edge enough as it is. Let us talk of something else. But I want to add that I intend to go to London for a repertory season. Come! Don't all look at me like that! I know, and have carefully considered, everything that you want to say to me."

"And I," said Arthur Meyer, kissing Sarah's hand, "think that those of us journalists who are your friends will do well to sharpen our pens to defend you. And where would lie the pleasure in doing it, my dear friend, if you always acted like a rational human being?"

"Come and kiss me, my little Meyer," said Sarah, moved to tears.

That eased the strain. There was no more talk of the Comédie Française, but . . .

. . . . .

("I think, Lysiane, that nearly all my friends, when they left the Rue Fortuny that evening, told themselves: 'She is quite mad. She says that her wings are itching, but she is in for a hard time.' ")

CHAPTER XXI

LONDON

FREE from all her shackles, and trusting in her good star, Sarah signed a contract with Meyer and went to England from May 24 to June 27, 1880. She engaged eight artistes, among them her sister Jeanne. No! She would never return to the Comédie Française! Nothing would make her alter her mind about that.

"It is going to cost you dear," people told her.

"The action against you is as good as lost," said others.

Even her own lawyer shrugged his shoulders. But she fiercely resisted all attempts at conciliation: this new tunnel was going to be a difficult one to get through, but she would succeed. And even if her wings did get scorched in the process, they would grow again.

"I would much rather fall down, be wounded, even burned, so long as I reach some other place in the end."

.   .   .   .   .

("And yet, grandmother, long, long afterwards, I myself heard people criticizing that caprice of yours.

" 'Sarah ought never to have left the Comédie Française to go and act in plays which were often worthless. She ought to have remained at the service of the classics and of the great modern dramatists.'

"And you were even criticized for playing Sardou! To a great many French people this second rupture with the Comédie amounted to desertion. Were they right who said that? What did you yourself, with your strict ideas about professional etiquette, really think about it? One day, rather timidly, I put the question squarely to you.

" 'The Comédie Française,' you replied, 'is and always will be the standard-bearer of the dramatic art of our country. I may have refused to serve in its ranks. Am I a deserter because of that? No. My own rôle was, perhaps, to make that standard float in the air of other countries, to make it known beyond the frontiers of France. Only posterity can judge whether I fulfilled my mission.'

"But what about Paris?"

"Paris was an indispensable springboard. I was always delighted to return to get a new take-off.")

.   .   .   .   .

This new London season was even more successful than the preceding one had been. A few French journalists had crossed the Channel, to give the *Figaro*, the *Temps* and *Gil Blas* an account of the new venture. Sarah Bernhardt declares in her *Memoirs* that the critics watched her with "the intentness of an Englishman watching a lion-tamer in the hope of seeing him eaten by his

SARAH BERNHARDT

animals". At any rate, these journalists, among whom was Francisque Sarcey, dealt quite fairly with her; they sent their papers, particularly at the performance of *Frou-Frou*, a series of such flattering articles on the Comédie Française runaway that Sarah congratulated herself on her escapade and cried "Victory!" prematurely.

"Victory!" sang her heart. Thenceforward she would be her own mistress, would organize her own tours, and would sign contracts in Paris for the duration of any play that happened to appeal to her. Victory! She opened the window of her London hotel and inhaled the foggy air, permeated with the scent of American tobacco. The sun playing on the river made Turner landscapes of it. Everything filled her with enthusiasm. What a pity it was that Maurice had not come with her!

He would like those calm Englishmen who were quite amusing when one got to know them, and were healthy, good-looking and courteous, and well dressed in clothes rather too big for them. He would have been able to ride in the Row and to flirt with English girls whose faces were like exotic flowers on a background of soft blonde straw.

However, Maurice was not concerned with the fashionable world, or the public, or the articles in the papers. He was proud of his mother and jealous of her; he was like a gardener with a rare orchid, who cannot bear curious people to thrust their commonplace features into its calyx. He sometimes wished that his mother could become plain Madame Bernhardt, as one becomes Mrs. Smith! On the other hand, he never suffered because of his irregular origin. His physical and mental qualities secured his position for him: no one ever ventured to make any allusion in his presence to what might have been.

Victory! Sarah's mind went back to the past. Just long enough to say to the London scenery, while conjuring up certain other scenery in Brussels, "My heart does not ache so much now."

Victory over that first unhappy love! Sarah wanted to mingle with the noise and population of the old City, to stroll in Hyde Park, to visit Madame Tussaud's, to run as far as the Tower of London, to send the Princess Royal dozens of roses to thank her for having come to her first night. She was so headstrong. She felt herself to be so young, so invulnerable! But her white dresses, her slimness, her gaiety, and her pranks once more made her a butt for her detractors. She was always doing something farcical, and these farces— as in *Beffa*, which she produced several years later—played her sorry tricks. She was not forgiven for buying a cheetah at the Zoo, nor for walking in Hyde Park with a bear on a lead, nor for having accepted as gifts six chameleons, three dogs and another monkey—animals whose extraordinary names constantly recurred in her conversation at all times, so that people never knew whether she was anxious about the health of a friend or that of a monkey or of a parrot.

Nor was she forgiven for ordering twelve trunks made of some rare leather, for receiving as many as sixty baskets of flowers in one day, for making the English roar their enthusiasm, for laughing at the women's fashions, for wearing three or four gold and silver belts one above the other and never wearing stays. Nor (and this last protest came from the women) for attracting the most handsome, the cleverest and the least impressionable of the men, in spite of the absence in her silhouette of those graceful curves in which, until that time, had consisted the charm of Eve in the eyes of Adam.

In short, she was not forgiven for being herself.

While Sarah was thus parading herself, parasites were once again at work on the rose-bush. In Paris, the Beloved Monster, kept informed of her movements by the Press and annoyed by her enthusiastic English reception, decided to turn a cold shoulder to its idol on her return to the Capital. It gave her to understand, in a dozen different ways, that it had had enough, once for all, of Sarah Bernhardt's turpitudes, of her thirst for advertisement and of her impossible character. Her true friends wrote her affectionate and anxious letters. She scarcely read them and continued to walk the tight-rope while shouting at the top of her voice. Then . . .

.   .   .   .   .

("One day, Lysiane, I returned from an amusing picnic at Maidenhead with some of the cast: Devoyod, Kalb, Mary Julien, your Aunt Jeanne, Pierre Berton and Dieudonné. Exhausted, but happy, I went home before the performance. We were playing *Frou-Frou*, and that play always aroused delirious enthusiasm among the English audience. As I entered my drawing-room in Chester Square (I had left the hotel for a small flat) I saw on the table a black-edged envelope. I knew that it contained bad news, not news of a death, but of something very vexatious.

"The letter was from my lawyer. It informed me, in legal terms, that I had lost the action brought against me by the Comédie Française. I was ordered to pay a hundred thousand francs damages with interest, and to suffer the confiscation of the forty-three thousand francs which I had confided to its care.

"I was expecting this, but the amount to be paid was far greater than I had bargained for. What was I to do? Was it true, as I had been warned by Louise Abbéma, Clairin and Parrot, that the Paris theatre directors, in a sort of moral conspiracy, would refuse to engage me on my return? Was it true that the Parisian public would boo me on my reappearance on the stage? Was it true that, for the moment, no author would dare to give me a part?")

.   .   .   .   .

At the end of her contract, Sarah returned to Paris with the feeling of a lion-tamer leaping suddenly into the middle of a cage to get his animals under control. But she encountered neither ill-will nor calumny. They had melted away, and with them disappeared the young woman's fighting spirit. The Press was silent, and there were no recriminations. Only the members of the Little Court remained with their disconsolate faces and sad expressions. Out of friendship for her, Arthur Meyer wrote a long article in the *Gaulois* on the return of Sarah Bernhardt. No one seemed to notice it.

At first, Sarah was amused by this silence. Then, after struggling against it like a wounded animal, fettered by that liberty for which she had cried so loudly, she became unnerved, ran into debt and fell ill. She sold her jewels, her bracelets, her gold belts and her horses. She was even on the point of being arrested for debt, but a respite was obtained.

Then one morning she refused to get up and lay in bed with her eyes closed, her mind a blank, while at her door moneylenders, creditors, a few faithful friends, sensation-mongers, and even sadists knocked and rang.

.   .   .   .   .

"You can't go on like this, Sarah. You must do something. You have always been so combative, so eager for the fray. But for the past week you have been lying there indifferent to everything. Would you like me to call a doctor?"

"No, mama. The doctors condemned me to death once. What could they add to such a definite diagnosis?"

"Do you want me to give you some money?"

"No, thank you. You haven't too much for yourself and I've already borrowed from you. No, only one thing really distresses me. When I go out of my house I have to cross the courtyard. To the left, near the stables of my own horses, or, rather, where my own horses used to be, there is a small stall, painted white, with a green shutter. Over the door is a name: *Nacelle*. But the stall remains empty because I have not kept my promise to the person whom I love most in the world. And now less than ever am I in a position to buy the pony. So I might as well stay in bed, so as not to see my creditors' ugly faces or the white stall."

Sarah, buried in a cloud of white lace, turned her hollow-cheeked face and her eyes wet with tears towards her mother.

"I understand that," muttered Madame Bernhardt, rising with some difficulty, as Judy had become fat, and suffered from shortness of breath. "But I don't understand your apathy."

"I am not apathetic, mama; I am merely waiting. I am waiting in the most comfortable manner possible—that is to say, in bed."

"What are you waiting for, dear?"

"For the event that will change all this. It cannot be far away now."

"I'm afraid you are pushing our belief in fate too far."

"It cannot be long now," repeated Sarah, closing her eyes.

With heavy footsteps Madame Bernhardt went down to the courtyard, passed by the empty stall and sighed. But never for a moment did she consider that her daughter was mad to expect "something" to happen, stretched there on her bed, ill, without a doctor, without will-power, with bills pouring in on her like snow and bailiffs constantly knocking at the door.

The next day Judy returned. She did not pester Sarah, but just smiled at her, taking turns with Madame Guérard and Maurice, who were unhappy and helpless, to keep her company. And on the following day Judy came again.

Judy's eyes held a silent enquiry. Sarah replied, "Nothing yet."

And Judy returned again that afternoon.

While she was telling Sarah, in an attempt to distract her mind, how Monsieur Berentz eventually got a wife in spite of his beard and his hair, which was now white, Émile knocked and entered, flushed and rather flustered.

"There's a foreign gentleman who insists on madame seeing him."

"Is he a journalist?" asked the sick woman.

"He's an Englishman. His name is . . . heavens! I've forgotten it!"

"It doesn't matter," said Sarah in a weary voice. "Send him away."

At that moment Sarah caught Judith Bernhardt's eye, and she called Émile back.

"Ask him what he wants."

"He wants to see you, madame. He gave me no reason and he was rather truculent."

A loud voice on the staircase broke in:

"Mademoiselle, my name is Jarrett and I am one of the greatest of English impresarios. I've come to bring you money and a contract for the United States. If you cannot see me today I will come back tomorrow or the next day. But this boy isn't going to stop me seeing you."

Maurice, in a rage, burst into his mother's room and declared that he was going to "throw the man out".

"Maurice," said Sarah, "tell this gentleman, very politely, first to stop talking on the stairs; and secondly that I shall expect him here tomorrow afternoon at three o'clock. And, Maurice, bear in mind that this gentleman has in his pocket a piece of paper which might well procure an occupant for Nacelle's stall."

Maurice shook his head. He did not like this business at all. Then he looked at his mother and his grandmother open-mouthed. They were now both smiling; they seemed to be calmly picking up the threads of life where they had dropped them some days before. Everything had been going so badly in the Rue Fortuny. No more money, no more time given to pay, no visitors received, bills, summonses; and the moving spirit of the house sick and as though plunged into a coma interspersed with nightmares. And now his mother flung off the bedclothes, colour returned to her cheeks and she quietly put on her slippers, stretched herself and embraced his grandmother.

"You see, mama, the event has taken place!" The arrival of the impresario now seemed something quite natural and foreseen. "I will inform my friends! Arthur Meyer will look after the journalists."

"You must be careful, my Sarah, you still look very weak. Well, Maurice, instead of standing there gaping, why don't you obey your mother? Go and see this gentleman and give him her message."

Maurice ran downstairs. Half-way down he found the Jarrett "event" sitting down. The Englishman got up; he was a tall, lanky creature, with white hair and frank, serious, blue eyes.

"All right, I'll come tomorrow, my friend."

He held out a sympathetic hand which the boy gladly shook. Maurice felt a sort of frantic glee coming over him. The bad dream was receding, and his mother was talking again. Oh, how he longed to hug her!

As soon as he had seen the impresario off, Maurice, guided by his mother's siren voice, hurried back to the drawing-room. His mother, with her hair tidy and her face made up, was already scolding her domestic staff.

"How stupid you are, Émile. Why are there no flowers in the house? You never do anything right. What were you waiting for? Money? Or for my death and for the wreaths? Félicie! Félicie! Iron out my satin and lace dress. Well, hurry up! Who came today? The same old lot. Anyway, that doesn't interest me. Take a cab and go and tell Clairin, Arthur Meyer, Parrot, the Comtesse de Najac and my sister Jeanne that I'm giving a dinner-party this evening at the Café de Paris. And, Maurice, go and tell Besson to harness . . . Oh yes, of course, the horses have been sold. Well, tell him to hire a carriage; and don't let Nick lie on the divan, he eats the cushion fringes. And now, mama, I will willingly accept your four thousand francs; give them to Jeanne to bring to me. I'll see you later. Heavens, how stuffy it is in here! Is there any reason, because I have at last found time to be ill for a few days, for all the windows to be hermetically closed? Félicie, burn some of the jasmine joss-sticks."

She was through the tunnel. Would the New World like her? Confident of her destiny, and putting her trust in the honest Jarrett, she signed a seven months' contract for America. She received a large sum of money on account, paid part of her debts, bought her son's pony, and got ready for her tour. The Press began to speak about her again. The public became alarmed by the impending departure of its neglected idol. Theatre managers offered her engagements immediately or on her return to France.

For some weeks all was flowers, flattery, protestations of friendship and of fidelity: Paris, repentant and affectionate, realized that Sarah was leaving it. And Sarah knew that it was her duty to go.

CHAPTER XXII

THE *AMÉRIQUE*

THE extraordinary Mr. Jarrett had chosen the steamship *Amérique* deliberately. However, this liner, if we may dignify her by such a stately description, enjoyed a very bad reputation. Bad luck seemed to attend each of her voyages. She looked terrible; the paint was scaling off her plates in large patches, as though she suffered from some monstrous disease, and when the stokers piled on too much coal an alarming throbbing sound rose from her old entrails. Her captain, whose name was Jouclas, declared that through the spluttering mouth of her funnel the *Amérique* declaimed the inglorious and completely ridiculous epic of the poor ship: once she had lost three lifeboats which were badly secured to their davits; and in the previous year the pumps had failed to function because they had been fitted upside down! And at each crossing, storms, mysteriously informed of the ship's position, waited for the *Amérique*, bearing down upon her with vertiginous speed, buffeting her with mountainous seas and wreaking upon her all the fury of gales and thunderstorms.

So, on the morning of October 15, 1880, Jarrett, who had struck a good bargain for the transport of his passengers, strode up and down the quays of Le Havre, waiting for his star; fearing Sarah's rather definite ideas of her own importance, he wanted to prepare her gently for the discovery of the *Amérique* with her jumble of decks, saloons and cabins which piled on each other higgledy-piggledy without any apparent method or idea of convenience.

But Sarah had other thoughts in her mind than those of the beauty of her ship. The idea of departure so upset her now that, having arrived at the wharf an hour too early, she was hiding with her son in a dock-side tavern.

"Mama, darling, you've still got half an hour."

"Will you write to me often?"

"Twice a week."

"I want to know what you are doing, what you are thinking about, and what you are saying. Go and see the doctor once a fortnight. Don't ride your friendU——'s horse Crack. It isn't safe. Be content with Nacelle. Promise me on your word of honour."

"I've already given it to you!"

"Give it to me again."

"Then, mama, it won't be a word of honour any more; it will only be words," said the boy, laughing. "Anyway, it's time we went to the boat."

Suddenly realizing that she was going to leave her beloved son for many long months, Sarah was overcome with grief. She took both his hands in hers and pressed them distractedly.

"Maurice, Maurice! I can't——"

"Come on, mama, take my arm."

A sound of uproar put an end to this touching scene. While Sarah Bernhardt and Maurice were approaching the embarkation stage, Jarrett was haranguing a group of people, emphasizing his remarks by waving his arms about.

"Idiot!" he cried, addressing Félicie. "You ought never to have let her leave without giving me warning. Madame Sarah Bernhardt is under contract to me!"

"Possibly, my dear fellow, but I am not yet your prisoner," replied a clear, rather sarcastic, voice.

Sarah had come up on her son's arm. She had not troubled to say where she was going and her companions, in alarm, had been looking for her everywhere for three-quarters of an hour. Dock-loungers, voyagers, emigrants and reporters were soon all involved in the argument. And it was in a complete uproar that Sarah and Maurice crossed the gangway, inadequately protected by Jarrett, who, with angry looks and set jaw, endeavoured ineffectually to keep them from being jostled.

"Mind the shooting-star!" exclaimed a journalist with a laugh.

When calm had been restored a small crowd followed Sarah as far as her cabin. Arrived there, Jarrett recovered his calm, opened the door and stood to one side. Sarah looked round and laughed gleefully. The cabin was decorated everywhere with red, white and blue flowers in the form of the initials "S. B." interlaced. These initials extended even as far as the bed-hangings, and on the bed lay her Mongolian rug, her clothes and her personal effects, all neatly spread out.

"You *are* a charming man," she said in English, with that pronounced French accent of which she was never able to rid herself, in spite of all her numerous travels to English-speaking countries.

Putting her head on one side and lowering her eyelashes, she gave Jarrett a sweet smile. No one could resist Sarah when she smiled like that. The impresario lowered his blue eyes in turn and with a wide sweep of his arm indicated the artistes, her friends, Madame Guérard, Félicie and the two stewards.

"These are the people whom you must thank."

There were farewells all round, then everyone left except Maurice.

"Mama, it is better that I should leave too. I am going on shore with Madame Chesnau." Here the young boy tried to clear his voice and to make it seem strong and masculine. "I have brought you something, a photograph of myself on Nacelle."

Maurice placed the framed photograph on the shelf over Sarah's bed and she went over and gazed at it.

"Thank you, darling. Come and kiss me."

But when Sarah turned round Maurice had gone.

She hurried on deck, crying "Maurice!" But the gangway was already being lowered, the siren was blowing and, on shore, people were waving handkerchiefs: seagulls circled round the ship and seemed also to be waving farewell to those on shore. "Maurice!" Sarah looked for her son among the crowd. Suddenly she caught sight of him. Where, now, was the handsome lad, so proud and so brave? All that she saw was a small boy whose shoulders shook with sobs as he ran back towards the town.

"Look after him, Madame Chesnau!" cried Sarah into the blue.

"Don't worry!" a phantom voice replied.

Sarah seemed to hear her name repeated several times. The ship was slowly gathering way and farewells from the shore were wafted up to her, muffled, indistinct. Like an automaton, she descended the companionway to her cabin and collapsed on her bed, abandoning herself to her sorrow. She had never felt so lonely, so deserted; she only hoped that the boat would split in two, so that they might all be drowned, she and the cold, hard Jarrett and all the passengers in that ridiculous ship. Then the gentle movement of the *Amérique* lulled her sorrow. In her imagination she was wafted along by a kindly giant who strode over the sea with a rolling gait. Then she thought, "I shall be hideous at dinner this evening at the captain's table, with my large mouth, swollen eyes and congested nose."

And on that note she fell asleep.

.   .   .   .   .

In spite of the ship's bad reputation, there were no accidents on the voyage. Sarah soon recovered her equilibrium and her gaiety and strode up and down the deck with the actor Angelo, while the sea air whipped her face. On the fourth day out she felt quite revived, young, splendid and strong. Debts, gossip, petty jealousies and hatreds all disappeared with the French coast. Only the image of her son remained ever present in her mind. The shelf over her bunk was filled with photographs of him. Maurice at six months, at a year, at the age of seven, at twelve. The last one which he had just given her showed him as a young man astride Nacelle.

"The captain says we're in for some rough weather. I hope you are a good sailor and have got good sea-legs."

"So far I've never crossed anything but the English Channel, where I behaved reasonably enough; anyway, the sea is quite calm."

Scarcely were the words out of Sarah's mouth than the ship began to pitch; huge black clouds came scurrying towards each other; the sea became dotted with foam-tipped wavelets crossing one another like sword-blades; ten minutes later the rain started pouring down in torrents on the upper deck from a threatening mauve-coloured sky, and a storm began to rage round the *Amérique*. The ship creaked and groaned, plunged whining into the sea and staggered out again, buffeted by the waves. Angelo wanted Sarah to return to her cabin.

"Certainly not, my dear fellow. It's a wonderful sight; I won't be sea-sick for another hour."

Angelo looked at her in surprise. Then, going hideously green, he fled below. Sarah continued her walk until she saw an elderly woman coming in the opposite direction, clinging to the handrail. The wind blew her about so much that she finally lost her balance and fell on her knees, and Sarah, going to her assistance, raised her up and, taking her arm, tried to reach the companionway with her. She had almost reached it when a larger wave came over the starboard rail and threw the two women on the deck; the other woman fell so awkwardly on the wet boards that she began to slide feet foremost towards the companionway. Sarah realized the danger at once; the other woman would be bound to crack her head at the bottom of the iron steps. Sarah flung herself at the old lady and grasped one of her arms with one hand, gripping the handrail with the other. It was a miracle that they were not both scuppered. Some deck-hands who witnessed the incident caught hold of the women. Sarah, who sustained a wrenched elbow, laughingly thanked them. The other woman was taken to the saloon and given brandy.

"Madame," she whispered to Sarah in French, with an American accent, "I have to thank you for saving my life." There was, however, a certain irony in the way in which she said this. "Will you be kind enough to tell me your name?"

"Sarah Bernhardt."

As though actuated by a spring, the American lady rose up. She gazed keenly at Sarah and her lips began to tremble. She acknowledged her introduction with a slight bow.

"I, madame, am Abraham Lincoln's widow."

And she left the saloon, refusing any further offer of help.

"Well," said one of their fellow travellers, "the old party has an odd way of thanking you!"

Sarah replied:

"Abraham Lincoln was assassinated by a man named Booth, an actor from the Washington Theatre. His widow has not forgotten that." And her eyes filled with tears.

"But, surely, today it is you, an actress, who has saved Mrs. Lincoln's life."

"No doubt Mrs. Lincoln is angry with me for having kept her alive, thus preventing her from rejoining her adored one at the first possible moment."

This incident upset Sarah considerably, but she was too proud to have it out with the famous President's wife, and merely avoided meeting her on deck; this was not difficult, as the storm, so far from abating, seemed to gain in intensity. Once more the *Amérique* had proved to be a magnet for bad weather.

One evening, Sarah was playing a game of *salta* with Angelo before dinner. The other artistes—those who had survived the ravages of sea-sickness— were playing cards; a young Frenchwoman was singing one of Béranger's songs, accompanying herself at the piano. Sarah, who was not very musical, but who made up for it by being a very bad player, was humming out of tune and accusing her opponent of using the pitching of the boat to move his pieces. Suddenly the girl at the piano uttered a loud scream. Following her gaze, the passengers saw, framed in the saloon doorway, an emaciated face with glittering eyes, belonging to a man of about forty. His left cheek was disfigured by a deep scar. Three other men's heads, each scarcely more reassuring, appeared behind him.

"Haha! You're playing and you're amusing yourselves," said Number One, with a strong Spanish accent, "while below the poor emigrants are being thrown about by the storm like ninepins."

The table at which Sarah sat caught his eye and, staggering over to it, he made the pretty mother-o'-pearl pieces fly with a well-directed blow of his fist.

"I can tell you one thing, and that is, if there is a shipwreck, we emigrants will save ourselves and the turn of you rich people will come afterwards. And you can always use these tables as rafts. And you, madame, who are so thin, you can easily fit into a drawer."

spire of the Church of the Trinity, the Post Office and the City Hall Park. The towers of Brooklyn Bridge were beginning to rise.

Their landing took place through a crowd of sightseers brought there by curiosity. Men and women stared unceremoniously at Sarah and she began to fear that her approach to the Beloved Monster in the United States would be less easy than she had bargained for. So she decided, after all, to give a reception to a few journalists at her hotel. But she soon grew so tired of their questions, and so bored with saying that she did not like cheese, that her son did not wear his hair long, that her own hair curled naturally, that her mother and sister really were her mother and sister, that she did not travel with her coffin . . . that at length she asked that any more reporters who asked to see her at the Albemarle Hotel should be sent away.

Jarrett again intervened: it was not necessary to receive them all, but she must have a word with the more important of them. So, without more ado, Jarrett ushered in the first of these gentlemen. Sarah, furious, threw herself face downwards on the ground, with her arms stretched out on either side of her. The terrified journalist fled and told his colleagues what he had seen. Another reporter came up, then another, then five more, all completely disconcerted by what they saw. Then Jarrett had an idea.

"Madame Sarah Bernhardt is very tired. If you like, gentlemen, I will talk in her place. She will sit in that easy chair where you can look at her at your ease, and, if you want to, make drawings of her."

The proposal was agreed to by both sides. Sarah curled up into an easy chair and the impresario replied tirelessly to all the questions put to him, however absurd they might be; where necessary he invented, sure of not being contradicted; for Sarah was sound asleep.

Sarah awoke at the moment at which a draughtsman was putting the finishing touches to a sketch of her, and she snatched the drawing out of his hand; it represented a skeleton surmounted by a nest of serpents. Without a word Sarah tore up the drawing and threw the pieces on the ground; but the draughtsman picked them up, put them into his pocket and made for the door.

On the following morning, most of the New York papers reproduced the skeleton with the serpent-wig.

CHAPTER XXIV

"THE BERNHARDT"

"The Bernhardt" was the name given Sarah by the Americans in the course of her United States tours in 1880, 1886, 1891, 1896, 1900, 1905, 1910, 1913 and 1916. They used the expression "the Bernhardt" as they would say "the Academy" or "the Theatre". In 1917 I accompanied my grandmother to the United States: the Americans still called her "the Bernhardt". She was then seventy-two.

When, on November 8, 1880, she made her first appearance in New York in *Adrienne Lecouvreur*, by Scribe and Legouvé, Booth's Theatre was completely sold out. The New York ticket agencies were more than grateful to Jarrett for having brought to New York this extraordinary, thin, eccentric person who received journalists lying flat on the floor in her hotel, and who bought dogs, materials and furs as other women bought powder, cosmetics or jewellery.

Yet the public as a whole hesitated to express its admiration for this foreigner who arrived preceded by a fanfare of trumpets. During the first act, certain people in the stalls thought each actress who appeared on the stage was Sarah Bernhardt. "There she is! There's the Bernhardt," they whispered.

Then someone in the third row of the stalls, annoyed by all this talking, leaned over to someone in the second row and said in a loud voice:

"Sh! Sarah Bernhardt does not come on in the first act."

The third, sixth and eighth rows and even some of the circle heard the remark. Someone who misunderstood it got up and made for the exit. Another followed suit, and then a score of the audience, all asking for their money back because "the Bernhardt" was not playing. An announcement had to be made from the stage to the effect that Sarah Bernhardt appeared in the other acts. Order was re-established and the curtain fell on desultory and perfunctory applause.

After five minutes of interval the public grew impatient and started stamping, clapping and whistling. For two months it had, by means of paragraphs and headlines in the Press, been promised a curiosity: and it was not going to brook any further delay. At last Sarah made her entry in the second act. The audience was silent, not knowing what to think. Sarah Bernhardt! But this woman was not even very pretty. Indeed, they had never seen anything like her. That slim outline, that proud, fascinating face, those eyes. And then Sarah began to speak. Her voice rippled out like a bubbling spring and held the audience spellbound with its music. Her nervousness could mar neither its purity nor its modulations. A murmur, swift as an electric current, ran through the audience and bound them together in their common surprise. They had not yet reached the stage of admiring her; they were still uncertain. They had heard so much of this transatlantic marvel! And here was merely a woman, more feminine than anything they could imagine or hope for.

Sarah Bernhardt herself admitted that she had more than once won over lukewarm audiences by her intense femininity. She could appear either lascivious, or quivering with fear, or in despair. Tears, real tears, were always near her eyes. She could make her voice metallic with terror or tender with love. Her expression could be either commanding, cunning or distraught with passion. Hands that shook with emotion, arms outstretched in token of surrender or of sacrifice. The bearing of a queen, of a coquette, of a mistress, of a mother, of a murderess; or floating over the earth like a fairy princess. She could interpret any feminine rôle, from the humblest to the highest, from the most malignant to the most virtuous. And that evening in New York, when Adrienne Lecouvreur, mistress of the handsome Maurice of Saxony, rebelled against the Duchesse de Bouillon, the hearts of the audience beat more rapidly. The spectators did not understand all the dialogue, but the inflexions of Sarah Bernhardt's voice, her gestures and her expression made them vibrate in sympathy with Adrienne's love and enthusiasm.

After *Adrienne Lecouvreur* Sarah gave *La Dame aux Camélias*, with the handsome actor Angelo in the rôle of Armand Duval. While attending the final rehearsals of this play at Booth's Theatre, Sarah recalled that July 19, 1870, was the day on which the younger Dumas, after escaping from the boisterous attentions of her puma and her dogs, had left his manuscript with her while the soldiers in the street were rejoining their regiments.

La Dame aux Camélias, Phèdre, L'Aiglon! Those were the mainstays of Sarah Bernhardt's dramatic and lyrical career. At the Théâtre de la Renaissance, and later at the Théâtre Sarah-Bernhardt, when a new piece did not come up to expectations, one of those three plays was quickly substituted for it, and either Marguerite, or Theseus's incestuous spouse, or the Duc de Reichstadt saved the situation, filled the box-office and made up the deficit.

On the first occasion on which she played the part of Marguerite Gautier in New York, Sarah, who never allowed herself to hark back into the past, could not help doing so for a moment. When, in the third act, Marguerite writes to her lover to tell him that he must renounce her, Sarah, excited by the hundreds of people who followed her movements and hung upon her words, imagined herself back in the little room in Brussels in which she had written that letter to her Prince. Would he be pleased to hear of her success in the New World? Would he even hear of it? She had sworn never to see him again, but not to stop loving him. In her innermost heart she carried a wound whose presence no one, save Madame Guérard, ever suspected. She laughed, worked and, in spite of this other memory, loved; no power on earth, no man, could prevent Sarah Bernhardt from enjoying the hour and the moment, or from listening to the ariettas, the songs and the hymns which life orchestrated for her. Sarah lived quite happily with her wound. She wore it against her side like a dagger, but, if she did not take care, the steel could still hurt her.

For a fleeting moment, Sarah, her face bathed in tears, showed her despair to the audience. There, in the proscenium, sat a fair young man who looked like her son Maurice; in the same way that Maurice himself looked like the Memory. But the evocation only lasted for a second.

Already Marguerite Gautier, proud in her act of renunciation, had sealed her letter and fled into the night. And the house rocked with applause.

·   ·   ·   ·   ·

Jarrett could be courteous enough if he tried. His star's dressing-room, sumptuously furnished and filled with flowers, was adorned with dwarf palm trees and other green plants, not to mention, of course, Sarah's personal possessions, make-up bottles, cushions and fur rugs, all carefully arranged by the deft hands of Félicie and the loving ones of Madame Guérard.

"I am taking you with me as piece of my native land," Sarah had told Madame Guérard before leaving France.

After the first performance of *La Dame aux Camélias*, "the Bernhardt", while removing her make-up, discussed finance with Jarrett. The receipts had surpassed their expectations and Sarah had been making plans: to pay her debts in France, to send some money to her son, to repay her mother.

"I'll be back in five minutes, madame. Don't forget that we are having supper with Abbey, the impresario, and a few New York notables."

"Yes," replied Sarah.

A tacit understanding existed between Jarrett and Sarah Bernhardt. Jarrett insisted on a minimum of co-operation from Sarah to maintain good relations with the battalions of reporters, and Sarah received their questions, their impertinences and their official dinners with unvarying good humour. "The fierce gentleman", as Sarah dubbed him, knew quite well, as gentle Mother Saint-Sophie had known in former days, the exact words to use to calm the actress's nerves, or to cope with her revolts, which were sometimes justified. But that evening Jarrett's patience was tried pretty highly. This is what happened.

Several American women, who had been to Sarah's dressing-room to congratulate her, returned to the front entrance of Booth's Theatre. When the people loitering there saw these elegant women, with their escorts in dress clothes, they thought that Sarah Bernhardt was going to make use of the front entrance and hastened to warn the crowd collected round the stage door. When asked about it, the amused visitors declared that, on the contrary, she would be leaving by the other door, where her carriage awaited her. So the crowd all returned to the stage door, collecting other people with them as they went. Several hundred people were soon stamping their feet in the cold, hoping to see the young woman and to accompany her back to her hotel.

The door opened on the brilliantly lit porch, and, warmly muffled in a beaver cloak, with hair covered with a silk lace scarf, Sarah appeared on Jarrett's arm; applause immediately broke out and cheers went up in the chilly air while police, holding hands, tried in vain to press the crowd back. Then Sarah's coachman, in trying to bring up his horses, knocked down a woman. Sarah screamed, but the woman quickly rose and ran up to her, saying, "Please sign my autograph book!"

This was a most unfortunate inspiration. As though by magic, pieces of paper began issuing from pockets and handbags: men thrust forward their cuffs or pointed to their shirt-fronts or even their collars. Sarah signed and went on signing. Elbowing her way roughly forward, a woman admirer approached the actress. She had fanatical eyes and full red lips. Sarah, still signing, turned towards her.

"And what about me?" asked the girl in a hoarse voice. "I want your signature too." And she held out her programme.

124

"Have you a pencil?" asked Sarah.

But the excited woman took a penknife from her pocket, pulled down her glove, cut her wrist and, tearing a feather from her hat, dipped it in the blood. All this occurred in less time than it takes to write down.

"Oh!" cried Sarah, revolted.

"What does it matter? It is only blood," replied her admirer, passionately.

"The girl's crazy!" exclaimed Jarrett, shocked.

Jeanne burst out laughing and quickly hid behind the group formed by her sister, Angelo, Piron and Jarrett. The more the crowd grew, the angrier the impresario became. Important people were waiting supper for them and there they were, hemmed in by these shoving men and hysterical women. It was perfectly ludicrous. The "fierce gentleman" called up a policeman and spoke to him in a low voice and then, turning quickly on his heel, he led Sarah back into the theatre.

"Aren't we going to supper, after all?" she asked, delighted that her admirers had succeeded in ruffling the usually phlegmatic impresario.

"We're waiting here for police reinforcements," replied Jarrett, crossly.

"I've an idea. Let's put my cloak and scarf on Jeanne and then leave by the front."

Jeanne, delighted by the idea, put on the beaver cloak and placed the lace scarf on her pretty fair hair and then, taking Angelo's arm, walked boldly out of the stage door. There she shook hands and signed autographs, delighted at the idea of impersonating her sister and playing a trick on everyone.

"Idiots!" she said to Angelo, who was protecting her as best he could. "They can't see the difference between the sun and the moon."

CHAPTER XXV

THOMAS EDISON

WHEN Sarah had been in New York for a month it was decided that she should pay a visit to Thomas Edison. From whom did this suggestion come in the first place? From Sarah Bernhardt? From Jarrett? From Abbey, her other impresario? Surely not from Thomas Edison himself, the inventor of the phonograph and of the electric lamp? This reserved, retired scholar had to summon all his courtesy to give a polite reception to the woman whose actions and gestures were daily reported in the Press, often with rather critical comment.

Sarah Bernhardt's hermetically closed landau rumbled through the darkness, followed by another vehicle carrying some of her friends, about fifteen people in all. The road between Menlo Park Station and Thomas Edison's property was not lit and Sarah dozed, numbed by the cold and by boredom. How much she would have preferred to be lying in bed, with her inseparable Mongolian rug pulled right up to her chin, in the wholesome oblivion that she sought each night, buried in her five pillows. She was aroused from this doze by cheers rising on all sides, and Sarah thought she was entering Paradise. The trees, the lawns, and the hedges appeared to her amazed eyes as though encrusted with precious stones: sapphires, amethysts, rubies, emeralds, diamonds and topazes sparkled everywhere. Branches shone in the reflection of carefully concealed lights, while the bushes seemed to bear golden fruit and clusters of silver grapes. The snow on the ground glittered like a bed of mother-o'-pearl. Sarah's carriage halted before the house, on the steps of which a crowd of people seemed to be waiting for her.

"Which is Thomas Edison?" Sarah asked herself.

It was as light as day; a woman came forward, and presented her with a bouquet.

"Thank you, madame," said Sarah, and walked towards a man who stood slightly apart from the rest. "Monsieur Edison? I am so happy, so proud to know you. I have much admiration for your work, your researches and your achievements."

Thomas Edison bowed and Mrs. Edison, who was much more amiable than her husband, suggested to her guest that she should visit the "workrooms" while awaiting supper. Sarah agreed and the scientist begged her to be good enough to follow him. They passed through several huge rooms; Thomas Edison, the genius of light, touched a button, pulled down a lever, or pressed a switch and flashes appeared all around them; flames shot up and he controlled them; lightning flashes entwined with each other and he separated them; blinding forks of light broke the darkness of the room and went out again at his command.

"This man may be a genius, but he thinks I am an idiot," thought Sarah, who wanted to make an impression on her host. So she exerted her intelligence, and possibly also her charm, to question him about illumination, in which she was, naturally, intensely interested. She discussed the importance of footlights and battens on the mind of the public which, in darkness itself, has an entirely objective attitude towards what happens on the stage. Gradually, Thomas Edison's stiffness melted like snow in sunlight, and he took the young woman into his study, where for half an hour he spoke to her of the two passions which filled his existence: light and Shakespeare.

When they returned to the drawing-room they were delighted with each other, and Sarah came to the conclusion that, although she needed the worship of the Beloved Monster, she also needed the respect of intelligent people. She remembered a talented young painter who, by his attainments and his hard work, had attained high honours and wealth. But, in the midst of the general adulation, his best friend watched his progress and criticized it. So, in spite of the appreciation he received from everyone else, the painter craved for the admiration of only one person: that of his friend. His friend's coolness and criticism gradually depressed him to such an extent that when the 1870 war broke out he volunteered and was killed, with the sole object of gaining the esteem of the only person who did not appreciate his qualities.

.   .   .   .   .

("You are still too young, Lysiane. Later you will understand the irritation, the misery of being among friends all of whom love you except one. It is precisely that friendship which one most needs, even if the person in question is stupid, or even despicable. But, when the name of that person is Edison, you can imagine how necessary it is that he should like one.")

.   .   .   .   .

On the following morning Sarah, accompanied by her two impresarios, by Jeanne and by Madame Guérard, arrived at Boston Station and drove to her hotel. In spite of the cold, Jarrett insisted upon the carriage being open during the drive. When the carriage reached Boston Drive a man waiting on the kerb sprang on the carriage step. He wore a large fur cap and an opossum overcoat, through the open collar of which showed a bright red tie, in which was stuck a solitaire diamond the size of an almond. Sarah instinctively shrank back and Jarrett shouted to the uninvited guest to get off.

"Please, sir . . ." began the man and continued in very bad French, beseeching Sarah to honour him with a visit to a whale captured with great difficulty by his men in the neighbourhood of the Gulf of St. Lawrence.

"It is still alive, but you must be quick. It might even die tonight. I have brought it to Boston especially for you. It has cost me a small fortune."

"But I never asked you to do anything, sir. And please get down. You will only break your neck and then I shall be blamed for that too."

"I beg of you, madame, to come tomorrow morning. Not only do I promise you a marvellous spectacle, but also an amusing one. Naturally, the whole of your Company is included in the invitation."

Just then the horses took rather a sharp turn, the man lost his balance and Jarrett kept him from falling off by grabbing his coat-collar.

"All right!" said Sarah. "I'll go."

Anyway, she thought, it would amuse the Company, and there was no reason why she should not accept. The man in the opossum coat leaped down and disappeared.

"That's rather odd!" said Sarah, looking at the "fierce gentleman".

"Extremely," he replied coldly.

Publicity by all means, but this whale episode was more like a circus parade. Jarrett was not at all pleased by it.

For months Sarah was to regret this impulse of hers towards an unknown man who wore large diamonds and dressed like a Fenimore Cooper hero. The man in the fur coat (whose name incidentally, was Henry Smith) wasted no time during the night, tipping off the reporters, the citizens of Boston and the actors, and all this by relays of drummers, of sandwich-men and of street-parades: "Come tomorrow, at 10 a.m., with Sarah Bernhardt, to view the largest whale in the world." And one board even declared, "The French prodigy is visiting the Marine prodigy." This was a happy thought and Mr. Smith might have produced some excellent publicity slogans as a result of it. Fortunately, Sarah never saw this advertisement, which was being paraded about the streets by a poor devil dressed as Neptune. But Jarrett saw it. At the time his carriage was travelling at a walking pace towards the harbour where the whale lay dying; he sprang nimbly out, went up to the sandwich-man, and threatened to "push his face in" if he did not go straight back and turn his sandwich-board in.

At Boston harbour a huge crowd was pressing round the turnstiles: the price of admission was one dollar. Then it dawned on Sarah that Mr. Smith had played a trick on her. She had intended to do a favour to a somewhat original fisherman, but at any rate a decent fellow, and she found that she was supporting what was nothing less than a financial organization. This visit of hers was going to net the man with the diamond a lot of money! She took a quick glance at Jarrett and caught a quizzical look in his eye.

Sarah and her Company walked along a wharf lined with policemen, until they reached a grey, motionless sort of mound in the water; this was the whale. Ninety to a hundred feet long, it nearly filled the dock; a small step-ladder, flanked by four men dressed in white furs, was fastened, heaven knows how, to the whale's back, which was encrusted with limpets and barnacles. At the imminent risk of falling into the water through wooden parapets hastily erected during the night, people were straining and elbowing one another on the banks. Sarah Bernhardt was going to mount the whale! The whole incident was ridiculous and pointless. One of the white-clad men, a tall French-Canadian, offered Sarah his services. Sarah, hampered by her furs, allowed herself to be half-carried by the man and, before she realized what had happened, amid the cheers of the crowd, she found herself on this enormous mass. The cold had been so intense during the night that the water in the dock had frozen round the animal and ice-floes struck and crackled against its huge body. But that was a minor matter: the whale's back was also frozen! At the first step Sarah attempted to take she slipped, dragging her companion with her. From every corner of the quay laughter and cheers broke out. And Sarah, white with fury, remained seated on the whale's back, determined to remain there until her impresario sent a barrow for her. Then she took a sudden resolve.

Lucien Guitry

Sarah Bernhardt in *Lorenzaccio*

Sarah Bernhardt and her daughter-in-law, Terka, in the studio on the Boulevard Péreire

"Lead me to the edge," she told the white-clad man.

"But, madame, it is dangerous. You might slip again."

"Do as I tell you."

Holding her firmly to him, the Canadian led Sarah to the extreme edge of this strange platform, to the point where the enormous mass of the whale disappeared in a gentle slope into the water. Before the white-clad man knew what was happening Sarah leaped on to an ice-floe, and from that one to another, with the object of reaching the quayside where the Company and the disappointed mob were watching and where Jarrett was striding furiously up and down, and wiping his eyes watering with the cold.

But Mr. Smith's spectators were to have their money's worth after all.

The floe supporting Sarah suddenly broke away, swung slowly round and, impelled by some treacherous current, began to float towards the harbour entrance. Sarah stood proud and erect on her little floating island, glad of having escaped from a comic situation (for other people). One thought only dominated her mind, in spite of the cold : to kill Mr. Smith. And she wondered why the crowd was getting excited and shouting. It was not until she saw two men hurriedly put out in a boat and heard Jarrett, leaning perilously over the parapet, shout to her to wait for help, that she realized that she was in any danger ; the quayside, black with people, was receding from her ; her islet, gathering speed, was making for the open sea, threading its way smoothly through the smaller floes ; people waved their arms frantically. Sarah smiled. Now it was she who was making fools of them.

Rowing strongly, the boatmen were fortunate enough to intercept the floe, colliding with it so heavily that the boat's gunwale cracked. One of the men seized Sarah and hove her on board. And for that day, at least, the whole episode was at an end.

Sarah returned to her hotel and retired to bed with quantities of hot-water bottles and fur rugs. Jarrett, in a rage, had left her at her door without a word. Later on, however, he came to enquire after his star's health ; Sarah, in excellent humour, was playing dominoes.

"Why are you so angry with me? I wasn't to blame for all this."

"You ought never to have gone on that ice-floe, madame."

"Come, my dear Jarrett, it's no good looking at me like that! Would you ever have forgiven me if I had died of shame? Wouldn't it have been far better for me to drown?"

"If you had drowned," answered Jarrett categorically, "you would have been a dishonest woman, because you would have broken your contract."

There was no answer to that. For a moment Sarah stared at the "fierce gentleman" open-mouthed, then she held her hand out to him.

"Don't sulk, Jarrett. It wastes such a lot of time in life."

"The incident is closed. But that rogue must have made a small fortune this morning. What a stunt!" added Jarrett, pensively.

But Sarah had forgotten him : she realized that she was in the wrong. Had an accident occurred to her, she would not only have been breaking her contract with Jarrett, but she would also have put an end to that loving contract which she had, as it were, signed with her son in her heart and with her

129

blood; her son who was waiting for her so wistfully in Paris, and who trusted her.

The thought that she would not be seeing Maurice for many more months made her miserable. She put her hand to her forehead.

"You must be feeling upset," said Madame Guérard.

"No! It's time to go to the theatre. Let's be off!" She felt that on that evening nothing but the beloved public could distract her from her great love.

CHAPTER XXVI

MAURICE BERNHARDT

FOR some days the Bois de Boulogne had rid itself of its counterpane of snow. A few pockets still lingered beneath the thicker bushes, but the milder weather gave pedestrians and horsemen the chance of meeting again along the Sentier de la Vertu and on the sanded rides. Maurice, riding Nacelle and followed by his dog Nick, left the house in the Rue Fortuny at about ten o'clock and trotted up the Champs Élysées; when he reached the Avenue de l'Impératrice (now called the Avenue du Bois de Boulogne), he put his pony into a canter. The winter sun shone on the trees and the grass between them; the air was keen and crisp. The boy, who had a good seat, was followed at a few yards distance by Émile, on a hired hack. Maurice was on his way to meet d'U——, L. Stevens and his Ker-Bernhardt cousins, at the entrance to the Bois de Boulogne.

The day before, he had received a telegram from his mother at Springfield, Massachusetts. Twice a week Maurice sent her a long letter recounting all the smallest details of his life—up to a point; soft-pedalling on his more precocious adventures, he emphasized everything that concerned his studies, his comrades, the life in the Rue Fortuny, Madame Bernhardt's health, and that of Madame Chesnau and of his cousin Louise Ker-Bernhardt, a charming woman who considered that she had proprietary rights over him; he gave Sarah long dissertations upon the dogs, the parrots and the horses. Reassured about his darling mother, with money in his pocket, a few good friends and one or two feminine faces to grace his life, Maurice, in spite of Sarah's absence, was enjoying his life and the advantages of being a handsome, intelligent and well-to-do young man.

The young people were waiting for him by the Chinese Pavilion, a relic of the 1878 Exhibition, and the little cavalcade set out for the Acacias; they were all good riders, and many a pretty young woman's head turned to meet the smiling eyes of these personable young men. Yet d'U—— seemed to be preoccupied.

"Let us ride on a little, I want to talk to you," he said to Maurice, and, putting spurs to their horses, they raced ahead of their companions.

"Do you happen to have seen, in the *Cri Parisien*, the reproduction of a water-colour drawing of your mother exhibited at the Salon des Incohérents?"

"No," replied Maurice, with a sudden sinking feeling.

"It's infamous," went on young d'U——. "I've got a copy of it here. Look at it at your leisure. Not now. Come and see me at home about six o'clock. My father will be at his club and my mother at her charity sale. We can have a quiet talk."

Maurice took the cutting and put it in his pocket-book without unfolding it: it weighed on him like a stone. He could not bear anyone to talk about his mother without admiration, nor that anyone should mention her name without respect. She was the most important person in his life. She was his past, his

131

SARAH BERNHARDT

present and his future. She was She. Sometimes, in the studio in the Rue Fortuny, he would come across traces of that amber and jasmine scent which he reproached his mother for using when she was at home, and yet of which he was always seeking traces when she was away. To carry in one's heart such pure and jealous filial love sometimes has its disadvantages when the object of it happens to be named Sarah Bernhardt.

When he reached home, Maurice, before even removing his riding-boots, retired to his room and took out the cutting from the *Cri Parisien*. When he saw it his whole soul was revolted. That his mother should be caricatured for her leanness, that her semitic characteristics should be exaggerated and that the eccentricity of her coiffure should be made fun of, these were only so many pin-pricks which he had to put up with. But this disgusting thing of which he held a reproduction in his hand made him shudder. It showed his mother only half clothed. He strode up and down the room, striking his boots with his riding-whip, trying to keep calm. But his anger increased as he turned the insult over in his mind, and finally he sent for Émile and changed his clothes. He had decided what to do.

Towards two in the afternoon, a smart young man in a blue suit, and wearing grey gloves, took a cab in the Rue Villiers. Maurice drove to the Salon des Incohérents. He did not enter the picture gallery; he could not have borne that; he merely asked for the address of Monsieur Langlois, one of the exhibitors.

"I have been commissioned to buy one of this artist's pictures," said Maurice smoothly.

The commissionaire shrugged his shoulders and looked suspiciously at Maurice.

"I haven't got the addresses of the exhibitors."

"That's a pity," said Maurice, "a pity for Monsieur Langlois." And he slipped a gold coin into the man's hand. The man still hesitated, then, singling out a man who was just leaving the exhibition, he said:

"Here! Do you know where Langlois lives?"

"No, but he can always be found at about six o'clock at the Café Blanc, on the Boulevard de Montparnasse."

For the rest of the afternoon Maurice strolled about the streets, bought some ties at Charvet's and a new walking-stick, sent some flowers to an actress at the Odéon and had a drink at Tortoni's. At five o'clock he made for Montparnasse on foot; in spite of his indignation he was determined to remain calm. He would ask that blackguard Langlois to remove his painting from the Exhibition. If necessary he would buy it, and destroy it.

"Is Monsieur Langlois here?" he asked the waiter in the noisy, smoky Café Blanc.

"He's not yet arrived, sonny."

"All right, I'll wait for him."

He ordered a small glass of madeira, which he did not drink. All around him the clients were discussing art or politics.

"These aren't artists," thought the young man, petulantly. "They are degenerates and wasters."

In which he was wrong. A great number of these young men were really

132

talented. A year later, Grimm, invited to the Rue Fortuny, recognized, in the young master of the house, the little fop who had made a scene in the Café Blanc.

"There's Monsieur Langlois."

The waiter pointed to a bearded man of about forty who had just come in.

The artist greeted a few friends and then, leaning against the bar, he ordered an absinthe. Maurice was brave enough, but he was shy. The "blackguard" had a nice enough face, with commonplace and rather coarse features; he was neither well nor poorly dressed and looked like an ordinary, not over-clean, Parisian of the lower middle classes. Maurice paid for his drink and fingered his pocket-book in which the cutting from the *Cri Parisien* reposed.

His courage and self-possession returned to him in leaps and bounds, and he flushed with anger. Going up to Langlois, he said:

"Monsieur, I would like a word with you. Will you be good enough to come outside with me?"

"What's on your mind, my friend?" asked the caricaturist calmly.

"Monsieur, it is difficult for me to talk to you here, with all this noise. What I have to say to you is a personal matter."

"You surely don't think that I am going out of my way to catch cold on the Boulevard merely to obey a boy like you?"

"I am not a boy," retorted Maurice, raising his voice. "My name is Maurice Bernhardt!"

"Don't know him," said Langlois, frankly.

"I am Madame Sarah Bernhardt's son."

"Oh? Well, what can I do about it?"

"I want you, monsieur, to withdraw from the Salon des Incohérents the insulting drawing you have made of my mother. I am prepared to buy it from you."

"Really? I can quite understand your being annoyed. But the picture is amusing and is very well suited to the exhibition. I am sorry, for your sake."

And Langlois turned his back on Maurice, who cried:

"Very well, monsieur, you will hear further from me, for I find myself compelled to send you my seconds."

Langlois roared with laughter.

"I don't fight with children and schoolboys. Wait until your beard begins to grow before insulting people. Look at that infant! A duel? And all because of a caricature of an eccentric actress——"

He did not finish. Maurice seized the glass of absinthe and flung it in Langlois's face. Then he took hold of his tie and shook him vigorously.

"You dirty cad!" cried the boy in desperation, now quite out of control.

The proprietor of the Café Blanc sent for a policeman, but long before he could arrive the other customers had pounced on Maurice and dragged him to the door.

"Look here, my boy," muttered a man of a certain age, kindly enough, "the more scandal you make, the more it will react upon your mother."

"Thank you, monsieur," replied Maurice, with tears in his eyes.

By this time the policeman had seized Maurice's arm, but he slipped away from him and, mounting on a table, shouted at the top of his voice:

"Monsieur Langlois, I will come for you on my twenty-first birthday. I swear it!"

Then he got down from the table and said to the policeman calmly, "I am ready now."

Immediately on his release, a quarter of an hour later, Maurice went to the d'U——s' house, where he recounted his adventure, or, rather, his misadventure, to his friend. His friend approved of what he had done, regretting that he, too, had not been there to lend a hand. What an amusing fight they might have had! In 1880, young men were, like mediaeval knights, quick to take up any challenge. If a woman they did not know was insulted they fought. If anyone looked at themselves or laughed at their conceit, again they fought. They were always fighting. They never thought of their near ones. It was a thoughtless generation. Men waged their little personal wars on the duelling ground, in the streets and in the restaurants.

"I have decided upon one thing," said Maurice. "I am going to join mama in Columbus."

"Are you sure she will allow you to?"

"I shan't tell her. It will be a surprise."

Would not his mother's reproaches be silenced at once in the presence of her son? Would she not be too happy, too stirred, when she embraced him, to have the heart to scold him?

The two boys burned the press-cutting.

"In five years' time you will be my second," repeated Maurice, as he left his friend.

"Let's hope your opponent will still be alive!"

In his youthful optimism he only foresaw death for others and yet d'U—— died at the age of nineteen, his skull fractured in a fall from the famous Crack.

CHAPTER XXVII

CHICAGO

SPRINGFIELD, Montreal, Baltimore, Philadelphia. The tour continued, punctuated by receptions which were more or less enthusiastic according to the temperature of the Press or, as for instance in Canada, the whim of the bishops, who constantly accused Sarah of producing immoral plays.

The Company toured Massachusetts, pushed into Canada, came back into Maryland, and passed on to New Jersey, trailing along in its wake its baggage, its reputation, and its successes to which were always being added speeches, banquets, anecdotes and situations which were sometimes critical and sometimes dangerous. The little platform at the back of their private car was always full of fading flowers. Packing-cases containing gifts, curios and souvenirs accumulated. There were full houses in every town, and if sometimes the public seemed a little cold at first, its hesitation soon changed to applause. Men and women often joined the Company, travelling with them from one town to another. Sarah was thoroughly enjoying herself; she was making a lot of money: "Gold, gold, gold!" The New World, hospitable, tumultuous, jovial and familiar, did not disappoint her. The youth of the United States provided a laughing, optimistic foil to her own vitality.

And so to the beginning of January 1881 and the departure for Chicago.

Only one black spot had marred this triumphant progress, namely the whale-man. The terrible Henry Smith, encouraged by his first success in Boston, dogged Sarah's footsteps, as it were, with his old dead whale, which by now exuded such a stench of rotten fish that people could not get near it without holding their noses. This did not worry Smith. He ordered thousands of scented handkerchiefs, embroidered with Sarah's motto, "Despite All", which he sold for a few cents to his thousands of spectators. Sarah implored Jarrett to bring an action against him, but the impresario shrugged his shoulders.

"The more attention we pay to Smith, the more money he makes."

When the train bearing the French Company entered Chicago station, Sarah hardly noticed the crowd that awaited her. She did not hear the band that attacked the *Marseillaise* as though it were a polka; her eyes were riveted to a cloth stretched above the station exit, on which was written: "Come and see Sarah Bernhardt's whale. The celebrated actress wears stays made from the monster's bones." Sarah, very smart in her ermine cloak and violet-trimmed toque, Sarah, who a moment before had been smiling and happy, became ashen; she removed her grey gloves and settled herself into a pullman chair.

"Have that notice removed, Jarrett, or I won't leave this train. I have had enough of the impostures and villainies of that wretched man. Besides, I have never worn stays in the whole of my miserable life."

The rest of the Company, gathered round her, were at their wits' end. All, that is, except Jeanne, who adored scenes and put her nose in the air, sniffing the atmosphere charged with electricity. They all dreaded one of those terrible rages against which no argument, no reasoning, could prevail. Jarrett met the storm without flinching, and endeavoured to divert it.

"You must get out now, madame. I promise you that I will deal with Smith."

But Sarah sat where she was, silent and stubborn; her eyes were dark with fury. The crowd on the platform began to get restless. Luckily a young Frenchman climbed into the compartment and created a diversion. He came to announce that the French Consul was waiting for his compatriot in the foyer. Jarrett explained the situation to the Frenchman in a few words.

"Madame Sarah Bernhardt is perfectly right. We have all been very shocked about this whale business. I will have the cloth removed immediately."

The young man got out quickly, had a word with a couple of workmen standing by, and in less than five minutes a ladder was brought. Sarah, seeing that her demands were being complied with, resumed her pearl-grey gloves, buried her hands in her little round muff and took Angelo's arm.

"Come along," she said, "we mustn't keep these good people waiting any longer."

And she swept past Jarrett without a glance at him.

"It seems that my star is angry with me," observed the impresario.

"I should think so, indeed!" retorted Madame Guérard, picking up Hamlet III, a Brussels griffon even more bad-tempered than his predecessors.

Sarah shook people's hands and received flowers, followed by Félicie and Jeanne, whose duties, on these occasions, consisted in carrying her bouquets or handing her a pencil, or in taking care of the souvenirs, vases, medals and addresses which people showered on her. Sarah was so occupied in talking, smiling and thanking people that she did not see Henry Smith in a sable overcoat and with a smug look of satisfaction on his face. Luckily Piron caught sight of the plutocratic fisherman in time. What a scene there might have been! Piron lost not a moment; he flung himself on the man and dragged him quickly out of the line of Sarah Bernhardt's sight.

"Begone, unhappy man!" cried Piron. "Begone at once! Sarah Bernhardt has sworn to kill you. She keeps a pistol hidden in her muff with the sole object of shooting you."

Piron's agitation was so convincing that the whale-man thrust the bouquet he was carrying into his arms and made off as fast as he could. Piron returned to the foyer and handed the flowers, exquisitely fresh camellias, to Madame Guérard. The little group now began to move towards the exit. Their carriages were drawn up before the front of the station because, ever since the New York incident, Jarrett and Abbey, fearing public demonstrations, had asked the police to meet them at each town and to look after them. But in this case either the impresario's message had miscarried, or the Mayor of Chicago had underestimated the drawing power of Sarah Bernhardt, for there were only four or five policemen round the carriages, while six other men, spaced out on the steps, kept back the sightseers, who were already jostling and abusing one another. When the two stage-managers appeared, followed by Jarrett and Abbey and then by Sarah, the crowd pressed the police forward so vigorously that they nearly met in the middle. Having completely lost control on both sides they began to shout and to strike at any back or stomach within reach, and the crowd began to panic. With no more police barrier to hold it back, the tide rose further and further towards the station.

Those enthusiasts whose agility or violence had enabled them to climb the station steps surrounded Sarah and cheered. A moment later she found herself at the bottom of the steps, pressed on all sides by people, and separated from Jarrett and from her Company.

"Please! Please!" she cried in a half-strangled voice.

She had a horrible fear of being trodden underfoot. She would never reach the carriage. Her legs were giving beneath her, while up above Jeanne and Madame Guérard were shouting: "Sarah! Sarah!"

And their voices still further excited the crowd, whose laughter now bordered upon tears.

A cold sweat broke out on Sarah's forehead.

"I'm going to die," she thought. "Maurice!"

She said that mechanically, hearing a sort of battle raging round her and a deep voice crying: "Stand back, you fools! You'll kill her!"

Somewhere, two fists were connecting with chins and stomachs. Three men went down. Then two powerful arms seized Sarah as though she had been a feather and she recovered her breath. She found herself hoisted on to the shoulder of an enormous man. He had only one eye, but Sarah did not notice this at the time. Holding his burden firmly with one hand, with the other he drove a passage through the crowd. His coarse brown hair gave out a strong smell and, in spite of the cold, the giant perspired under his threadbare overcoat.

The police reinforcements arrived just too late. Quietened, silent and rather abashed, the bystanders watched the passage of this young woman in her ermine cloak; her pretty violet-trimmed toque had fallen off on the steps. Pale with emotion, with her deepset eyes and her tousled hair, she looked like a little nymph being saved—or ravished—by a Cyclops. Dominating that sea of heads and shoulders, Sarah felt that she had been given a new lease of life. A few more steps and the carriage would receive her and take her to Palmer House to rejoin her comrades. So she smiled sweetly as though to apologize for having caused so much trouble: at all costs she must keep the sympathy of the crowd.

The giant put her down.

"Come with me, please, monsieur," she begged.

During the journey Sarah examined her companion and thanked him for saving her life. The one-eyed man seemed to be very uneasy. Cowering back into the corner of the carriage, he took a worn, greasy cap from his pocket and pulled it down over his forehead. His solitary eye looked nervously to right and left.

"He looks crazy," thought Sarah. She was frightened of this silent man.

The manager of Palmer House, who was expecting a cortège to arrive, paid no attention when the landau stopped before his hotel. He was quite shocked when a ragged man and a hatless woman without any luggage entered. Going quickly forward he addressed this strange couple abruptly:

"What do you want here?"

"I am Mademoiselle Sarah Bernhardt," a clear voice replied. "Yes, I understand your astonishment, sir. But your fellow-townsmen have nearly torn me to pieces; and without the help of this gentleman I should never have made the acquaintance of Palmer House. My friends will be here shortly."

137

What? Could this charming but dishevelled woman really be "the Bernhardt"?

Somewhat abashed, Mr. Palmer bowed.

"Oh, madame! I am at your service. Please follow me. The Press is waiting for you."

"My dear Mr. Palmer, please be kind enough not to inform the Press of my arrival. At least not yet. First show me to my room. And have a light meal served for this gentleman and myself."

Mr. Palmer led his guests to the suite that had been reserved for Sarah; it had blue silk hangings and was furnished with gilt furniture upholstered in petit-point.

Still without uttering a word, the giant dashed to the window as soon as the manager left. Then he suddenly fell on his knees as though to hide his presence from the outside.

"What is the matter, my friend?"

"This man is mad," she thought. "I must call the chambermaid."

"No! No!" he cried in French. It was as though this strange person had read Sarah's mind. "Above all, don't be afraid. I won't do you any harm, madame. Only they are already there."

"Who, 'they'?"

"The police, the detectives. They are going to recapture me. Oh, it doesn't matter now: I've been wandering about for a week, and I can't go on any more. If they had not come here, I would have given myself up. I must tell you the truth. I have escaped from the Joliet prison. Ten years ago I committed a crime; for a woman; I was mad with jealousy; I was sent to prison. Once my crime was purged, I went back to work and made some money. I sought the woman out again; she married me, then she began to be unfaithful to me again. My business went to hell, she tormented me and left me. This time it was not the man I killed, but her."

"How did you kill her?" asked Sarah, scarcely daring to breathe, and involuntarily staring at the enormous hands which had saved her.

"Yes, as you think. So I was condemned to death. I escaped, but I was recognized among the crowd. Oh, have no regrets, madame; I am a doomed man. I do not regret what I did this morning: it will be a memory to me . . . until the day when I shall be hurtled into the other world."

The waiter brought a tray laden with food.

"Sit down, monsieur," said Sarah, "let us lunch."

The man stared at her. No doubt he could not believe his single eye; taking his place at the table, he devoured the ham and fried eggs with a good appetite.

Sarah could only nibble at her food. She had but one idea in her mind: to be delivered from this ordeal; not to be left alone with this condemned murderer. The stranger's enormous hands broke the bread and handled the fork clumsily yet gently. The horrible atmosphere surrounding this one-eyed man was intolerable to her. Where on earth were Jarrett, Angelo, Piron, Jeanne, Guérard? Why had they deserted her like this? Yet she had only to stretch out her hand and ring the bell and the detectives would rush in and seize their quarry. But she had not the courage to do this. Sarah felt so uncomfortable that nausea overcame her. It only needed her to be sick to put the finishing touch to the adventure.

A quick step echoed in the corridor, there was a knock on the door, and before Sarah had time to say "Come in" the "fierce gentleman" entered precipitately and took Sarah's hands in his own. Jarrett was visibly moved, and his steely eyes shone with unaccustomed gentleness.

"I have been so alarmed for you, madame! Thank God you are here and safe!"

Then only did he condescend to notice the presence of the giant. He stared at him for a moment, then the one-eyed man put down his napkin, rose heavily and bowed to Sarah.

"Thank you, sir," she said in a flat voice. "Thank you for your kindness to me."

The man went to the door and opened it wide. Sarah just had time to see two detectives seize hold of him before she fainted in Jarrett's arms.

When Madame Guérard and Jeanne arrived at the hotel and were received by the over-excited Mr. Palmer, they hastened to Sarah's apartment and stood spellbound on the threshold. The still unconscious Sarah was stretched on the sofa, while the impassive Jarrett ran between the dressing-room and the sitting-room with damp towels to place on Sarah's forehead. He wrapped her like a baby in the eiderdown from the bed; he slapped her hands; he abused the chambermaid who was too long bringing hot bricks, and when he saw Jeanne and Madame Guérard framed in the doorway he shouted furiously at them:

"Do you realize that Madame Sarah Bernhardt was nearly killed this morning and that it is my fault, all our faults? We ought never to leave this woman, even for a minute."

Madame Guérard, accustomed to her friend's fainting fits, held smelling-salts under her nose, rubbed eau-de-Cologne on her temples and introduced a few drops of melissa water between her lips. She soon came to herself and smiled. But Madame Guérard and Jeanne seemed to have forgotten Sarah. They were staring at the puritanical, abstemious Jarrett, who, in one corner of the sitting-room, poured himself out first one and then another bumper of neat whiskey which he drank at a draught. Then he made for the door, walking a little stiffly.

"This evening, at the theatre, there will be a general rehearsal at seven o'clock. Please be punctual."

Jarrett was himself again.

.   .   .   .   .

A few days later the Mayor of Chicago begged Sarah Bernhardt to be kind enough to entertain the convicts in the Joliet prison. Sarah refused. The Press would certainly find in it a new pretext for poking fun at her. Her rôle was to be a great artist, not a curiosity like Smith's whale. Although no prejudice could ever prevent Sarah from transforming a wish into a reality, she had learned to avoid grotesque exaggeration and idle scandal. No. She would not play to the convicts. Jarrett supported her in this decision.

Then the prison governor paid Sarah a personal visit. Quite amiably she pleaded previous engagements, fatigue and the refusal of her impresario. But the governor was persistent.

"I would have been so glad, madame, to give my men this splendid distraction from their troubles. An intelligent entertainment can do so much good to those prisoners who have some chance of becoming decent citizens again. And you would have met among us an old acquaintance, if you do not mind me referring to him as such. Do you remember the one-eyed man who saved you from the over-enthusiastic populace on the morning of your arrival in Chicago? The unfortunate man is shortly going to be hanged and he has asked me, as a last favour, to try to get you to come and play for us."

Sarah flushed. She often thought of the giant, the man who had himself recaptured because of her.

"Sir," she said, "I promise to have another talk with my impresarios and to see what I can do; I may not act without their authority; I am not free . . . either."

The "fierce gentleman" required a lot of persuasion, but, as Jarrett was at the time in rather a difficult position—as will be seen in the next chapter—as regards the American theatre managers, he thought it more diplomatic to meet the wishes of the officials of the great American cities. So, when the Mayor of Chicago returned to the charge in support of the prison governor's request, Jarrett agreed, on condition that his star should be escorted by plain-clothes detectives. The Company was to play an act of *Hernani*.

When she arrived at Joliet prison, Sarah's heart suddenly sank. Prison seemed to her to be an unnecessary mental torment. The governor showed her all the smallest details of his kingdom, all the latest humane or penal innovations; he described the whole working of his institution to her.

Before the curtain rose, Sarah asked to be allowed to look at her strange audience through the curtains.

In an enormous room, ranged on iron benches, sat between six and eight hundred convicts, clad in the usual American prison dress, of alternate white and black hoops. At the back of the room a wooden platform held other prisoners crowded together, either seated or standing. Round the room warders, armed with rifles, formed a hedge, and lastly a little box, fitted up actually on the stage, was reserved for the governor and a few members of the prison personnel. Sarah gave an involuntary shudder as she looked at these outlaws, murderers and thieves who were at the moment quietly awaiting her appearance on the stage. "The Bernhardt!" An actress who was always being abused by the Press. "The Bernhardt", who had recently been saved by one of their number, a convict, a real criminal, a strangler.

When the curtain rose, the audience in its black and white uniform showed its appreciation by shouting and whistling, but the performance itself took place in complete silence. Not a sound, not a whisper interfered with the acting. The convicts did not let themselves go until the end, when the curtain fell for the eighth time on their applause and their cheers.

It was over.

The inmates of Joliet left the room in pairs. Some of them turned to take a last look at Sarah. What a contrast for them! They were returning to their reflections, to their companions in misfortune, their fetters, and their gloom.

The vision must endure for those who wished to take it with them. Sarah remained on the stage until the last two convicts had disappeared.

"For twenty-five per cent of our number," the governor subsequently explained, "the performance you have been kind enough to give us will merely whet the basest appetites. For several hours, perhaps several days, the discipline of this minority will deteriorate; the instinct of vice will leap in among them like some horrible wild beast leaping out of the darkness into the revealing light of day. But for the other seventy-five per cent of my prisoners such a performance can do only good. It will bring them hope and light and will give them patience; it will bring happy memories back to them and remind them that their miseries will one day end. And now, with your permission, madame, Number 729 will read you the usual address of thanks." And the governor added, "We are hanging him the day after tomorrow and this is his last favour."

The giant came forward, his chest filling out his hooped uniform and his single eye fixed on Sarah. He read a little speech of welcome in a halting voice, though it did not shake as much as Sarah's when she thanked him and shook him by the hand.

On the day on which 729 was hanged, Sarah was so upset that she was quite prostrate and Jarrett suggested cancelling the evening's performance. Sarah refused to allow this, but for some nights afterwards the giant's face haunted her dreams. She would wake with a start in her pretty bedroom in Palmer House with the words ringing in her ears: "You whet the basest appetites. Twenty-five per cent will be only more resentful."

Sarah thought only of that minority. She decided that never again would she play to convicts. And yet, in February 1913, thirty-two years later, she gave another performance at the Saint-Quentin prison, before two thousand prisoners.

CHAPTER XXVIII

IN A TENT AT COLUMBUS

SAINT LOUIS, Cincinnati, New Orleans, Mobile, Memphis, Louisville and, as the next step, Columbus.

After warming themselves in the New Orleans sun, where they had to contend with floods, the Company left Kentucky for Ohio. Louisville today bears no resemblance to the little city of 1880, which had been founded in the eighteenth century under the name of Falls City, above the Ohio rapids. On either side of the main street the country still retained its unspoiled charm, and cattle-tracks had not yet been entirely replaced by roads.

Having relinquished her private railway coach at New Orleans, Sarah went to the Louisville Hotel after the evening performance. Bad news awaited her. Among her correspondence Sarah found a black-edged letter informing her of the death of the venerated Mother Saint-Sophie at the Grand-Champs Convent. Her dear little saint had left this world. "We will always meet again," the Mother Superior had told her favourite pupil.

"Now it will be in Heaven!" cried Sarah, in tears. "And the news does not surprise me. Some fool threw a piece of heather at me yesterday, and the ill-omened flower stuck to my cloak."

In her large, cold, gloomy room Sarah, nestling down among her five pillows, slept badly. Madame Guérard, who occupied the adjoining bed, contributed to this sleeplessness by waking up in the middle of the night uttering piercing screams. Ever since visiting New Orleans, where she had found some inoffensive grass-snakes crawling through her dressing-room, she thought she saw snakes even in her mattress.

Sarah, herself, liked snakes. They did not repel her at all. In 1916, while playing the title-rôle of *Cleopatra* in England, she used to thrust a real snake (it was only a grass-snake) into her bosom, but after a short time the reptile died. The stage-manager replaced it by another snake which he obtained from no one quite knew where. It happened that one of the Zoological Gardens officials, knowing Sarah Bernhardt's passion for animals, came to see her at the theatre and to ask her to come to visit the Gardens. Out of curiosity, he lifted the cover of the basket containing Sarah's new serpent. He uttered an exclamation and quickly replaced the cover.

"This reptile is a horned viper and is extremely poisonous. Luckily it is dozing in this warm dressing-room. Otherwise, madame . . ." And he wiped his brow.

On awakening that morning in Louisville, after a restless night, Sarah asked Félicie to order her tea immediately.

"Why did you let me over-sleep?" she asked. "We are leaving at eleven."

"Oh, no, madame! You may go to sleep again. Mr. Jarrett has just told me that we are not playing at Columbus until tomorrow. So we're taking the afternoon train."

"What! Aren't we playing this evening?"

"Apparently not."

"But it's ridiculous, revolting! What's the reason of it? Jarrett! I want Jarrett!"

"Jarrett," said Madame Guérard with a yawn, "will be back at eleven. There! It's raining again."

At that moment the floor-waiter brought in the breakfast tray. Wrapped in her white satin dressing-gown, Sarah, in a decidedly bad temper, pointed to the fireplace.

"*Firé, please,*" she said.

"What, madam?"

"*Firé,* my friend, *firé!*"

"I beg your pardon?"

The waiter retreated a few steps with a look of alarm on his face.

"*Firé! Firé!*" screamed Sarah. "Don't you understand English? *F, I, Fee, R, E, Ré, Firé!*"

But Sarah's accent was beyond the poor American waiter, and, in a profession which attracts people of so many different nations, it was really bad luck that this one happened to speak only English. The more Sarah repeated the word *Firé,* pronounced as in French, the more confused the poor man became, until, in the end, he opened the door and fled.

"The idiot must be deaf!" said Sarah, sniffing at the jam. "I hate marmalade. The toast is cold, the tea is too strong and the milk is sour."

She went into the corridor and began to shout out:

"*Au feu! Au feu!*"

In a few moments the hall porter, the head waiter and the manager all dashed along in a panic.

"Good God, madame!" said the manager. "Where is the fire?"

"There isn't a fire, but I want one in my fireplace and your waiter is stone deaf. Your hotel is an ice-house, sir! And I want some strawberry jam. It's absurd to make jam of oranges with their skins on. It smells like floor polish."

Sarah retreated to her sitting-room and stood in the doorway with her hand on the door-handle.

"Guérard," she said in a hollow voice.

"What is it, Sarah darling?"

"Do you realize that we're in room number 13?"

"Oh! We got here so late and so tired!"

"Yes; well, we've got room number 13. It's madness. It's another joke of Jarrett's, but I'll make him pay for it. He knows how I hate that number and he chose it for me deliberately."

"Perhaps he didn't notice——"

"Then what on earth is he thinking about?"

At this point Jarrett arrived on the scene. Sarah strode up to him like a cat going into a fight.

"This town is impossible. I want to take the first train out of it. The hotel is freezing, the public is lukewarm and even the tea is cold. And, as if this wasn't enough, you put me in room number 13. I don't want to be unpleasant, Jarrett, but, if any misfortune befalls me, my son will never forgive you. Besides, my lucky star cannot always be fighting against evil spirits, particularly when you make it work overtime by strewing thirteens across my path. Have some tea. It's undrinkable!"

Jarrett waited patiently for the end of this diatribe. He drew a chair up to the now blazing fire and held his hands out to the flames.

"You're not looking any too cheerful yourself," said Sarah; "what has happened to us now?"

"The United States entertainment business is annoyed with me. The managers of the theatres in which we haven't played are furious. So are the others. They are all furious because we have made a lot of money. They are trying to boycott us. Winslow has played me a dirty trick in Columbus. We can't get a theatre there."

"No theatre? Didn't you hire one?"

"Yes, but the manager never sent me the agreement. I thought his letter, having missed me at Mobile, would catch me up at Memphis, or here."

"Let's cut Columbus out, then, and go straight to Dayton. On second thoughts, no! Don't let's be defeated by such dirty tricks."

"Particularly," added Jarrett, "as the house is completely sold out. And now we'll have to refund the money, all because of that filthy Winslow. I could, of course, make another suggestion, but you are not bound to accept it."

"Well? What is it?" demanded Sarah, sharply.

"Well, I have half made arrangements with . . . with a circus, the Torito, which happens to be in Columbus at the moment. Jeff Torito owns a magnificent tent capable of holding two thousand people. For a fairly substantial fee he is prepared to let us have his tent ready set up. But I repeat, madame, you are not bound to accept. It is stipulated in our contract——"[1]

"For the moment, I don t care a fig for what is stipulated in our contract, my dear Jarrett; all I care about is not to let the Columbus show fall through. On the contrary, I am highly amused by the idea of playing in a tent. Quick, be off with you! Go and fix it all up!"

"I'll go at once," replied Jarrett, kissing Sarah's hand, "and I promise you a record house, madame. You will follow with the Company by the two o'clock train."

Box-office receipts were the only things that were able to excite the "fierce gentleman". Jarrett could not bear anyone to speak lightly of the box-office. His whole existence revolved around it: the weather, friendship, humour, health, the beauty of a view, the gaiety of a town. He chewed it like chewing-gum, putting it sometimes in his cheeks and sometimes in his mouth, but never forgetting it.

"In spite of the 13 on my door, I am glad to be going to Columbus," declared Sarah a few minutes later; "but I really don't know why."

* * * * *

The rain continued to fall. If the sky cleared for an instant, scurrying clouds would almost immediately cover up the exposure, as though they had been commissioned to keep the soil and the river banks and the air in a permanent

[1] The same thing occurred many years later: Sarah Bernhardt and her Company had to play for two days in a tent at Dallas.

Sarah Bernhardt in her studio

Sarah and Maurice in 1896

state of mud and flood. Roads became streams, streams rivulets, and rivulets rivers: the land of Ohio appeared or disappeared beneath lakes, and water sprang up on all sides. The beautiful American countryside was grey and desolate. Trees appeared here and there, their branches protruding from the water like outstretched arms. In small railway stations at which their express train did not stop the employees stood gloomily watching the carriages flash past.

The train drew up at a little Kentucky station. From her compartment Sarah noticed that the passengers were crowding on to the platform and arguing with the guard, who was shortly afterwards joined by the engine-driver.

Before going on a long train journey Sarah always had a superstititious habit of having the engine-driver introduced to her. Was the man married? Had he any children? How long had he been on the footplate? And on their arrival one of the stage-managers would give the driver a tip, to which Sarah often added a small souvenir for his wife or his children, sweets or some other trifle. And on this occasion she noticed that when they left Louisville their driver seemed to be particularly depressed.

"Our driver doesn't look very pleased with life," observed Jeanne, who always took a positive delight in bad news.

"There's nothing to be particularly cheerful about in this sort of weather," replied Sarah, drily.

She was annoyed with her sister. At luncheon-time at Louisville, Jeanne was nowhere to be found.

"I overslept," she explained, as she climbed quietly into the train.

To tell the truth, except during working hours, no one ever knew exactly where Jeanne was, or even where she slept or ate. In America, as in Paris, she continued to lead her secret, independent life, which caused her sister constant anxiety.

"You might at least consider mother!" cried Sarah one day. "She would never forgive me if anything happened to you. I'm getting tired of you!"

This was not quite true. Sarah really loved her sister, and all the more since the death of Regina. And Jeanne, in the depths of her secret soul, was very fond of Sarah, though she only showed this affection in sudden remarks such as "I love no one but you . . . !" and would then lay her pretty head with its grey eyes on her elder sister's shoulder, and for a few effusive minutes Sarah would forgive her her selfishness, her mysterious ways, her unkindness, and her constant pessimism.

"I'm going to take Hamlet III for a walk," declared Félicie.

On the platform the engine-driver, a thickset little man, shrugged his shoulders and then, tired of arguing, he looked towards Sarah's compartment, gave her a toothless grin and hurried back to his engine.

"Is that one married?" asked Jeanne, teasingly.

"He has two wives and five children," replied Madame Guérard.

The train started off again on its shining wet rails.

"Let's play four-handed dominoes," suggested Angelo.

"Certainly. Go and fetch Piron. Are you going to play, Jeanne?"

"Yes, if you keep your temper and if I can be your partner."

"Oh no," objected Madame Guérard, "you know you'll only quarrel."

K

"Not at all. It's only that our star is inclined to cheat, and I prefer to profit by her gifts to having to suffer from them."

Jeanne gave her sister a kiss, and the ivory dominoes began to click against one another on the little table fixed up between the seats. Abbey went off to smoke a cigar. Hamlet III, outraged at having been made to go out in such weather, sulked on Sarah's lap, preferring to burst rather than to pander to the wishes of such impertinent people. The hours went by, and the engine whistled monotonously as the train drove through the mist.

"It isn't a tent, it's an ark that Jarrett ought to have hired for the Columbus show."

Hardly were the words out of Jeanne Bernhardt's mouth than the passengers were precipitated against one another: the train, suddenly braked, halted in the middle of a flood.

"The driver's crazy!" cried Madame Guérard, removing herself from Piron's knees.

"Something must have happened," said Sarah.

"Didn't you tell me that your room was Number 13?" put in Jeanne, picking up the dominoes. "In any case, it's a piece of luck, as we were certain to lose that game."

"That's enough of that," ordered Sarah. "And you, Angelo, go and see what's happening."

Before Angelo could open the door, the engine-driver appeared in the corridor, followed by Abbey. The little man was shaking his head gloomily and the impresario, whose cigar had gone out, was scarcely more reassuring.

"We can't get across the Ohio River," declared Abbey. "We've been warned that one of the arches of the bridge has been strained by the pressure of the stream. We'll have to get back to Cynthania and take another train through Gallipolis. Jarret was lucky!"

The engine-driver shook his head again. The Gallipolis bridge was cut. Then he muttered, looking from the impresario to Sarah Bernhardt and back again.

"I can do it! I can do it!"

"What?" asked Sarah, irritated. "What is it he can do?"

"He says," said Abbey with a shrug, "that he is prepared to get us across this tottering bridge, in spite of everything, if we undertake to give him enough money for his widow."

"For which one?" asked Jeanne.

"If all goes well," went on Abbey, ignoring the interruption, "he will return the signed undertaking at the other end of the bridge."

"Bravo!" cried Sarah, delightedly. "That's the way to talk. Only, if we all go to the bottom of the river, this man will no longer have any guarantee. So one of us must remain behind. You, Guérard. Yes! Yes! You must think of my son too. And you, Jeanne."

"Don't get excited!" cried Abbey. "Do you think we're alone on this train? And that all the travellers are going to risk their lives in this mad attempt? We must tell them the position frankly; those who don't want to go on with us will get off. I'll arrange it all with the guard."

"Good," said Sarah. "And now send the whole Company to me."

Abbey, assisted by the guard, went quickly through the train. Ten other people had been allowed, because of the floods and the altered time-tables, to travel in the express train reserved for the French Company, and seven of these agreed to attempt the crossing. Of the artistes themselves, only two elected to stay behind, a young actress and one of the stage-managers. The rest no doubt trusted in the good star of their leader.

A paper guaranteeing the sum of two thousand five hundred dollars to his wife in case of accident was handed to the driver, and a copy of this was deposited with the stage-manager, who remained behind. Meanwhile another scene was taking place in Sarah's compartment. Sarah, having given up trying to get Madame Guérard to get off, now turned to her sister.

"As for you, Jeannette, I won't even argue the question with you."

"Of course," replied Jeanne calmly. "What would mama say if anything happened to me?"

"At least give me a kiss."

Jeanne gave her a peck, grabbed her valise and jumped off the train.

"I'm glad she isn't coming," muttered Sarah; but there were tears in her voice.

Madame Guérard, busily brushing Hamlet III, also muttered something; then she raised her head. The train gave a jerk and started off. The two women leaned out of the window in spite of the cold. The travellers who remained on the platform waved hearty farewells and Sarah called gaily to them: "*Au revoir!*"

At the windows of the neighbouring compartment Abbey, Angelo and others of the Company kept their eyes on the Ohio River. The Ohio was spread out like a cheerless lake without any precise limits; some way on, the line took a bend and then the bridge appeared with its latticework of iron arches, a fine feat of engineering. And yet, among those arches . . .

"I wonder," said Sarah, "whether the driver will cross the bridge very slowly or very fast."

"Very fast," replied a quiet voice behind her. "He told me so."

Sarah turned round and the blood rushed to her face; Jeanne was gravely replacing her valise in the luggage-rack.

"What! *You* back?"

"I never had the least intention of remaining in that horrible station, but you know how I loathe family scenes."

Sarah shut the window without replying. Making herself comfortable, she told her sister to come and sit beside her; then she took Jeanne's head and laid it on her shoulder. Jeanne let her have her way. All she said was:

"If I had known that we were going to play divers, I should not have put on my lace petticoat."

Abbey lit a fresh cigar, which was strictly against Sarah's rules, and sat down next to Madame Guérard.

"Well, well!" he said, rubbing his hands together.

But Sarah thought he looked a little anxious. Then Angelo appeared, and Piron, and Madame Demeria and other members of the Company. They came along to be with Sarah. For no other reason. Then the train gathered speed.

"What a sharp bend!" exclaimed Abbey, pretending to be thrown against Madame Guérard.

They all knew that the bridge followed immediately after the bend. The rain pattered on the windows. The engine-driver opened the throttle wide and the train went faster and faster.

"We're on the bridge!" said Madame Guérard in a stifled voice and she crossed herself, as did many of the others, including Sarah.

"Mother Saint-Sophie, who must certainly have reached Heaven by now, protect us and protect my son!" she prayed inwardly.

Wrapped in mist, the waters of the Ohio swirled along with a roaring sound. Through the windows the travellers could see the narrow iron parapet dripping with rain.

"The driver is going too fast," muttered Piron.

Sarah said nothing. Divine Mercy had given her a star of destiny: so she waited in resignation and full of confidence. Jeanne's hair seemed to her to be paler than ever in that watery light and a smell of cinnamon and amber rose from it.

"Dear God! Have mercy upon us!"

Madame Guérard crossed herself a second time.

There was a rumbling sound. It was impossible to decide whence it came. It was just a rumbling sound, that was all. This was swiftly followed by a jar which shook the train as though the parapet had gathered it up and shaken it in its iron arms. The train continued its mad career and suddenly the compartment assumed a different level. Sarah, Jeanne and Demeria, seated facing the engine, appeared to be lowered in relation to those who sat opposite. The train shuddered like a racehorse a few yards from the winning-post, seemed to make a final effort, slowed down and came to a halt, panting; a silent ghost in the icy shroud of the mist.

"We're over!" cried someone further up the train. "We're over!"

But the end of his sentence was lost. A noise like thunder, or of an explosion, and a great rushing of water broke the silence of the dismal countryside: behind the last waggon the defective arch had collapsed and had fallen into the Ohio, folded over on itself.

With his face streaming with rain, sweat and coal-dust, the driver ran the length of the train. He was laughing. Sarah shook his hand through the open window.

.　　.　　.　　.　　.

The two thousand five hundred dollars were handed to the little man as a reward. When they arrived at Columbus, Jarrett, as a matter of principle, abused Abbey, Sarah, and Angelo for having risked their lives . . . without him. But after the "ordeal" by bridge, as Jeanne called it, the whole Company was very merry. Let it rain as much as it liked. Nothing could damp the general good humour. The artistes were full of enthusiasm over the huge tent. Jarrett sulked for a few minutes, then he showed Sarah into two warm little rooms, scented with red roses and entirely lined with furs: seal, prairie-dog, buffalo and others, all kindly lent by the accommodating Torito.

"Your dressing-room, madame!"

Other surprises awaited her, too. In a basket placed on the dressing-table, on which Félicie was unpacking her bottles, a lion cub a few months old, with a blue ribbon round its neck, stretched itself and yawned into the face of the delighted Sarah. "Hernani", which was the animal's name, was naturally adopted on the spot. And that was not all: while kissing the nose of the baby lion, Sarah caught sight of a blue envelope on the table.

"What's this, Guérard? A telegram, and no one told me?"

And her heart beat fast as it always did when she received a telegram. When she opened it her face became as white as a sheet.

"No, no! It's not possible. Maurice! Maurice!"

"What? What's happened to him?"

"Nothing, nothing!"

She stuttered and laughed with such intense pleasure that the two women could not understand a word she said. Sarah, in tears, handed them the telegram with a shaking hand.

"Read it!"

"*Arrive Columbus Tuesday. Your Maurice.*"

"The little imp; the little imp! He's over here! He's come here all by himself!"

Madame Guérard was in floods of tears. Félicie trod on one of Hamlet III's paws, starting him off yelping, and the three women and the dog made such a noise that soon the entire Company was aware of the great news, including Jarrett, who bowed, kissed Sarah's hand and said:

"You deserve this happiness, madame. Don't scold the boy, even if he has come here without our permission."

"As if I could be angry with my son for loving his mother! Of course I won't scold him, my dear Jarrett. Later, I'll tell him . . . How on earth do I know what I'll tell him?" And she broke into clear youthful laughter. "I must pull myself together now and try to be calm. I've got to act properly, otherwise poor *Frou-Frou* will be beneath contempt, and you haven't deserved that, Jarrett," she added, pinching her impresario's cheek, an unexpected piece of familiarity which took that worthy man completely aback.

At what time was Maurice arriving? The telegram had been sent from New York to Louisville and redirected. When the crimson velvet curtain hanging at one side of the ring rose at half past eight on the first act of *Frou-Frou*, Maurice had not yet appeared.

Each time she left the stage Sarah looked enquiringly at Madame Guérard, who replied, "Nothing yet." Sarah acted the first act of the Meilhac and Halévy play a little too quickly, but she pulled herself together in the subsequent acts and threw herself wholly into her part, being capricious, gay and jealous by turns. "You have taken my child, my husband, everything! All right, keep them! I am leaving!" cried Frou-Frou to her sister Louise in a paroxysm of rage and sorrow. (Let anyone try to touch Maurice!) Her voice rose and fell on silken wings.

The public, crowded into the tent, had been informed of the situation by the Press and by Jarrett. By which I mean that it was fully aware of the fact that Winslow had refused to let his theatre to Sarah Bernhardt.

Cries of "Long live Sarah! and Long live Jarrett! Down with Winslow!" came from the audience. And the same thing was repeated at each interval.

When the curtain fell on the last act there was still no sign of Maurice. The whole Company tried to spot him among the audience, without success. They could not see him where he sat in the back row of the topmost tier, hidden behind the Beloved Monster, and watching, in feverish excitement, *Frou-Frou*, his mother, his mama, die on the stage.

Sarah left the stage, or, rather, the ring, after several curtain-calls. She was beginning to be worried.

"Stage, please, madame, once more," said the stage-manager.

But the curtain rose only half-way. Coming from the wings, a tall fair lad ran towards Sarah. He had patiently waited his turn. The public must now release his mother. It was his own hour, his love-tryst.

PART THREE

CHAPTER XXIX

FRANCE AND ROMANCE

DAYTON, Indianapolis, Saint Joseph, Detroit, Quincey, twenty-six towns in all. The first American tour was coming to an end. Since she had got rid of Henry Smith and had been reunited with her son, Sarah's troubles seemed to be at an end. She travelled through the United States with a singing heart, triumphant and rich. "Gold! Gold!" Whatever the future might have in store, the soil of America would always remain for her a fertile soil, a source of wealth. Thenceforward, the rose-bush of her life would be hardy enough to resist all attacks by the green-fly.

"In a fortnight, Maurice, we shall be back in France!"

The young man did not share his mother's pleasure. He was thoroughly enjoying his adventures in the New World. He rode, fished, hunted and flirted, and in the big cities never missed a single theatrical or variety performance.

"Do you know, mama, that Mr. Jarrett has taken our passages on the *Amérique* again?"

"That does not surprise me about the old skinflint," replied Sarah, with a smile. Nothing could ruffle her good humour. "Captain Jouclas ought to be pleased——"

"Oh," interrupted Maurice, quickly, "Captain Jouclas is dead!"

"Dead? Oh, I am sorry. What did he die of? Who told you?"

"A man at the club yesterday. . . ."

And Maurice suddenly got red and confused and interrupted his explanation.

"Where were you, then, yesterday evening?" Sarah asked him suspiciously.

"With Jack Felton. You introduced me to him yourself. After the Music-Hall he asked me to go to the club with him. I couldn't very well refuse, could I?"

"Certainly you could. A young man has no business to go to gaming-houses."

"But, mama, it isn't a gaming-house. It's the smartest club in Baltimore."

"All clubs are gaming-houses, and the smarter they are, the worse the gambling that goes on in them."

"If I had refused to go it would have made me look like a small boy."

Sarah stared at her son. Was he not a small boy any more? Alas! He was already repudiating his childhood and wanted to appear to be a man and was dreaming of responsibilities, mistresses, quarrels and debts.

"Did you play?" she asked severely.

"Well—that is, I——"

"Answer my question, yes or no?"

"I put three dollars into Felton's bank. You don't think that very wicked, do you?"

"It is not the amount that is wicked but the fact of gambling at all."

"I'm sorry, mama."

Maurice went over to his mother and kissed her hand.

"I hope he is not going to promise me never to gamble again," she thought.

Sarah was quite well aware that a boy brought up like Maurice, with many distractions but very few occupations, would almost inevitably acquire bad habits. She, whose whole life and whose entire efforts and aspirations had only her art as their end, could not understand people being unable to resist the desire to drink, to gamble, and to make love. Still less did she understand that anyone could promise to forgo all these things and then start again the next day.

However, Maurice made no promise and this was a relief to Sarah. Clairin often used to tell her, "give your son less money and more responsibilities". She would either tell him to mind his own business or would agree with him. But Maurice would come in a few minutes later and Sarah immediately forgot her resolutions. "Mama, I want to buy this new gun, if you don't think it is too expensive . . . Mama, I want to go to Normandy with d'U—— . . . Mama, I've seen a lovely tilbury, a real bargain. . . ."

"Well," said Sarah, to change the subject, "what about Captain Jouclas?"

"He killed himself."

"What?"

"Yes, after a heavy loss at cards."

Under his mother's steady gaze, Maurice felt extremely uneasy. The more he went into details, the more involved he became. He swore to himself never to touch another card. And, that day in Baltimore, he really meant it.

.   .   .   .   .

With a new captain, the *Amérique*, creaking in every joint, sailed for France. The day was fresh and sunny. The ship pitched slightly. Sarah and her son were talking on deck, stretched on deck-chairs. The gold pieces in the little strong-box in the cabin tinkled gaily in Sarah's imagination. This first tour of hers in the United States had brought her in the respectable sum of nine hundred thousand francs. She was already spending it in her mind: furs, carpets, the redecoration of the house in the Rue Fortuny.

"I need a new carriage. You must see to that, Maurice. I also want a pair of chestnuts. What do you think of turning the round room off the studio into a study for yourself?"

"What for?"

"When you have finished your studies you will have to work, of course."

"Oh!" replied Maurice.

The only work that appealed to him was writing. But his mother, of course, wanted to make a lawyer, or a doctor, or an engineer out of him, as is the way of mothers all over the world. Perhaps even a soldier. His father would be pleased and the story of his birth would thus take on a much more romantic aspect. His father . . .

"This Spring I shall take a villa a few miles from Paris. At Viroflay, for instance."

"Oh!"

Maurice thought that Spring was a hundred more times beautiful in the Champs-Élysées, at Longchamps and in the Bois de Boulogne, unless . . .? Maurice looked at his mother. How young she looked!

"I know, mama! Let's spend a fortnight at Sainte-Adresse, without anyone from the Little Court: just you and I. You need a rest after this long voyage. The villa belongs to us and we never go there. We could go straight there after landing at Le Havre. Why not? Do let us!"

"But, darling! I must go to Paris first, to find out what is going on."

"Then everything's gone to hell!"

"Maurice! Moderate your language!"

With his lean face bronzed by the sun, Maurice looked like a sulky little boy.

"I know what to expect in Paris. Bores, authors and rehearsals."

"Very well! We'll go to Sainte-Adresse, my sweet. Kiss me and give me your arm. I've time to walk at least three times round the deck before being sea-sick."

.   .   .   .   .

When the ship reached Le Havre on May 15, 1881, the port was as animated as the bay of the Hudson River had been ten months before. About a hundred boats of various shapes and sizes, all flying French colours, were cutting through the waters of the Channel. Sarah could hardly believe her eyes. She and the French people had parted rather coldly, so this demonstration could not possibly be in her honour.

"Look!" said the captain. "All this is for you, madame."

"I don't think so," replied Sarah. "It's probably a public holiday today."

This modesty and total absence of affectation remained with Sarah Bernhardt throughout her life. Proud she undoubtedly was; and her pride protected her like a shield against abuse, jealousy and slander; but she was never vain. Even at the peak of her fame she preserved her simplicity of soul, her delight at being praised, her shyness and her fear of not giving the public, her friends, her fellow-artistes and her family, what they expected of her. In this way she was never satisfied with her work and always tried to surpass her best efforts.

When the journalists came on board the *Amérique* they confirmed the fact that the flags and bunting had been waiting for Sarah Bernhardt since the morning: crowds were gathered at the quayside, gazing at the old ship with her scaling sides.

Leaning against the ship-rail, Maurice listened to the cheers and acclamations; his mother was drifting away from him again.

Sarah and Maurice spent that night at Sainte-Adresse. In order not to disappoint her son, she dined alone with him on the terrace of the villa. All the rest of the Company and the staff, except Félicie, had taken the train to Paris. Maurice smoked a cigarette and gazed at the sky spangled with countless stars.

"Are you cross with me for being . . . famous?"

"No, I admire you, mama. But fame is a very difficult dish to digest in the family circle."

"You're talking like a small tradesman's son."

153

"That's how you brought me up. I am flattered and proud of your glory, but I sometimes regret not having a mother like those of my friends."

"I try to satisfy your smallest whims."

"That's quite true. Other children don't always get what they want, but they have got just what I want, an organized, simple life."

"Maurice!" cried Sarah, in anguish. "You're not happy!"

"It would be very ungrateful of me not to be. I am the most pampered son in France. But I would so like to remain a little longer at Sainte-Adresse. Mama, may I ask you a question? Promise you won't be angry!"

"Ask me whatever you want to, darling," replied Sarah, anxiously.

"Are you ever going to get married?"

"Maurice," replied Sarah severely, "I cannot allow your conventionality to ruin our happiness. I can understand that you find my art a little too exacting, but that you should think of getting me married, merely to hear people say 'Monsieur and Madame Bernhardt', which would not be very flattering for your step-father, or to be able to say to your friends 'This evening I am going out with papa and mama,' that really does offend me. You're nothing but a little snob."

Maurice's clear young laugh interrupted this harangue. He gave his mother a hug.

"Don't be stupid, mama! The reason I asked you that was that I wanted to be assured that you would never marry. Do you imagine that I would be able to bear the gentleman for twenty-four hours?"

Sarah, rather taken aback, thanked Heaven for having given her this son. But the old wound reopened, and the Prince's face appeared to her, outlined in the starry sky.

.   .   .   .   .

Paris: June with its wealth of flowers; its swallows flying in circles; its women dressed in muslin and organdie. For a month now Sarah had resumed her restless life. She was preparing for an extensive European tour, to include Russia, Austria, Spain, England, Switzerland, Belgium, Holland and the Scandinavian countries.

Victorien Sardou brought her a drama in four acts, entitled *Fédora*. He read it to her in the little garden of the Rue Fortuny where, to quote Clairin again, "there were more flowers than there was garden". Sarah was delighted with it.

"As soon as I return we will put your play on."

But where? She did not know yet. She was determined, as was Sardou, to find a theatre. They discussed the matter light-heartedly. Around them the rose-bushes shed their petals one by one; the garden wall was hidden by zinnias and nasturtiums, and the lawn was gay with poppies and buttercups. Sardou could not move his feet without crushing a flower.

"I want someone to play opposite me; Angelo won't come. You haven't got a juvenile lead up your sleeve, have you?"

"As a matter of fact, I have. He's a Greek."

Sarah made a face.

"No foreign accent, handsome as a Greek god, a good actor and a thorough man of the world. Nothing of the barnstormer about him."

"Where did you come across this prodigy?"

"At the Greek Legation. His name is Jacques Damala and he is a friend of some friends of my wife, who have asked me to give him a chance. He comes from an excellent family, but he's ruined himself at cards, and has taken up the stage. He's 'resting' at the moment. There's no harm in your having a look at him."

"How old is this protégé of yours?"

"Twenty-six."

A week later, Sarah, after a hurried luncheon, was interviewing scene-painters and costumiers. A number of costumes and dresses needed replacing, as, before her departure on her tour, she was going to give a fortnight's performances of *Hernani*. Where? Negotiations were taking place with the Variétés, the Ambigu and the Porte Saint-Martin Theatres. She wanted to get back into contact with the Beloved Monster.

("Paris is necessary for me as a springboard. I always returned to it for a fresh take-off.")

Sarah interested herself in every detail of her tours. Nothing was ever done without her supervision. Her own dresses were designed by painters, and were actual pictures, some of which, by Geoffroy, are still in existence. From the pictures the costumier would model the skirt and bodice in silk or velvet. These would then be put into the hands of the embroiderer, the lace-maker, the gold-thread worker and the ribbon-weaver. Special care was given to the pearls on Dona Maria de Neuburg's robes, to Adrienne Lecouvreur's mantle, and to the brocades of Marguerite Gautier and of Frou-Frou. Sarah, who, in her private life, wore long dresses of plain or figured satin, trimmed with fur and circled by her characteristic gold girdles, always took particular care that her stage costumes should be right according to their period, while at the same time giving vent to her natural taste for sumptuous materials. Each time she put on a new period play she would spend hours turning over the pages of Racinet in her search for new details of costume.

Rehearsals took place every day, either at the house in the Rue Fortuny or on a hired stage.

Nowadays a crowd is represented on the stage by a few people going through a few conventional gestures; in some theatres animation has become stylized. In 1881, a period play was a vast production with anything up to a hundred and fifty extras who came on, went off, ran about, danced, shouted and died on the stage. The combined movements and the choruses were patiently rehearsed in the most minute detail for days and days. I am not criticizing the present-day theatre: I merely want to say that the public—as I remember it in 1912—was more enthusiastic, more responsive, more excited than it is now. The real devotees left the theatre with splitting headaches, because they had been to a "pageant". They had assisted at something which would afford them a subject of conversation for weeks.

Sarah was rehearsing her part in the little garden of her home. The front-door bell rang.

"Darling," said Madame Guérard, "there's a gentleman here sent by Monsieur Sardou."

"I never have a moment to myself," replied Sarah, crossly. "What is he like?"

"Not bad. Good manners. Well dressed."

"Yes, he would be like that. I want a good actor and not a tailor's dummy. Well, I suppose I must see him. Tell him to wait a few minutes in the round room."

She went on with her rehearsing and she was suddenly startled by a melodious voice taking up the cue, giving the lines following those which she had just declaimed.

"Really, monsieur," protested Sarah, "will you please be good enough not to interrupt my work?"

A young man appeared at the garden gate and bowed respectfully.

"Pardon me, madame. My name is Jacques Damala. I could not resist answering when I heard your voice. Please forgive me!"

Sarah cast a jaundiced eye on Sardou's protégé. Slim and elegant, he wore a small, glossy, black beard, and close-cropped hair. Apart from that he had intelligent eyes and a well-shaped nose.

"Without that beard," thought Sarah, "he would seem much younger."

"Well, monsieur," she said aloud, "since you know the part of Don Carlos so well, let us go over that scene again. Will you?"

Her momentary irritation subsided. Soon she was asking Damala to try his hand at something more modern, in the part of Armand Duval. At six o'clock that evening Sardou's protégé was still there, courteous, admiring, self-effacing.

"I want you to make a note, monsieur, of the parts in which you will have to play opposite me: *Adrienne Lecouvreur, Ruy Blas, Hernani, Phèdre, La Dame aux Camélias, Frou-Frou, L'Aventurière, L'Étrangère* . . . and don't forget the part of Vladimir in *Fédora*. No, rather study the part of Loris," she said, as an afterthought, pouring him out a glass of white port.

"Am I to understand, madame, that you are engaging me for your tour?"

"But of course, since Sardou sent you. I could see at once that you had talent. You want to be more objective, but that will come in time. Are you ready to leave in a month's time?"

"Certainly, madame. Thank you, madame. I feel so honoured."

"As for terms, you must see my manager. I can't bear that side of it myself. I shall expect you here tomorrow, and, of course, every day, for our private rehearsals. You seem already to know half the parts. Excellent. Consider yourself engaged. *Au revoir*, monsieur."

He kissed her hand and Sarah looked appreciatively at the smooth brow bowing over it.

"Guérard," she cried, "I am delighted! The boy is charming. He has talent and he is handsome. His gestures are a little stilted, but I can soon smooth that down."

"You're not ill, are you, Sarah?"

"Me? I've never felt better in my life. Why?"

"Your eyes seem rather bright and your hands are hot."

"I'd like to see what you'd be like in my place. I've been rehearsing for three hours!" replied Sarah, indignantly.

CHAPTER XXX

THE NEW HAMLET

IN this European tour in 1881 and 1882, Belgium and Denmark were the first countries to benefit by Sarah's amazing charm. Jacques Damala also had his share in her success. His partner's acting developed his own lyrical instinct and added fire to his own acting. Sarah was well aware of his success and was not in the least jealous. Whenever she came before the curtain she always had Damala beside her with his hand in hers. She liked to share her personal triumphs with him. After the Scandinavian countries, the Company had a setback in Russia. Kieff and Odessa applauded her as an actress but disapproved of her as a woman. Anti-semitic demonstrations had taken place and Sarah Bernhardt's Jewish ancestry might have put the public against her. So the Company cut short its season in Odessa and went to Moscow. Anyone who knew Sarah would realize that this initial rebuff would not make her abandon Tsarist Russia. A good soldier never deserts his post.

And indeed Moscow, and especially St. Petersburg, covered her with glory. In the presence of a brilliant audience, the Tsar Alexander III himself led the applause. He organized parties for Sarah Bernhardt. The aristocracy and the diplomatic corps turned up to pay her homage in her apartment, which was a mass of flowers. Sarah's individual art, her acting, her voice, and even her reputation made a profound appeal to every class of the Russian people. Yes, even to the workers, who followed her sleigh and caught the flowers she flung to them and kissed them ecstatically.

The French Ambassador came to dine with her. She spoke to him of his important functions.

"Madame," he replied, "there is but one ambassador here: Sarah Bernhardt."

The tricolour flag flew constantly beside her. It followed her through the towns, it awaited her in the theatre wings, and during the night it floated from her balcony. The Imperial Court and all the audience of the Alexandra Theatre greeted it every evening as they bowed before Sarah.

After that came Austria, meaning Vienna. Then Hungary, with its Magyars. The overlords left their estates to hear and applaud the artiste who brought tears to the driest eyes and touched the hardest hearts with a gesture, turning their first indifference to enthusiasm.

Then Italy. The land of love owed it to itself to acclaim Marguerite Gautier, Dona Sol, Dona Maria de Neubourg, Frou-Frou, Ophelia and Phèdre. Sarah interpreted the passions of her heroines with a realism and a sensitiveness which delivered her to the public breathless, in tears and with her face either twisted in agony or calm in death. Her daintiness enchanted these Latins; her gestures disturbed their senses. Her cries tore at the heartstrings of women in Genoa, Parma, Venice, Florence, Rome and Naples. In the last-named town she arrived as though escorted by the fascinating romances which she brought back to life. But she was unaware of the fact that in the midst of this singing, dancing throng the sweet poison of love was entering her own heart. The orange-groves and the romantic nights were too much for that traveller with her wandering soul which hitherto had always claimed to love without being in love. And now she was in love.

Jacques Damala, whom the public applauded for his talent, his good looks and his dignity, ceased to be for her merely one of the actors in her Company and an agreeable companion. "Very polished," Madame Guérard called him. Beneath the mask of the actor, Sarah loved the real expression of this attractive young man. On the stage, she longed for Armand to fall in love with Sarah. She told him so.

Damala did not resist his partner's charm—why should he? But he showed no desire to commit suicide after a tiff, or any signs of being jealous, or racked with passion. He remained reserved and "very polished". Neither the perfumes of Italy, nor the beauty of Florence, nor the Roman churches, nor Raphael's frescoes had any effect on this Greek born under the skies of Hermopolis. He was just quietly flattered. And Sarah, who was now thirty-eight, had neither the time nor the patience to wait for Jacques to fall desperately in love with her. She was not content to bind this man to her with wreaths of roses, stage kisses or laurel branches. She made a very conventional resolve, namely, to get married. Yes, but when would she marry him? And where? Paris was calling her; after her tour she wanted to direct the Ambigu Theatre.

Suddenly, at Trieste, while making up in her dressing-room before the performance of *Hamlet*, she uttered a shout of triumph. Madame Guérard, startled, asked her what was the matter. But Sarah made no reply. Jacques and she would be married in London, where the formalities were quick and very simple. No one need know it was going to happen; in some things it is better to put people in the presence of an accomplished fact; their indignation may be greater, but it is over more quickly. She was playing Ophelia, and her long pale green dress seemed hardly to cover her. Impatient and excited, she reached the wings before her call.

Hamlet, played by Damala, was on the stage with Horatio. How handsome he was in his black doublet and hose! She loved looking at his face and his fine hands. The young man in the black doublet? The sight of him brought back so many memories. The Prince! The Bruces' mansion, the Lignes' home with the ancestors in the corridor. Her great, her first love! Sarah waited for the wound to reopen. But no! It was healed now. Only love can cure love. She blew an invisible kiss to this new Hamlet who was already ogling a haughty brunette in one of the stage boxes. There are two different persons in each man: a healer and a torturer. Sarah offered her life to the healer in the black doublet and hose—her life which, in the years gone by, the Brussels torturer had refused.

．　　　．　　　．　　　．　　　．

On April 4, 1882, in London, before the priest of Saint Andrew's Church and before God (man being still unaware of her intentions), Marie Henriette Sarah Bernhardt married Jacques Damala. They left the parish church at about eleven in the morning and dived into a waiting cab. Sarah was happy and in a hurry. Damala felt happy, too, but a little awkward. After England, they were due to go to the South of France. There was no question of a honeymoon: they had to get on with their tour, and they were already behind with their time-table.

Damala felt very embarrassed at the thought of having to inform his friends and relatives of his marriage, to say nothing of his immediate family, with whom his relationship was in any case rather cold.

He explained this to Sarah.

"Leave it to me," she said, "I'll see to it all."

The scene is worth putting on record. On the afternoon of her wedding day, Sarah collected all her Company, a few London celebrities and representatives of all the important London newspapers, and gave a large reception at her hotel. She was gloriously happy and flitted gaily from group to group: but Jacques was not at all at his ease.

Taking advantage of a momentary pause in the conversation, of a "gap", as they say in the theatre, Sarah approached the editor of the *Illustrated London News* and said:

"Really, my dear, England is an adorable country. Just think, this morning my husband and I . . . yes, my husband, Monsieur Damala . . . as I was saying, we were leaving Saint Andrew's Church when a small flower-girl gave me a little bunch of pinks."

Sarah turned to the sound of a cup breaking; the faces round her were expressionless. No one said a word. Someone upset a brandy-and-soda. Sarah continued.

"I wanted to give the girl some money, but she said: 'Oh no. You're a bride!' "

At this point, Piron said:

"But, Madame Sarah, we didn't know. We ought to have congratulated you. Why all this secrecy?"

"Pooh!" replied Sarah. "One is so pushed around. I meant to invite you all to a wedding breakfast, but we are expected at Nice and there was all the packing to be done. So Jacques and I suddenly decided to find a couple of witnesses and to get it over; after all, it isn't of much interest to anyone else. Anyway, now you all know. Tell me, my dear," she added, addressing Ellen Terry, "what are your plans for the coming season?"

Sarah stopped talking. The journalists jostled each other at the door of her apartment in their hurry to be the first with the news.

"It didn't go off badly," said Jacques Damala after the reception. "I only felt slightly ridiculous."

"I am not afraid of London, or the newspapers, or Paris . . ."

"Maurice, eh?"

"Yes, Maurice."

.   .   .   .   .

She interrupted her journey south for a few hours to break the news to her son in Paris, hoping to forestall the English newspapers. When she arrived, Maurice greeted her with his usual tenderness.

159

In the course of talking of this and that, Sarah confessed to herself that by a single glance Maurice was capable of making her lose all control and of destroying her peace of mind. At the end of an hour, she blurted out:

"Maurice, I've got something to tell you."

"I know, mama. You've married Monsieur Sarah Bernhardt."

That was Maurice's only bitter remark.

"Are you angry with me? Do you think you will get on with Jacques?"

"Don't be afraid of that. And don't forget that you brought me up very well. Let's talk of something else. Let's talk of you, since we can no longer talk of the two of us."

"You're hurting me."

"Let us hope that Monsieur Damala never will." Maurice's clear blue eyes hardened.

"He grows more like his father every day," thought Sarah.

At this point Émile came in to announce that an impresario wanted to see her.

"Von Stirtz, of Berlin," said Maurice, reading his card.

Sarah rose at once. "Tell the gentleman I cannot see him."

"It isn't necessarily to play in Germany, mama. Besides, who knows? Herr von Stirtz may have forgotten. We will refresh his memory."

"Very well, then. Ask the gentleman to come in, Émile."

If she and Maurice expected to see a Uhlan in civilian clothes they were disappointed. Herr Stirtz was dark, inclined to stoutness, with mild features, quiet manners and hardly any German accent.

"Madame," he said, "I have an interesting proposition to put before you. I, and my colleagues in Berlin, Stuttgart, Munich and Frankfurt, wish to book you for a tour in Germany for next Spring."

"I am sorry, monsieur," replied Sarah coldly, "but my engagements do not permit me to accept."

"I hope I can persuade you, madame. Such a tour would be of great political interest."

"I am sorry, monsieur, and I regret that you should have put yourself to any inconvenience."

Von Stirtz's expression changed. He suddenly became less affable and his features hardened. Clicking his heels together, he bowed to Sarah.

"Your price shall be ours, madame, whatever it may be," he persisted.

Sarah gazed at him for a moment, then she said sweetly:

"Very well, monsieur. My price is five thousand million francs."[1]

The German said something in his native language, but in an inaudible voice, because Maurice was quietly advancing towards him.

---

[1] The amount of the Franco-Prussian war indemnity.

The Coliseum, London
Sarah Bernhardt in *Theodora*

Sarah Bernhardt and her granddaughter Simone

Sarah Bernhardt and her granddaughter Lysiane in 1922

CHAPTER XXXI

COMPLICATIONS

A YEAR later a use was found for the study in the round room in Paris. Maurice had been appointed by his mother Director of the Ambigu Theatre. So this lad of eighteen had two offices, one in the Rue Fortuny and the other at the theatre. And these two offices cost a great deal of money.

For the third time Sarah had to go through a tunnel. Being older now, she needed exceptional confidence in her lucky star, and this time in her art, to reconquer the Beloved Monster which was prepared to hate her for having loved her too much. The struggle was a hard one. Sarah was not diplomatic, her tempers laid her open to attack, she easily lost control of herself, betrayed her private life in wishing to defend it and defended it badly in trying to preserve it.

After the famous performance of *La Dame aux Camélias* at the Vaudeville Theatre, for the benefit of Madame Chéret, in which both Sarah and Damala scored great personal successes, Sarah found herself on a dangerous downward path, and she was too tired, too sentimental and too hurt in her pride, to try to pull herself up.

First there was the deficit at the Ambigu, of which Maurice had made a hopeless failure. Too polite with some, too overbearing with others, how could this youth of eighteen manage a big Parisian theatre properly? So, in spite of the success of *Fédora*, the enterprise was wound up at the end of 1883 with a loss of 350,000 francs. Then Sarah took the Porte Saint-Martin Theatre, where she put on two plays by Jean Richepin, *Nana Sahib* and *La Glu*; these were both expensive productions and were both failures. But Sarah played in Richepin's plays to console herself for not playing with Damala any more.

Jacques had recaptured his liberty. The young Greek, who had never been much in love with Sarah, immediately fell in love with every woman he met. Sarah's pride suffered, but as her pride had grown less haughty with the years, so her suffering was more sincere and deeper. To make good this fresh deficit Sarah revived *La Dame aux Camélias*. This was a happy thought. All Paris flocked to the theatre to pity the misfortunes of the sincere and romantic consumptive. The box-office receipts kept things going for a while, but Sarah did not know, nor would she ever know, how to hold on to money: it dribbled away or ran through her fingers like golden sand. For the second time she sold her jewellery, her silver, her horses.

At the theatre, Marguerite Gautier kept looking for someone over the glare of the footlights. The same orchestra stall was always reserved for Jacques Damala when he was not acting with his wife. Sarah wanted, if only for a moment, to gaze on Jacques' finely chiselled features. But the stall remained empty. And yet he had promised to come that evening. She fretted and forgot her lines; the prompter gave them to her in such a loud voice that too many people heard. Sarah kept on glancing towards the empty stall, until eventually the audience noticed it and began to whisper among themselves.

L

Then, at last, it flashed on Sarah that she must sacrifice her love if that love was not to sacrifice her. If she were to allow herself to go on suffering, soon she would have only three faithful followers left: Old Age, Desertion, and Poverty, the triumvirate of the weak. And her son would judge her, even be sorry for her. Oh no. Never! She woke up that night in a cold sweat. She chased away the ghosts and took a sleeping draught, but her magnificent command over sleep seemed to have deserted her. She seemed to be struggling among a thousand financial difficulties made even more bitter by her disappointment in love. She must hit on something. Where was that splendid fatalism which, only three years before, had made it possible for her to go to bed to wait for something to happen to save her? And besides, another fact added to her worries, a fact which was a very painful one for Sarah to bear: the Beloved Monster was losing its love for her. Her performance in *Macbeth* (translated by the great poet Jean Richepin) did not improve matters. The critics were pitiless. Sarah cast about her. The tunnel was dark and long. In these critical hours who would stretch forth a helping hand? Fresh dangers seemed to crop up at every turn. She did not lack courage, but . . .

. . . . .

("I lacked confidence, Lysiane. The Press, with a few rare exceptions, would not leave me alone. Audiences tittered as they applauded me, because of the stupid rumours that were current about me; people no longer fought to see me as they had once done. Then the flash came and I saw that I would have to start all over again.

"My husband had spurned the affection and love which I had lavished upon him. And now I wanted to recover from that love. I decided to separate from Jacques Damala. As soon as I put this scheme into operation I recovered my faculty of thought. Jacques took an engagement in South America. His departure saved me; it was as though I had been exorcized. I sent Maurice back to his friends and his horses, and as he had professed a desire to write I gladly encouraged him in his ambition."

"So as to find a use for the round room!"

"Don't forget, Lysiane, that he is your father."

"I'm sorry, grandmother."

"At the same time I recovered my sense of fatalism. I decided to take *Macbeth* off on November 12. But in the meantime a fresh position arose. Really four important events occurred in my life: four events of which the first caused me deep grief.

"Judith Bernhardt, your great-grandmother, died. She was discovered one morning lying on her yellow sofa, dressed in a pretty négligé, with her head on a lace pillow. Her beautiful hands held a small tray-cloth which she had been embroidering. She was smiling, a coquette even in death. And I was so upset that I fell ill.

"The second event ought to have killed me; morally, I mean. It was horrible."

"Why?"

My grandmother glossed over the subject. It had to do with an abominable book written about her by Marie Colombier, a jealous, spiteful, hypocritical actress who divulged all the secrets of the woman who had been her intimate friend. And Sarah had certainly been very indiscreet! When one has to deal with a bitterly envious woman, one must either get rid of her or try to convert her. Sarah did neither, but allowed her to go on nursing her hatred, to collect tales about her, to invent rumours and even to buy up her letters.

(In later years, whenever the name of Marie Colombier was mentioned in the house, there would be an awkward silence and blank looks would be cast at the person who had thus dared to rake up the past. One day I asked my father about it. He recoiled as though he had been bitten by a snake.

"As soon as the book appeared," he said, "I went to see the authoress of the infamy to ask her if there was anyone who would be answerable for her. She laughed in my face. Then your grandmother came in, accompanied by Richepin. They must have followed me. I can still see her, holding a riding-whip in her hand, hurling herself on Marie Colombier, who was white with fear. Once, twice the riding-whip rose and fell, and before I could intervene the woman fled into the neighbouring room. I tried to persuade my mother to leave the house. She smashed everything: the china was reduced to smithereens, all the pictures were slashed to ribbons: Richepin attacked the chair and table-legs, which he demolished methodically, one by one. Of course, all this came out and there was a scandal. Octave Mirbeau defended your grandmother in an article in the Press. Anyway, what possessed you to ask me about this today?")

"And the third event, grandmother?"

"The third event was called *Théodora*. How I loved that part! In 1884 I had gone to Ravenna to bask in the atmosphere in which the strumpet empress had lived, and to gather local colour. I wanted to steep myself in the scenery in which she struggled and triumphed. During the rehearsals I was sometimes fascinated by the thought that I was interpreting this part better than any other, and at other times I was in despair. I was afraid of how the public would receive the play. The Marie Colombier incident had robbed me of my glamour, leaving the crowd to gloat over horrible little tales about me.

"Théodora! Ah, Lysiane, what a first night that was! The public was cold, even hostile. But, after the first act, I felt that its heart was beating in tune with mine. I wanted to dominate the house and to persuade it that nothing mattered except Art. After the second act the curtain rose to cries of 'Long live our Sarah!' Then I whispered to Angelo: 'They're coming back!' That was all I could think of saying: 'They're coming back!' Angelo understood and pressed my hand. Yes, the public was coming back to me."

.   .   .   .   .

Thus Marie Colombier's treachery did her no good. Worn out, bitterly hurt, but nevertheless triumphant, Sarah, clad in Théodora's heavy tunic, emerged from the long tunnel and found herself in a new meadow full of flowers. And Jarrett was there! Jarrett with his cold eyes, his loyalty and his contract in his pocket. This time he proposed a South American tour. The soul of the wanderer began to flap its wings. That was the fourth event.

After giving a few performances of *Marion Delorme* and of *Hamlet* (in the part of Ophelia), in 1886 Sarah Bernhardt crossed the ocean once more, her head held high like a conqueror. The future certainly held further trials in store for her: but from then onward nothing was ever able to turn her aside from her two loves: Maurice and the stage.

She might give her heart again, but she would never abandon it to anyone or anything.

CHAPTER XXXII

PRESENTIMENTS

DURING the year of this American tour Sarah Bernhardt and her Company visited Brazil, Mexico, Chile, Canada and the United States. To the repertory which I have already listed, she added Georges Ohnet's *Le Maître des Forges*. Maurice went with her and surrounded her with love, affection and filial devotion. He tried to make her forget Damala, and, as it were, mounted guard over her.

The voyage, in his eyes, became one of adventure and enchantment. In Chile he persuaded Sarah to take a lease of the Reforma ranch, not far from Concepcion, and to live there with her Ker-Bernhardt cousins from Valparaiso, Jean Stevens and five or six of her friends. There they led a splendid life, in close communion with the land and with Nature. Photographs show us Maurice Bernhardt at the ranch, among his friends and the overseers; leaving for or returning from shooting swans, duck or ostriches, or camping on the bank of a lagoon, or, later, in the woods of Villa Mercedes in the Argentine.

Whenever she could manage to do so, Sarah would go and stay with her son and hunt with him. In later years in the Boulevard Pereire, I was daily confronted with a large wapiti which she had shot in the course of the tour and which then stood in the hall. It was a beautiful animal, with fine horns and coarse, dark fur. My grandmother and my father never agreed about the shot that killed it. Whenever my grandmother claimed to have shot the animal entirely by herself my father would smile faintly behind his little moustache, without saying a word. That year, too, in South America, there was a famous crocodile hunt, in the course of which my grandmother nearly fell into a river while escaping by the skin of her teeth from an enormous alligator which she had shot at and missed.

She was always a keen sportswoman. I remember that on Belle-Isle-en-Mer she used to creep along the privet hedges with my father while I acted as beater. My father used to warn me particularly to keep at a safe distance from my grandmother's gun, which often went off by itself. I have shot with it myself, at romping Breton rabbits and harmless wheatears, of which I knew my grandmother was very fond, although when they were cooked the little birds shrank so much that they looked more like kidneys *en brochette*.

My grandmother also shot teal, ravens, blackbirds and larks. She imported hares and rabbits from the mainland, which she set free on the island, but they completely disappeared, which is, to say the least of it, curious. She also used to shoot at grey mullet which came up in shoals at high tide round a little jetty on the Penhoët beach. One day when some trippers had invaded the property and refused to go away and shouted abuse at us, Sarah's damascened gun went off as though by accident; half the lead spattered on the boundary wall, while the other half buried itself in the intruders' buttocks. The local Press got hold of the story and said that my grandmother shot off cannons "for fun". The amusing thing is we were actually very proud of a small cannon, of

165

what calibre I do not know, which Émile used to salute the arrival of important guests or to celebrate July 14.

. . . . .

Sarah returned from this triumphant and lucrative tour with another million francs and fresh laurels. But in the ship which brought her back the incident occurred which was to have such such grave consequences in the future.

All her life Sarah had an uncanny sense of presentiment and intuition. She could always feel whether the people who came near her were lucky or unlucky to her. She rarely made a mistake, and if she did occasionally harbour traitors in her house like Marie Colombier, she was seldom unconscious of the fact. She was quite aware of all the meanness and jealousy which surrounded her, but she continued to brave them in a fighting spirit, or sometimes from pure affectation and often even only to tease and annoy her Little Court.

From presentiment to superstition is but a very short step. Sarah had always been superstitious from childhood. But when she declared that heather brought the Bernhardts bad luck, it was not because anyone had told her so. No. That pretty, rather pathetic little flower, which is exactly the same whether it be fresh or dried, always brought trouble and misfortune to our family. Which may explain what happened on this voyage.

On the fifth day out, Sarah was about to enter the first-class saloon, when she suddenly felt faint; her legs gave way, and she stumbled and fell on the threshold, which was covered with studded copper. It was never quite clear whether she had been thrown off her balance by a sudden lurch of the ship or whether she had really felt faint owing to overstrain due to her exacting tour. Or, as she declared afterwards, did she receive a sudden shock which "deprived her of the use of her limbs"? However that might be, Sarah picked herself up quickly, leaned against a table and rubbed her knees. The other passengers ran to her assistance, but Sarah thanked them and left the saloon. On a table near the one against which she had leaned she had suddenly seen a beribboned pot of heather with its mauve-brown flowers and dark foliage.

In her own cabin Sarah examined her knees: one had a slight bruise, but the other, her right knee, was red and rather swollen, and very painful.

"We must get the ship's surgeon," said Jarrett, who had been sent for.

Sarah shrugged her shoulders.

"It isn't worth it. It will be gone in an hour."

She rubbed her knee gently with camphorated spirit. Half an hour later her kneecap disappeared beneath a cushion of water. Jarrett sent the doctor to her.

The doctor was young and nervous and on his first voyage. When he was told that this celebrated passenger needed his attention he put on his cap and knocked at her cabin door. This doctor may, in later years, have become a good practitioner. In 1887 he had one serious failing: dirtiness.

After fingering Sarah's leg and knee with his black-nailed fingers, he asked her to bend the knee, which she did with rather an ill grace, as she took a poor view of his obvious timidity. Suddenly her eyes fell on the doctor's hands.

"Don't dare to touch me again, sir. You hurt me and you'll probably give me blood-poisoning." (Sarah was talking like Judith Bernhardt now.) "What is the matter with me? What ought I to do? For heaven's sake say something, doctor!"

The unhappy doctor muttered something incomprehensible. The more Sarah questioned him the more confused he became. But finally he was understood to say that ignipuncture would be necessary.

"If ignipuncture is really necessary," cried Sarah petulantly, "I'll wait until we reach Le Havre. It's a disgrace for the company to have such a dirty doctor on board. Have you ever seen anything like it, Guérard? Send for the captain at once."

"He's on the bridge at the moment."

"Yes, he would be, when I want him! Félicie, bring me the camphorated spirit, a piece of cotton-wool and some oil-silk; I'll bandage it myself."

At the last moment she substituted iodine for the camphorated spirit, and painted it all over her knee.

"You'll burn yourself if you're not careful," said Jarrett, apprehensively.

"What does it matter if I do? The tour is over. So I can burn myself as much as I like."

She was in a shockingly bad temper.

"It's that heather. I went into the saloon and it was all over the place. People must be mad to sit among all that danger, just playing and talking."

"Was it the sight of the heather that made you fall?" asked the "fierce gentleman", provocatively.

"Yes, and let us hope that this will be the only manifestation of that ill-omened weed. And don't mention that sawbones to me again."

"Very well," said Jarrett cheerfully. "But you must get looked after as soon as you reach Le Havre. This isn't the time to be ill."

"And why not, pray?" asked Sarah, aggressively.

"I'm trying to arrange a world tour for you. I did not want to talk to you about it earlier, as I knew that you were longing to get back to your own people. But you are at the zenith of your career, and I want to take you across the world: Europe, Africa, Central America, Australia, and perhaps India."

"No, Jarrett, I have much less tiring plans in view. I have here," and she slapped her forehead, "an idea for a play. I'm going to rest and to write it in the company of my son and" (she dared not say her husband) "my dogs."

Sarah wanted to see Jacques Damala again. Moreover, Abbéma had written to tell her, with secret satisfaction, that he was in very poor health, and out of work. "He has left the army." Sarah's affection for the Greek began to haunt her again. Would it be possible for her to recapture her married life? To live with him and Maurice? But ever since the purple heather episode she had suffered from a haunting fear that something had happened to Jacques. . . . Unless it was to Maurice.

The next morning Sarah woke up in her cabin.

"It's a beautiful day, madame," Félicie told her. "How is madame's leg?"

"We'll have a look at it." And Sarah unwrapped her poor knee from its covering of wool.

"Well, it's still swollen, neither more nor less than yesterday, but the iodine has burned the skin. In any case, it doesn't hurt any more; it's only a little stiff. I'll see Dr. Taride in Le Havre; he's a charming man and his hands

167

are clean. Go and fetch my sister. When I'm dressed I'll go on deck; I want 'my' sea to put me right again. Doctors are asses: they don't understand that two days on deck are enough to put new life into me and to cure me of all my weariness. In the old days they used to want to send me to the mountains. I hate mountains with their huge bulk which robs the plains of sunlight, every day at the same moment and at the same place. Besides, the medical profession has ceased to be interested in me: my blood-spitting has stopped, no doubt because I am too old now to be called a young tubercular patient. Give me your arm, my dear."

. . . . .

On the morning on which Sarah had her unlucky fall, Maurice Bernhardt was fighting a duel.

He had left his mother at Santiago de Chile, on the plea that he had received a summons to appear before the Military Service Board. Sarah let him go. On his coming of age, Maurice had received from the Prince de Ligne a sum of money and authority to bear the name of the de Lignes. Maurice refused this offer, which, he said, came too late: his mother's name was the only one which suited him. However, in order to please his father, he agreed to enter a hussar regiment, the colonel of which was a great friend of the Prince's.

But the real reason for his return was quite a different one. It will be remembered that, five years earlier, Maurice, having challenged M. Langlois to a duel, had been scoffed at by him as being a beardless boy. Another attempt at the beginning of 1886 met with no better success. But now Maurice, having been told that Langlois was in Paris, and having reached the age of twenty-two, wanted satisfaction for this double insult. So he took leave of his mother (who, of course, knew nothing about the affair) and sailed for France.

As soon as he reached the Rue Fortuny he sent his seconds, Messieurs A. Schneider and Léopold Stevens, to the caricaturist, who, although a good swordsman, seemed very reluctant to fight, went away, came back and went away again. He hated having to appear on the field of honour to settle such an old quarrel, but he was forced to do so in the end, for fear of being thought a coward and of goading Maurice into doing something rash. Here is the official report of the duel:

"As arranged, an encounter took place at half past ten this morning at Ville-d'Avray, between Monsieur Maurice Bernhardt, assisted by Messieurs Schneider and Stevens, and Monsieur Langlois, assisted by Messieurs Colonna d'Istria and Colonna de Cesari.

"The weapons chosen were duelling swords, with permission to wear a fencing glove.

"In the first bout Monsieur Langlois received a thrust through the right flank and was slightly hit on the left breast and the left hand.

"The wound sustained by Monsieur Langlois having been judged by the doctors, Messieurs Haubussier for Monsieur Maurice Bernhardt and Chapelain for Monsieur Langlois, as putting the latter in a position of flagrant inferiority, the fight was stopped. Everything took place in accordance with the accepted Code of Honour."

CHAPTER XXXIII

LONELINESS

ÉMILE announced Dr. Taride. Sarah, her son and a few friends were resting in the Villa de Sainte-Adresse before returning to Paris.

For the space of half an hour Dr. Taride, the guest and doctor of the Villa de Sainte-Adresse, examined and felt Sarah's knee. When he had finished he said:

"You must look after yourself very carefully, madame. Your fall might have the most serious consequences. The ship's surgeon was right: it is essential that you should have ignipuncture. It is a pity that you didn't take immediate advantage of his good offices. You must consult a specialist the moment you reach Paris. I am afraid it's a case of severe dislocation. The play of the knee-cap seems to be impeded. I implore you not to treat this accident lightly."

Sarah promised. After a rather painful treatment, she rejoined her guests in the dining-room. This dinner in celebration of her return was to have been a very gay one. Clairin, Abbéma, Richepin and a few other faithful members of the Little Court had come down by train to be able sooner to greet their "Pretty Lady", a name given her by Clairin, and which was adopted by all her friends. But towards the end of the meal Dr. Taride, looking quietly at Maurice, put his foot right into it.

"Well, Maurice," he said, "it seems that Langlois was an adversary to be reckoned with. The old devil knows how to fight. My friend Haubussier tells me that he nearly wounded you in the chest!"

The more kicks Taride received under the table, the more his neighbour pinched his elbow and the more Maurice glowered at him, the more Jeanne tittered and the more the doctor floundered deeper in the mire with the calm unconcern of the determined suicide who refuses to be saved.

Sarah's reactions were prompt. Her presentiment had not deceived her after all! One dear to her, the dearest of all, had been in grave danger. When she recovered from the first shock she took all her friends to task, venting her anger upon them and heaping them with reproaches. No one had warned that her son was going to fight a duel! Was there no one upon whom she could depend? Their collusion was sheer treachery! Clairin, deeply offended, threw down his napkin and left the table. The others followed his example. Maurice, thoroughly upset, tried in vain to appease his mother, who wept and embraced him by turns.

"Only to think that if you had been killed that morning I would have lived another five days; five days more than you!"

"But, mama, everything went off all right. We must go and apologize to our friends. What's the matter with you?"

"Nothing. My knee. Tell me, have you had any news of—of Jacques Damala? You're the only person I can trust, Maurice; all the others are so stupid, so jealous!"

She cajoled him to try to get round him, to make him tell her everything, to show him that she considered him to be grown up. But Maurice evaded answering her questions.

"He's been very ill. I haven't seen him."

"What's the matter with him?"

"I don't know."

He knew quite well. Everyone knew what killed Jacques Damala. But it was not for Maurice to give his mother details. Now that Jacques had disappeared from his horizon, the thought of his stepfather no longer worried him and it would have been unchivalrous of him to trample on his fallen enemy.

"Very well," said Sarah. "I'll see about that when I get back."

This did not worry Maurice. In any case, his mother could be little more than a nurse at a sick man's bedside.

"Mama, I want you to promise that you'll consult a specialist about your knee."

"Of course I will," she agreed. "Besides, I'm going to write a play and I shall be able to rest while I am doing it."

.   .   .   .   .

The approaches to the house in the Rue Fortuny were blocked by reporters, friends and curious sightseers. All these people were jostling one another, laughing and chattering. In the porch of the little house Émile, who had arrived from Sainte-Adresse in advance, was giving orders to the staff and getting the luggage carried upstairs.

"I have to shake my people up," he used to say at times of great stress.

The cook, the footman, the butler, the secretary, and the housemaids ran about and got into each other's way. They had been expecting Madame Sarah for nearly an hour and Madame Sarah had not appeared. At last a carriage drew up before the house and Maurice, springing nimbly to the ground, quietly told the journalists:

"Messieurs, my mother has had to visit a sick relative. She will be here shortly."

Then he entered the house, followed by Sardou, who was sceptical about this sick relative. Maurice explained:

"Mama has gone to see . . ." (he never knew whether to say "Jacques", or "Monsieur Damala", or "my mother's husband", or "my stepfather") ". . . you know whom . . . he is very ill."

Victorien Sardou shrugged his shoulders.

During the short journey from Saint-Adresse to Paris Sarah was obsessed with the idea of seeing Damala as quickly as possible. Jacques may have been unfaithful, but he had never promised her to be anything else. It was she who had married him and had then deserted him to devote herself more thoroughly to her art. She felt a pang of remorse; perhaps it was returning love! She owed it to herself to help Jacques and to look after him.

Most of the people who were waiting for Sarah did not know what time her train was due and had gone to the Rue Fortuny. So Sarah had a very quiet reception at the station and immediately entered her carriage with Maurice and Madame Guérard.

"Are you glad to be back in Paris, Sarah dear?" asked Madame Guérard.

"Yes, darling," replied Sarah, whose mind was far away.

When they got as far as the Rue de Rome she could bear it no longer. "Go back! Go to the Rue Saint-Honoré," she told her coachman. "I must see Jacques," she told Maurice and Madame Guérard, rather unnecessarily. "I only want five minutes, just long enough to look at him."

The carriage went along the Rue Tronchet, the Madeleine and the Rue Royale. When Jacques and Sarah separated, Jacques rented three rooms on the corner of the Rue Boissy-d'Anglas. The carriage stopped and Sarah, in a grey dress and an orange-coloured, lace-trimmed mantle, her face hidden by a dove-grey veil over a little grey hat surmounted by a pigeon's wing, stepped lightly out. At the age of forty-three she was still slim and erect; to avoid tripping she lifted her dress in front, showing her beautiful ankles. She might have been any pretty Parisian woman hurrying to an assignation.

"Mama's knee seems much better today," observed Maurice.

The young man's lips parted, showing his fine, regular teeth; then his blue eyes grew serious. Up there, his mother was going to learn the truth. Up there . . .

A window opened on the third floor. Sarah put her head out, called "Guérard!" and disappeared again.

One or two people in the street looked up at her. Did they recognize her? They hesitated. What was Sarah Bernhardt doing in that modest apartment in the Rue Saint-Honoré, on the day on which the public eagerly awaited her return?

Madame Guérard climbed the stairs and was met by Sarah at the apartment door.

"Tell Maurice to take a cab and go to the Rue Fortuny to warn them that I shall be late. You, take another cab and fetch Dr. C——. Tell him to come at once and to bring a nurse with him. Jacques is very ill."

"But what is the matter with him?"

"Come in and see for yourself."

Jacques lay flat on the bed. His face was the colour of wax and his eyes were bright with fever. His eyes followed Sarah about the room and he smiled at Madame Guérard. The room was in a state of indescribable disorder. The floor was littered with books and newspapers, all mixed up with clothes and scent-bottles. Madame Guérard hesitated on the threshold, nauseated by the smell of verbena and medicines; she questioned Sarah with a look and Sarah suddenly lost her temper; she placed some little glass tubes in her friend's hand.

"That is what the matter is." Sarah's voice became very hard. "Hypo-dermic syringes and ampoules of morphia. What utter folly!"

Damala continued to smile from his bed.

.   .   .   .   .

This devotion of Sarah's lasted for two days. Then, bored by this deliberate invalid, tired of this patient who did not want to be cured, Sarah decided to have no more to do with him. Her sudden passion soon cooled in the presence of that body riddled with needle-marks, some of which were already beginning to fester, and by that fixed cynical smile, and by that face whose beauty had disappeared beneath layers of unwholesome fat.

She confided Damala to the care of Dr. C——, who made him enter a sanatorium near Paris. There he was cured, recovered his good looks and became almost normal. But he relapsed into his bad ways and died in the summer of 1889.

On her return to Paris Sarah put on a new play by Victorien Sardou, called La Tosca, at the Porte Saint-Martin Theatre. As in the case of other plays by the same author, the critics were very severe, not only about La Tosca itself (which, moreover, ran for a hundred and thirty performances), but about the whole of Sardou's work.

Sarah felt free again. She had done her duty towards Jacques and she had got him out of her system. For the first time in her life she thought of rest and of a quieter life. Maurice, her stage companions, her friends, Suzanne Seylor (of whom more later), Madame Guérard, Abbéma, Madame Grau, whom she called Nénette, and a few others who had joined the Little Court, surrounded her with their affection. So long as the run of La Tosca continued, why should she trouble about the future? Sarah was rich. She was so rich that she bought a property in Neuilly and took a lease of a house at No. 56, Boulevard Pereire. Once more Clairin and Abbéma got together to decorate the house.

As soon as she was installed, Sarah got to work; just as she had decided to do in the ship "in the company of her son and her dogs".

"I've already got the title of the play, L'Aveu [The Avowal]. All I've got to do now is to write it," she confided to Harraucourt.

Her knee only troubled her intermittently now; the swelling had almost completely disappeared and she congratulated herself on having followed Dr. Taride's treatment.

"When I have finished writing my play," she declared, "my knee will be cured."

She gave orders to illness, and illness seemed to obey her commands.

For some time now Sarah had noticed that Maurice had been rather quiet. In the afternoons he went out on mysterious errands. His mother smiled at this, a little jealous, but quite indulgent. Some new conquest occupied all her son's days; in the evenings he accompanied his mother to the theatre, sometimes happily and sometimes preoccupied. He avoided the hilarious society of his friends, young men of good family who frequented restaurants and theatres and other places of amusement. These young men drove in coaches to all the big race-meetings, fought one another, played practical jokes and manfully defended the honour of ladies of whose honour they were not always the official guardians.

In October 1887 Maurice fought a second duel. He sent his seconds to Paul Alexis, who had written an insulting article about his mother. The adversaries met in the afternoon at Villebon. In the fourth bout Paul Alexis received "a sword-thrust in the right biceps, which gave him a wound five centimetres in depth". The doctors stopped the fight.

Sarah Bernhardt knew nothing of the duel, but during her son's absence an agitated young woman called at the Boulevard Pereire and caused Sarah considerable anxiety.

"She is asking for news of Monsieur Maurice," explained Émile.

Sarah realized that her son must be in some danger, and told Émile to ask the stranger in; but when Émile went to fetch her she had vanished.

When her son returned safe and sound Sarah's thoughts went back to the girl.

"Who was that woman?" she asked Maurice.

Maurice flushed. Sarah thought it prudent not to pursue the matter and changed the subject.

"I've finished the first act of my play. But there are too many distractions here. So I have a suggestion to make to you, Maurice dear: as soon as the receipts from *La Tosca* show signs of falling, let us go to the South of France, just you and I. . . . to Nice or to Mont-Boron. You will be able to enjoy yourself and I will rest. I'll even let you go to the Casino. On condition, of course, that you are sensible."

She was trying him out. Maurice's eyes evaded hers and he replied in monosyllables. Sarah felt something clutch at her heart. She had hoped it was only a passing affair, but she read the real trouble in her son's face; she could read his soul; Maurice was in love. Sarah refused to believe it and continued to fight; she went on talking about the South of France, and of their journey.

Suddenly she felt she had had enough of this, and changed her tone.

"You're not listening to me, Maurice. What's the matter with you? You're keeping something from me."

The same young man who, scarcely two hours before, had been fighting for his mother's honour, bravely and naturally, as it was his right to do, now dared not bare his heart to her. He was afraid.

A ring at the door put an end to this awkward situation. Maurice glanced at the clock, rose abruptly, and said:

"Mama, I want to introduce a friend of mine to you. I asked her to come here before your reception so that you might see her and talk to her. Will you do so, mama?"

The young man's eyes were full of entreaty. He was no longer afraid now that "she" had arrived, now that "she" was in the house. He wanted his mother to understand that this was no ordinary day: something magnificent had happened to Maurice, and he wanted to tell her about it at the moment chosen by himself, after his duel and before the arrival of the Little Court.

Sarah changed her tactics. In one of those sudden revulsions of feeling of which she held the secret, she smiled at her son, put her head on one side and closed the manuscript of *L'Aveu*.

"Go and look after the girl," she said. "Because it is a girl, isn't it? And send Félicie to me with a powder-puff and a comb. And bring the girl up to see me in five minutes."

As on board ship, she always allowed herself half an hour before being sea-sick, so now she gave herself a few minutes before crying.

·   ·   ·   ·   ·

"Mama, I want you to know Mademoiselle Terka Jablonowska. Her mother, Princess Jablonowska, was a close friend of your own friend, the elder Dumas," added Maurice to relieve the tension.

The girl bowed to Sarah, who was immediately struck by her strange beauty. Of middle height, and admirable proportions, Terka wore a little otterskin jacket over a light chestnut-coloured skirt and a blouse of crêpe voile of the same shade. On her brown hair, drawn back to a chignon low on her graceful neck, was perched a minute toque which set off her oval face and finely moulded ears. A fresh white camellia was pinned to the toque. Two enormous eyes, speckled green and gold, a straight nose and white regular teeth: that was Terka Jablonowska. She stood there, respectful but quite at her ease, waiting for Sarah to address her.

"I am happy, mademoiselle," said Sarah, "to make your acquaintance. Look upon this house as your own. Maurice, don't leave Mademoiselle Jablonowska standing. Go and ask Félicie to serve tea at once. Run along! Are you fond of the theatre, mademoiselle?"

"I have seen you four times in *La Tosca*, madame, and I have the deepest admiration for you."

"And the deepest love for your son," added Sarah to herself.

"Maurice ought to have told me about you before. Have you known him long?"

"For about four months. I ask your pardon for this afternoon, madame: I ought never to have come; I frightened you," she added quickly. "I was afraid that Maurice——"

"Mademoiselle, since you knew . . . it was only natural. But, tell me quickly, quickly, before my son returns, is there anything else you want to tell me?"

The little Princess looked straight at Sarah, then she knelt before her. Sarah embraced her.

"My child! My child! Will your parents consent?"

"I think so."

"Then, tomorrow Maurice shall go and ask for your hand."

She embraced her again, and it was in that attitude that Maurice discovered them on his return.

.   .   .   .   .   .

Maurice was accepted by Terka's parents, and his engagement was immediately announced to the Little Court. Charles Jablonowska was a Pole. His wife, the stately Louise, ex-Lady-in-Waiting to the Empress Eugénie, and well-known in Parisian society, was of Hungarian origin. In those early days Sarah had no time to be sad. She had too much to do. The preparations, the wedding breakfast at the Avenue Pereire, the wedding itself, the invitations, the presents, her dress.

Maurice and Terka were married on December 29, 1887, at the Church of Saint-Honoré d'Eylau. A crowd of friends and sightseers invaded the church. The young couple rented an apartment in the Rue de la Néva, in the same quarter in which Sarah Bernhardt lived.

"I'll come to see you every day, mama, as before."

That evening, when the last lamp in the reception rooms had been extinguished, Sarah sat in her boudoir with Seylor, Jeanne, Abbéma, Nénette Grau and Clairin.

"They don't want to go," she thought. "They are afraid to leave me alone, sad unto death. Today I have given my son away in marriage."

"Why don't you turn Maurice's room into a little study, Pretty Lady? Look! What do you think of my plan?" And, to distract Sarah's attention, Georges Clairin placed a drawing before her.

"You are very kind," said Sarah. "I will think it over. The idea isn't bad, but we must find room for a divan in the room . . . in case Maurice. . . . Come, my friends, you must go away now. Suzanne, send Félicie to me."

She wanted to cry. Yes, it would be good to wet her five pillows with tears, to mourn this well-beloved son, the most attentive, the most chivalrous of children! He had deserted her. He had broken their contract.

But would they leave her to her tears? Certainly not! They still delayed their departure. Clairin talked at random, while Nénette, without caring what she said, held forth on men, women and children in the most entertaining manner.

At last they left. Lying in her bed, Sarah pretended to go to sleep and Félicie left the room on tiptoe. Sarah could feel her sobs rising already. To-morrow she would be ugly, but she had to cry: her sorrow needed a counter-irritant: tears, hiccoughs, handkerchiefs soaked in tears. Anything rather than oblivion or calm.

Suddenly the front-door bell rang so violently that her dog, Moustache, started barking.

A rapid step ascended the stairs. Had something awful happened? Sarah anxiously forced back her tears.

"Madame! Madame! Are you asleep?" whispered Émile.

"No."

"It's Monsieur Jarrett. He says it's urgent.'"

"Ask him to come in."

She was torn between anger at this intrusion and the hope of salvation close at hand: Jarrett! A little more and she would call out "Help!" to him.

Jarrett entered, accompanied by Émile holding a lamp. The "fierce gentleman" pretended not to notice that his star had been crying. He apologized for the inconvenience of the hour.

"Tomorrow morning," he said, "I am catching the boat-train to London, in answer to a telegram. You are at the apex of your career. I want to take you across the world: Africa, America, Europe, perhaps even India."

It was almost word for word what he had said in the ship.

"Very well," said Sarah, submissively. "What are the terms?"

She rested her head on the pillows and listened. Of course she would go. Her quiet orderly life had lasted but a moment; just long enough to write one act of a play and to marry off her son.

"I think, Monsieur Jarrett," said Émile in a low voice, "that you had better come back tomorrow. Madame is asleep."

"I know," replied the "fierce gentleman", relentlessly. "That is as it should be! Tonight, sleep at all costs. Tomorrow, work!"

He looked at Sarah, now fast asleep, and his eyes softened.

CHAPTER XXXIV

PARIS 1894

MAN proposes, God disposes. Jarrett returned in two days' time with a new project, which Sarah accepted as she had accepted the first one, with fatalism and resignation. This time it was a question of a European tour only, which meant that she would have to wait in patience for her world tour, for she categorically refused to go to Germany, which was to have been the first stage of the larger tour; so Jarrett had to reorganize that part of his expedition.

Four days later Jarrett caught influenza, and Sarah, at a loose end and inactive, started writing her *Memoirs*.

At last the day of departure arrived. Jarrett had recovered, but he confided his star to the care of another impresario. He himself was visiting Prague and St. Petersburg, working on Sarah's behalf and putting the finishing touches on the famous World Tour. After carrying off fresh laurels in Belgrade, Vienna, Prague, Bucharest and Sofia, Sarah crossed France and went on to North Africa. On her return, in January 1890, she created *Jeanne d'Arc*, *La Passion* and *Cléopâtre* on various Parisian stages.

Another incident that occurred in the same period was that Maurice Bernhardt fought a third duel, as a sequel to an argument with a certain Gabriel Mourey.

Sarah spent a great deal of money on herself and on her loved ones—much more than her plays brought her in. And yet, as Jarrett said, "she was at the apex of her career". Twice a week she gave large luncheon parties in the Boulevard Pereire. Seated in her throne-like chair, she presided at a table weighted down with gold and silver plate. Society, Art, Finance and Politics considered it a pleasure, if not an honour, to be invited to Sarah Bernhardt's house; the guests were sometimes ill-assorted, but they were all interesting personalities. Besides, the fare was excellent, and Sarah's quick wit saved the most embarrassing situations. Thus, on one occasion a young banker and his wife, recently divorced, found themselves face to face in the Boulevard Pereire. Someone told Sarah of this and she went up to the disunited pair.

"I hear you are divorced," she said. "You must have so much to say to each other. I won't interrupt you."

Completely disarmed, the couple burst out laughing.

Sarah was often a little vague and, while trying to give each of her friends a special sign of affection, would become confused and say the wrong thing. One day her old friend, Maître Clement, on his arrival at the Boulevard Pereire, apologized for not having been able to be present at her luncheon the day before.

"You know how I counted on your being there!" said Sarah, reproachfully

"Had it not been the anniversary of my wife's death, I would certainly have been there, my dear Sarah."

"What? Your wife is dead? I never knew it. You never told me, you oldest friend. It's very unkind of you!"

176

She was almost in tears, but Maître Clement quickly interrupted her. "But, my dear Sarah," he said, "she died three years ago. You were at her funeral!"

But Sarah never turned a hair. All that she said was: "I know, my dear. But I still cannot believe it to be true."

At last Jarrett reappeared, more of a "fierce gentleman" than ever; carefully planned in every detail, that extraordinary World Tour was to last for fifteen months. In March 1891, thinking that she had regained a firm enough hold on the Beloved Monster, Sarah was ready, even impatient, to be gone. She looked after everything, supervised everything; she bought furs, "travelling dogs", dresses, dresses and more dresses, while Émile "shook his people up" in the Boulevard Pereire.

Then Sarah embraced her son and her daughter-in-law, hugged little Simone, and left France for the ninth time in eleven years.

.   .   .   .   .

This 1891 World Tour proved to be a gold-mine, marred, however, by the mysterious complaint from which Sarah Bernhardt suffered; at times her knee appeared to be cured and at other times it gave her great pain. She carefully concealed these attacks and treated them with ignipunctures and massages by her doctor, who for over a year had accompanied her on all her travels.

In the course of this tour an unpleasant incident occurred while they were in Brazil. I had all the details from Suzanne Seylor, whose name will recur often in the pages to follow. Suzanne met Sarah Bernhardt in 1886. A native of Nantes, this slim and delicate girl with her violet eyes was completely captivated by the great artiste; she made her first appearance on the stage under her aegis, lived with her for a long time and accompanied her on all her tours. Here is the story.

On arriving at Rio de Janeiro, the Company split into two columns: one lived in the town, while the other, centred round Sarah Bernhardt, was accommodated in a private house situated in the garden of Botafoga, on the enchanting bay of Rio. As this villa was some way from the centre of the town, some of the members of the Company, namely Angelo, Darmont, Deschamps and Decori, thought it would be more prudent to stay with Sarah and her two companions, Madame Grau and Suzanne Seylor. All the more because in 1891 the Brazilian police was not so efficient as it probably is today. So altogether ten or twelve people, counting the doctor and the domestic staff, lived in the Botafoga villa, in addition to the dog, a fourth Brussels griffon named Moustache.

One evening, after the performance, Sarah and her friends drove back to the villa. It was a beautiful night, and the bay of Rio, dotted with lights like a piece of coruscating embroidery, glittered beneath the clear sky. It was good to be alive, and everyone was in gay mood. *Cléopâtre* had had a magnificent reception: the warm, cadenced acclamations of the Brazilians still rang in the ears of the artistes. The receipts had been phenomenal and the advance booking for the following day was most satisfactory.

A meal was served on the villa terrace.

M

"What is the wine like? Drinkable?" enquired Sarah, seeing Angelo make a face.

"It tastes funny to me."

"It's the wine of the country," put in Decori. "It isn't really bad at all." And they all drank it.

"Tomorrow morning there are no rehearsals and no duties, so I'm going to sleep late," Sarah announced happily.

Shortly afterwards she retired to bed, and said good night to Suzanne, while Émile silently went through the daily rite. This consisted of placing Sarah's travelling-bag, which weighed over a hundred pounds, at the foot of her bed and attaching the key to Sarah's gold belt, which he then laid on her bedside table. Then Suzanne and Émile locked Sarah into her room, as they did every evening. The door, which was a double one, was surmounted by a glass fanlight.

For a few minutes the sound of doors opening and shutting echoed through the house, then all the lamps and candles were extinguished. The silence of Botafoga enveloped the villa, broken only by the hoot of an owl, a ship's siren in the bay, or the song of a belated horseman passing on the highway.

The following morning the French manservant knocked on Émile's door. Émile's sleep usually resisted the most incredible din, but at last he opened the door, his eyes heavy with sleep.

"What on earth is the time?"

"Seven o'clock."

"You're crazy! Madame isn't getting up until midday."

"Madame's travelling-bag is on the stairs."

Émile stared at the servant through narrowed eyelids. His intelligence, dulled by the torpidity of his dreams, was slowly returning.

"Madame's travelling-bag is on the stairs," repeated the servant.

With a fierce oath, Émile pulled on his duck trousers and hurried out after the servant.

The famous bag was lying on the staircase; a doeskin bag which had contained three hundred thousand francs' worth of jewels lay open. The cotton-wool in which each piece of jewellery had been wrapped still littered the stairs; from among these pieces of cotton-wool Émile indignantly picked up a revolver. A glovebox containing five thousand francs in gold pieces had been left behind, emptied, naturally, of its contents.

Émile scratched his head, as he always did, then he decided on the desperate course of action of waking Sarah Bernhardt—a resolve which he carried out with some difficulty.

"What? My bag? What do you want with my bag? Why am I being disturbed?"

The usually noisy Moustache, instead of yapping, went on sleeping, curled into a ball.

Soon everyone was aware of the fact that Sarah had been robbed.

The burglars had worked quietly, without having to use violence. The police arrived shortly afterwards, arrested all the staff and found nothing. It was never discovered who had taken the key of Sarah's door from Suzanne Seylor's room and subsequently replaced it, nor how the criminals had made their entry, nor at what time this unfortunate nocturnal visit had taken place.

The inhabitants of the Botafoga villa had been put to sleep by drugs introduced into their wine and their food. A cabman gave evidence that on the previous day he had driven a manservant and the little dog to the house of a man who turned out to be an anaesthetist. There, too, the police arrived too late. The bird had flown. The cabman could not identify any of the servants in the house and Moustache, when he finally awoke, began to bark again.

Although this story has no moral, it has a sequel. Eight years later, in St. Petersburg, Sarah Bernhardt recovered her gold belt from a jeweller's shop, which proves that all roads lead to the receiver of stolen goods!

.   .   .   .   .   .

In 1893, after her World Tour, Sarah decided to settle down in Paris. She took the Théâtre de la Renaissance and inaugurated her management on October 6, with *Les Rois*, by Jules Lemaître.

Her great ambition was to manage a theatre. She worked for sixteen hours a day. But at the same time, as often as possible, she gathered her family around her, or sent for her grand-daughter Simone and played with the child. Maurice, although a young married man and a young father, kept his promise: he visited his mother every day, either at her home or at the theatre, where he helped her in her work. During the whole of Sarah's long life he always remained near her, affectionate and attentive: Sarah Bernhardt never had a more loyal defender, a more faithful knight, than her own son. He was a good swordsman, an excellent rider, and had a sound knowledge of the theatre. He wrote two books: *Monsieur Cupi* and *Impressions d'Amérique*. He subsequently became a dramatist with *Nini l'Assommeur*, at the Porte Saint-Martin Theatre in 1902, *Le Maquignon*, with Messieurs Josz and Dumur, at the Théâtre Sarah Bernhardt in 1903, *Par le feu et par le jeu*, with Monsieur Kozakiewicz, after Sienkiewicz's novel, at the Théâtre Sarah Bernhardt in 1904; and two one-act plays in collaboration with Henri Cain: *Une Nuit de Noël sous la Terreur* and *Cléopâtre*, created by Sarah Bernhardt in 1912 and 1913 respectively.

But to return to 1894. Sarah had reached the age of fifty and remained astonishingly young: her skin retained its fine texture, her eyes their deep melancholy and quizzical humour. She might have lost some of her slimness beneath her gold and turquoise belts, but Sarah still held herself erect and carried her head high.

From the very beginning of her stage career, thirty years before, Sarah never uncovered either her neck or her arms. She wore long sleeves that half hid her hands: small, adolescent, unfeminine hands. When she had to wear evening dress, she so arranged it that she showed only her shoulders, which still preserved their youthful grace. She seemed amazingly young. She always had a smile of welcome on her face, and that smile lit up her face, idealized her features and prevented her from seeming old.

Sarah put on three plays at the Renaissance Theatre: *Izëyl*, *La Femme de Claude* and *Gismonda*, with the fascinating Lucien Guitry, who was then thirty-four years old. Though the receipts were a little irregular, Sarah's renown was so great and her personality so firmly established that each first night became a memorable occasion. Lucien Guitry was a partner worthy for her, the only one who suited her perfectly, even more than Coquelin, Mounet or de Max. Those who saw them act together never forgot the experience.

The Press was loud in its praise of the two artistes. Sarah smiled, thinking of the battles of yore. The green-fly were now floundering at the roots of the rose-bush, and still occasionally delivered feeble attacks, but the roses of success flourished "despite all". Certainly, scandal may not have been dead, but it was growing very weary.

Besides, the Press in 1894 was busy with more important matters than Sarah's eccentricities, Sarah's extravagance, Sarah's hair, Sarah's private life.

A political issue was working France up into a passion, breaking up families and separating lovers: the Dreyfus affair. I do not intend to go into the question —not at length, at any rate. When the Dreyfus affair flared up, I was not even born, so I can only speak of it from hearsay. All that I know is that my grandmother was on the side of Dreyfus and that the meals in the Boulevard Pereire often suffered from divergent views on the affair. Georges Clairin, who was later to be my godfather, was anti-Dreyfus. He even went to Rennes to be present at Dreyfus's degradation; he returned from it so pro-Dreyfus that he went back to the same town in 1906 to be present at Dreyfus's vindication.

My own impression of the Dreyfus affair is as follows:

The scene is laid in the Boulevard Pereire in 1905, that is, eleven years after the affair. I was seated in a high chair next to my grandmother, who was diluting the wine in my glass with water. Around the table sat a dozen people: my father, my mother (who was keeping an anxious eye on me), my sister, the Charpentiers, the famous publishers, Madame Maurice Grau, Louise Abbéma, the Comtesse de Najac, Arthur Meyer, whose whiskers fascinated me, Georges Clairin, tall and dry, with his fine head and dark eyes, and my sister's god-father, Edouard Geoffroy, a stout, choleric gentleman, but a worthy man for all that.

The luncheon was proceeding gaily when suddenly the name of Dreyfus was mentioned, referring to the manager of one of the big Paris shops. There was a moment of tension. Remember that there was no question of the Dreyfus of the "affair", but merely of a Dreyfus who had just died in an accident. Then Geoffroy muttered:

"It's a pity it wasn't the traitor."

Georges Clairin told him to hold his tongue, and my grandmother exclaimed:

"We're not going to start that again!"

My father told Clairin not to be rude to Geoffroy; my mother implored my father to be quiet. The Charpentiers began to gesticulate. Madame Grau . . . in short, it started all over again!

The butler no longer dared pass the dishes. Geoffroy accidentally knocked the salad all over Abbéma with his elbow. My sister began to giggle nervously. My grandmother poured me out another bumper of white wine, then, at a remark by my father (her son), she broke her plate in two. Her son (my father) took offence at this and got up and began to pull my mother away from the table by her hand. Then my grandmother broke my plate on Geoffroy's arm and Geoffroy became purple with fury. The Charpentiers got up and the whole party scattered with screams of rage.

I was left alone in the dining-room, perched on my high chair and drinking white wine until the moment when my mother came to fetch me, in tears. She was the only one who had expressed no opinion on the Dreyfus affair, and precisely because of that she had just had a "wigging".

CHAPTER XXXV

"L'AIGLON"

For three years Sarah never left Paris except, in the summer, to go to her property of Belle-Isle-en-Mer, there to enjoy a short rest among her family.

In 1895 she played in *Magda*, by Sudermann, and in this connection it should be recorded that Maurice Bernhardt sent his seconds to Monsieur Edmond Lepelletier, the author of a disagreeable article about his mother in the *Echo de Paris*. But Monsieur Lepelletier preferred to return a letter of apology.

On April 5 of the same year the first production of *La Princesse Lointaine* took place.

Edmond Rostand was only twenty-seven years old when he made Sarah Bernhardt's acquaintance. And thus a great poet, a marvellous dramatist and a great friend came into the tragedienne's life. The lyricism of Rostand's verse gave Sarah the opportunity of creating a new emotional orchestration of her golden voice, putting harps and zithers into it, with, here and there, the roll of drums.

When my grandmother spoke of Edmond Rostand, she referred to him as "my poet", and she was right to do so. From that moment the Rostands were a part of my grandmother's life. As soon as they entered the house it became a scene of animation and gaiety. Rosemonde Gérard's beauty (she was Madame Edmond Rostand); Maurice's laugh and his way of expressing himself with careful preciosity; the reserve and wisdom of Jean; Edmond Rostand's wit, his mildly quizzical expression, his monocle, his elegance and his button-holes; all these fascinated me. This enchantment continued for a long time. My sister and I were nearly the same age as the Rostand boys. I think that Maurice and Simone flirted a little, while Jean paid no attention at all to me. Flowers, fruit and laughter preceded and accompanied the Rostands into the dining-room of the Boulevard Pereire. I used to watch for their coming from the window, for they were always late. Even their excuses were poems. As soon as their carriage drew up in front of the house I would cry, "There they are!" and my grandmother, already seated on her "throne" at the end of the table, would order Émile to serve luncheon.

They all came in and sat down. And after luncheon at least one of the four Rostands would recite the verses he had written the day before or even that very morning; except Jean, who listened and who looked like his father, like a silent, disillusioned Edmond. Maurice charmed me; Jean scared me; he looked as if he could read one's mind. Today Jean is a great scientist who reads the secrets of nature.

After *La Princesse Lointaine*, Sarah spread her wings again. Trunks were fetched from the cellars, and packing-cases from the attics, for a European tour. In 1896 another American tour. Antonio de la Gandara had just finished a magnificent full-length life-size portrait of Sarah in profile showing her in a white dress, standing proudly erect. The painter's brother, Edouard de la Gandara, accompanied her on her tour.

On her return to Paris, Sarah created the name-part in *Lorenzaccio*, a curious study of sixteenth-century Florentine mentality; she was perfectly at ease in the beautiful costume of the young Italian, which set off her finely modelled legs with their high sensitive calves. Very few women could have carried off this costume, but Sarah had the intelligence and the judgment only to attempt male rôles in which masculinity took a second place: Le Passant is a poet; Lorenzaccio, Hamlet and Bohemos are intellectuals; L'Aiglon (whom she called the White Hamlet) an unhappy prince in exile, and when, in 1907, she gave *Les Bouffons*, the hump which she wore beneath her doublet kept one's mind off everything save Jacasse's verses.

Edmond Rostand had just completed a new work, *La Samaritaine*. The religious emotion contained in this play, in which divine pity rubs shoulders with human love, procured a fresh triumph for Sarah and for her poet; they both gathered the laurels, and each offered the other the finest branches. It seemed at that time that Sarah could climb no further up the garlanded ladder, which was beginning to lose itself in the skies. And yet. . . !

She first gave herself the pleasure of appearing on the stage with the great Italian actress, Eleonora Duse, in a soirée in honour of the younger Dumas, who died in 1895. "The Duse" had an enthusiastic reception from the public, and this enthusiasm continued with Sarah's appearance; Sarah, at the age of fifty-three, played the part of the young Marguerite Gautier.

In 1897, after *La Samaritaine*, Sarah acted in a socialist play, *Les Mauvais Bergers*, by Octave Mirbeau. Wearing a black woollen dress, she moved about the stage in a scene of misery and want. She was bullied by the labourer, Jean Roule, a part interpreted in a masterly manner by Lucien Guitry. She played the part with beautiful pathos, and the Beloved Monster was amazed by the adaptability with which its idol showed the facets of her talent, like a woman turning a diamond ring round her finger.

1898. *La Ville Morte*, by Gabriele d'Annunzio. But Sarah was ill and had to undergo an operation which left her exhausted and weak. Preliminary signs of kidney disease began to show themselves and her knee frequently gave her pain. These ailments were not, at the time, very serious; they did not prevent her from working or loving or living or laughing; but the hidden enemy was there all the same; he disguised himself so well that his victim became careless and undertook new and arduous labours, the heavy bill for which she would have to pay some years later.

1898. Maurice Bernhardt, having had an altercation in the Renaissance Theatre with Félicien Champsaur, sent him his seconds.

In April, Sarah, now cured—or at any rate not so ill—returned to the stage in a play by Romain Coolus. The author chose as its title the name of Sarah Bernhardt's grand-daughter, *Lysiane*.

. . . . .

And now I must apologize for speaking about myself. After leaving the Rue de la Néva, in 1896 my parents rented a house in the Rue Scheffer, and it was there that my mother waited for the birth of her second child. I must admit that our family hated girls; my grandmother was no doubt permanently disgusted by the thought of her half-dozen aunts and, as Judith Bernhardt never seemed to be able to bear male children, the arrival of my father into the world was regarded as a happy event. Because of this, my poor mother was expected to have nothing but boys. So there was great disappointment when my sister appeared. Everything was blue to receive her, nursery, cradle, layette, and all marked "S.B.", as the baby was to be named Serge. But my grandmother and my parents consoled themselves because Simone was pretty.

Then my turn came.

Terka, wrote my grandmother from the United States, a month before my birth, *I've decided upon a name for my future grandson. He's to be called Louis. I have arranged for his layette: I hope it has come by now. Go and look at classical art and walk in the Louvre, and be very careful of yourself.*

My mother's care for herself and her contemplation of Greek statuary did not prevent me from being born a girl, and rather a wrinkled one at that. *It's another girl and she looks like Monsieur Thiers*, cabled my disconsolate father. And my grandmother cabled back from Colorado: *So much for Louis. Kiss my Lysiane for me.* My mother, to be on the safe side, had also chosen a girl's name.

My sister was dark, with large eyes and a neat little mouth. Two months after my entry into the world, a meagre tuft of platinum hair stood up on the top of my skull, and I looked like all the Bernhardts, with light blue eyes set wide apart. On her return from America, my grandmother, who had no doubt prepared herself for the worst, uttered an exclamation of pleased surprise on seeing me and gave me an affectionate hug. And afterwards she used to stop her carriage nearly every morning in the Avenue du Bois de Boulogne, where my nurse was giving me an airing, and then go on to the theatre for the rehearsals of *La Samaritaine*.

To return to 1898. After *Lysiane*, after *Medée* by Catulle Mendes, Sarah sold the Renaissance Theatre and rented the Théâtre de la Nation, in the Place du Châtelet, from the Paris municipality. She spent fabulous sums on the redecoration of the auditorium and of the stage and had her name put on the front of the building, and the Théâtre Sarah Bernhardt opened in 1899 with *Dalila*, by Octave Feuillet, shortly followed by Marcel Schwob's version of *Hamlet*, one of the most curious and most beautiful of Sarah's creations.

All these artistic productions cost a great deal of money. Sarah needed money, a great deal of money, so she decided to go on another tour.

Some days before her departure Rostand offered her a new play which filled Sarah with intense excitement.

Ah, that part, that part! She could think of nothing but that. All the time she was travelling through England, Scotland, Belgium, Holland and Switzerland one name was constantly in her thoughts, a proud, sad name, and she seized the opportunity of visiting Schoenbrunn, still haunted by a white wraith: "L'Aiglon! L'Aiglon!"[1]

· · · · ·

[1] After 1814, Napoleon's son was called the Duc de Reichstadt, but has always been referred to in France as L'Aiglon (The Eaglet).

The first performance of L'Aiglon, on March 15, 1900, created a sensation. Yet one critic wrote, "The play will not run for ten nights." L'Aiglon! A glorious work which has been played a thousand times, revived and revised. L'Aiglon, which has been played almost as often as many of the old French classics. What was in the mind of that tea-leaf prophet? The Eaglet, whose white uniform has been seen in every country in Europe, Africa and America; as a play, in opera and on the screen.

The play was acclaimed by an enthusiastic audience, which emphasized the more impressive passages, stamped its feet at the invective and followed with bated breath the marvellous rhythm of Rostand's verse and his fascinating juggling with words. L'Aiglon was a huge success: the Eagle's son, after becoming an Austrian duke, sent out an appeal to French heroism, and cast his spell upon the excited audience; the poetic tilting of L'Aiglon touched the heart of the Beloved Monster as with a rapier point.

Yes, the Beloved Monster was delighted that a poet like Edmond Rostand, and an actress like Sarah Bernhardt, should take the responsibility for this polished chauvinism, and the public instantly applauded the Eaglet's despair and his love for France.

"On the stage, to be natural is good, but to be sublime is always better," said Sarah Bernhardt to those who would have preferred her to play more realistic parts.

She also claimed that, from the strictly commercial point of view, a mediocre play which glorifies great love, or sorrow, or horror, or murder, brings in more money than a much better play which is more discreetly human.

It was during the successful run of L'Aiglon that my first conscious meeting with Sarah Bernhardt took place, that is to say the first picture I have of her, my first memory.

I was a very small child. Before going to Corsica with my sister, my parents confided me to Sarah's care.

"But Lysiane has a cold," protested my grandmother.

"It's nothing," replied my mother. "She hasn't a temperature."

Nor had I, then; but a week later I had bronchial pneumonia and was given up by Dr. Robin; my grandmother was frantic; her darling Maurice's child was going to die. She telegraphed daily to Ajaccio. Maurice and Terka could not return because my sister Simone had caught whooping-cough. One day, at seven in the evening, the doctor came to the Boulevard Pereire.

"She's very bad," he said. "But if she gets through the night we may have a chance of saving her life."

Sarah sent for a sculptor and said to him:

"If the child dies, you are to take a mould of her face."

Then she went to the theatre; the public was waiting for the Duc de Reich-stadt, but Sarah's thoughts were with the child, growing weaker and weaker in the large bed.

After the third act her carriage took her home. It was the time at which my injection was due, and although my own nannie and a hospital nurse were with me, she wanted to be present too. Beneath the huge Mongolian rug lay the pale child with her drawn features, listlessly tugging at her fair hair.

"Her temperature hasn't risen for five hours," observed the hospital nurse.

The Eaglet bent over. The aiguillettes on her cape brushed the sick child, who opened her eyes and smiled faintly at this vision; she was not frightened, as she was used to this anxious, loving figure. Sarah let a tear fall on the poor little face. She kissed her and left, wondering whether she would ever again see her grandchild alive.

At the theatre the audience found the interval too long and began to stamp and even to whistle. The stage manager appeared before the curtain.

"Madame Sarah Bernhardt asks your indulgence. Her grand-daughter is dangerously ill."

The curtain rose. The Duc de Reichstadt broke the mirror in which Metternich had just proved to him that he was, in fact, nothing but an Austrian Eaglet. The audience was very quiet. Some of the mothers may have been thinking of their children. At the end of the play the Beloved Monster roared its applause.

That evening, perhaps, it was not voicing its enthusiasm for the interpreter of more than fifty parts, but, far more, its admiration for the woman who played this stormy part to its bitter end in spite of her agonizing anxiety.

The "Duc de Reichstadt" got into her carriage with Suzanne without changing her costume or removing her make-up, and she spent that night at the small child's bedside, with the sculptor, the nannie and the hospital nurse. Dr. Robin arrived in the early hours of the morning. He looked at Sarah, huddled in an easy chair, ashen beneath her greasepaint and her fair wig, draped in her white mantle, broken, aged. He touched her arm.

"Madame, I think she is saved."

Sarah stared at him, then rolled to the floor, overcome by weariness and emotion.

CHAPTER XXXVI

BERLIN

In 1900 Sarah's sister Jeanne died, which was a great sorrow to her. Jeanne was carried off in a few months like little Regina Bernhardt. Jeanne left a daughter. I remember that strange young woman with her grey eyes, fair, amber-coloured hair and delicate colouring. Saryta, as she was called, painted, smoked a great deal and spoke very little; suffering from a chest complaint, she died, in her turn, in 1905.

After Jeanne's death, Sarah Bernhardt crossed the Atlantic for the fifth time. At the age of fifty-six she was afraid that her age would cool the affection the American people had for her. But the American public hailed her as "the most illustrious artiste in the world". Reassured by the reception of the first productions, by the first receipts, the first articles, the first cheers, she vowed to the New Continent the grateful friendship which she was always to feel for it. Paris was her springboard, but the United States remained for her a constant encouragement, a source of energy . . . and of dollars.

(While she was away on this tour, Maurice, who was managing the Théâtre Sarah Bernhardt in Sarah's absence, sent his seconds to Monsieur Muhlfeld, following an offensive article on his mother. But the seconds settled the matter and the duel never took place.)

On her return to Paris, Sarah Bernhardt played the name-part in *Francesca da Rimini*, by Marion Crawford.

One afternoon a telephone call came through from the Ministry of Foreign Affairs. The Minister wanted to come to see Sarah Bernhardt. As there was some question of decorating her with the Legion of Honour (in her capacity as theatre manager, whereas she wanted it in her capacity as tragedienne), she imagined that the Minister's visit had something to do with this. She was soon disillusioned.

"It would be a good thing for you to go to Germany on your next European tour," he said; "and that as soon as possible."

Sarah bowed. She could not refuse. Might France live in peace! Anything undertaken to avoid another war was a sacred duty.

Her visit to Germany took place in 1902. What had happened to Jarrett during all these years? I confess I do not know the exact year in which he died. After him, after Abbey and Grau, a French impresario offered to manage Sarah's tours for her, and he was accepted.

When the train drew into the Berlin station Sarah had an intuitive feeling that her German reception would be a cold one. And yet Emperor William II sent an official representative to greet her; and the Empress sent her a bouquet of camellias ("a very small one", my grandmother told me). She was treated as a diplomat, with deference, and not as a woman and a famous artiste. Pitou showed her cuttings from the German Press, respectful, reasoned articles. No criticism, no enthusiasm.

The German Press is like a praying mantis [she wrote to her son]. *It devours me in silence.*

The manager of her hotel had arranged for flowers to be put in his guest's apartment, accompanied by "very honoured and very respectful sentiments". The director of the Schauspielhaus sent her a bouquet accompanied by his card and his "very respectful and very honoured sentiments". All this was very correct. Sarah was asked whether she would like to be shown round Berlin and she replied that she was "very honoured".

In her dressing-room she felt more at ease, in that theatre atmosphere which was so near to her heart. She had been given a mission to carry out and she must fulfil it to the best of her ability. She would face the German public on the following evening and she would compel it to unbend.

"Germans are receptive to Art," she declared. "They don't care what trade mark it bears."

She imposed silence on her memory. 1870 was already entering the distant past.

"We mustn't think any more of yesterday's drama. We must think of the future. And we must think of Holbein, Bach, Wagner, Goethe, Schiller and Heine."

Alas! Although she found comfort in surrounding herself with phantoms, although she derived energy from hoping for an eternal understanding between the two peoples, and although, during her visit to Germany, she had but one watchword ringing in her ears, one command, Peace, nevertheless a painful reality made her task a difficult one. For the past month her knee had never given her a moment's rest.

"It feels as though an animal were gnawing my nerves and my tendons," she complained quietly.

At her son's request, Sarah had consulted several scientific luminaries. These pundits refused to admit that they had no idea of what was the matter, so they shrugged their shoulders in Pitou's den and prescribed remedies and cures at watering-places. And Sarah decided that they were all mountebanks.

"Madame," said one professor caustically, "we are not magicians."

"That's most unfortunate," she replied. "But at any rate tell me what the matter is."

More shoulder-shrugging. Some diagnosed arthritis, others tuberculosis of the bone.

So Maurice and the Little Court had implored Sarah to profit by her visit to Berlin to have herself examined by Professor Scheinfurt. The day after her arrival the eminent scientist called to see her. He was an extremely ugly, but an interesting-looking, man. When he removed his tortoiseshell-rimmed glasses his eyes were so handsome and intelligent that they seemed to light up his face. Sarah told him so. He looked at her with sympathy and respect; a great scientist and a great artiste. Science and Art have affinities which know no frontiers. Then Professor Scheinfurt felt the injured knee with his long, white, supple, gentle fingers and, while he talked, a secretary took notes. Suzanne, who had taken the place of Madame Guérard, for whom the continual moving from place to place was now too tiring, grew impatient and vainly tried to read a diagnosis in the Professor's face. Finally the scientist replaced his glasses and his expression again became inscrutable.

"Madame," he said, "I cannot give a definite name to your complaint. The femoro-tibial articulation is suffering from an affection, certainly tubercular in origin, which is attacking the femoral joints; these attacks provoke crises, accompanied by dropsy."

"And what is the proper treatment for it?"

The professor hesitated; then he removed his glasses and his magnificent eyes reappeared.

"Six months of complete immobility, with the leg in plaster of Paris. Then X-rays to decide the exact position of the evil, then a surgical operation. I do not promise that after that you will be able to run about or to use your right leg like a young girl. I was going to say 'like a young woman', but I see that you really are a young woman."

"Six months!" muttered Sarah, paling. "Six months! When ought I to begin this treatment?"

The professor replaced his glasses and said, curtly:

"Tomorrow, madame!"

.   .   .   .   .

"Tomorrow," he said, and Sarah was playing at the Schauspielhaus! Berlin was waiting for her; perhaps it is no exaggeration to say that Berlin was lying in wait for her. So the possibility of not appearing could not even be contemplated. Sarah interpreted Professor Scheinfurt's orders to suit herself. After Berlin, she would go and rest at her property of Belle-Isle-en-Mer and would remain there for three months. On her return, she would consult her friend Professor Pozzi, and would ask his opinion about the necessity for an operation.

The following day, at five o'clock in the afternoon, Sarah went to the Schauspielhaus. She was in such pain that the set was altered to save her any unnecessary movement. The last straw was when Dr. C., having had a slight heart attack, was unable either to massage Sarah's knee or to relieve it by ignipuncture. As for calling in another doctor, it was out of the question, as she always tried to keep her strange malady a secret.

At six o'clock the French Company began to feel nervous. The formal correctness of the director, of the theatre staff and of the stage hands got on Sarah's nerves.

"These idiots are laughing at us from the wings!"

After a meal in her dressing-room Sarah, contrary to her usual habit, asked all her Company to come to see her, and said:

"I think there is going to be a fight. A psychological fight. I am sure we shall win. Tonight, my friends, you must give everything that is in you."

Sarah hated silence, and everything in that theatre was silent. The stage hands set up the scenery and arranged the set noiselessly. The curtain was due to rise at eight o'clock, and Sarah was already dressed at a quarter to eight. And yet there was none of that cheerful animation that usually preludes an important evening at the theatre. The stage manager, sent to investigate, reported that the house was empty and that the foyer was not even illuminated.

So far only three people had entered the theatre. Sarah turned pale at the insult: an empty house!

"I won't play to an empty house," she declared. "Send for that director with a head like a chess-pawn."

But before the director could arrive she changed her mind. This evening, it was not a question of Sarah Bernhardt, but of France. Very well! She would play before an audience of three. When the director arrived she gave him a sweet smile.

"We don't seem to have much of an audience, monsieur."

"Not much of an audience!" replied the man, in amazement. "But, madame, the house is sold out!"

"Possibly, but the stalls are empty. Or perhaps only ghosts are coming this evening."

She went on smiling.

"The theatre is packed from top to bottom, and we have just added dozens of chairs!"

"Madame Sarah," cried Germain, the stage manager, entering precipitately, "the theatre is quite full! The audience all arrived at the same time, within ten minutes of each other!"

"You're an idiot, my dear Germain," Sarah observed quietly. "Excuse me for having disturbed you, Herr Direktor."

She gave him her hand, and the German bent his pawn-like head to kiss the Frenchwoman's fingers.

.   .   .   .   .

("The first act, Lysiane, passed in the most complete silence. When the curtain fell there was a little polite, desultory applause, very little. The second act was received in the same discreet manner. I began to be thoroughly amused. My fighting spirit kept me going: not that I was scared, but my knee was hurting me and I was afraid of limping on the stage. During the third act, not a sound interrupted my scene with Armand Duval's father and yet it seemed to me as though a half-suppressed mutter rose from the stalls. The curtain fell on the same polite applause. In the fourth act I seemed to hear that muttering again. When I entered the stage on Varville's arm, in my black dress with its camellias, I whispered to Decoeur:

" 'They will either whistle or applaud.'

"I was really lying, as I knew that the mutter was one of admiration. But there was neither a shout, nor a cheer, nor a curtain-call at the end of the act.

"At last the curtain rose on the fifth act. From the very beginning of the act I was sensible of a tremor in the audience. I knew that tremor well: the audience was stirred. I do not say it was thrilled, but it was clearly moved. I could feel the familiar waves of that emotion: programmes slipped to the floor, arms fidgeted on the arm-rests, feet shuffled nervously. But no one coughed or whispered or blew his nose. It was as though this German public was getting rid of its constraint.

"Then came the scene where Nanine tells Marguerite Gautier that Armand has returned, that Armand is coming to see her, that Armand is there! I turned to hold my arms out to my beloved, and, as luck would have it, in spite of the careful arrangement of the set, I tripped. My leg gave under me. I held on to the bed, and instead of calling 'Armand!' I gave a terrible scream, a cry of love, but also one of pain. With great presence of mind, the young actor who played the part of Armand sprang towards me and held me close to him, thus preventing me from falling.

" 'It's me, it's me, Marguerite!'

"And I whispered to him:

" 'Don't let go for a moment. Help me to the sofa.'

"And so, my child, that night your grandmother not only knocked the properties about but also took liberties with Alexandre Dumas's text!

" 'But the public?'

"The public? Well, the public roared and stamped. It prevented us from speaking. All the more unbridled because for two hours it had suppressed, first its animosity and then its——"

" 'Its admiration!'

"Very well; if you like. When the end of the last act came, the stage manager who controlled the curtain danced with glee as he watched it go up and down and counted: 'Three, four, five recalls, Madame Sarah! Nine, ten, eleven . . . thirteen!'

"Thirteen times my fellow-actors and I had to make our bows.

" 'And the German Press?'

"It was very correct. Anyway, I did not care. My mission did not consist in having sweet nothings said to me by the German Press, but to stir the German soul! And the German soul went out to me.")

PART FOUR

(UNPUBLISHED article by Sarah Bernhardt, a rough copy of which was found among her papers.)

"I quite see that we professional actors are really the amateurs. That is why our comrades, the actors of real life, judge us so severely. They are very wrong to do so.

"For us, the struggle is renewed every day, and every day we have to triumph. It is generally believed by the public that actors slacken off after ten or fifteen performances. Personally, I always live my own parts completely. Sophie Croizette, after the poisoning scene in *The Sphinx*, remained ashen-white for some minutes, and gnashed her teeth; sometimes she lost consciousness altogether. And this happened all through the hundred performances of the play.

"The tragedian Beauvallet wept bitter tears in the forest scene from *King Lear*. Mounet-Sully sometimes suffered from real hallucinations in the madness of Orestes. Morain's heart beat so fast in the fourth act of *La Dame aux Camélias* that he was often unable to speak his lines, and during the hundred and fifty performances of *Fédora* I myself felt for a hundred and fifty times that my last moment had come. Iponoff, blinded by rage, strangled me more realistically than Pierre Berton would have liked. And I have never played Phèdre without being stirred to the depths of my being or spitting blood. After the fourth scene of *Théodora*, in which I kill Marcellus, I am in such a nervous condition that I return to my dressing-room sobbing. Even though I do not shed tears I often have an attack of nerves, which is much more dangerous for the furniture. The interval is a little long and the public get restless; yet it is not really my fault. My great comrades, the actors of real life, think that this is not great Art. 'To interpret properly,' they say, 'one must feel nothing.'

"Diderot said so, and so has Coquelin. They are no doubt both right, and the proof is that Coquelin, an admirable actor, is a very great artiste, but I am only a woman and I like being in the wrong.

"I visited Aimée Tessandier in her dressing-room after the sleepwalking scene from *Macbeth*. She was icy cold and still trembled. And yet it was her fiftieth performance. Many of us belong to that emotional school. We live our parts, we weep, we laugh, we suffer and love with them. Our real life is down there in the ardent home of all the passions lived and dreamed. It is a daily battle. It is a perpetual heartbeat, incessant brainwork, the regret of never being perfect and the hope of becoming so, and the price of exultation. So our nerves suffer when we fall back into the real acting, that of real life, and we become scatterbrained. We sometimes do foolish things and our great comrades of real life are not indulgent with us: they call us mountebanks."

Sarah Bernhardt and the artist Georges Clairin

Sarah Bernhardt in America, lunching in her private car at Dallas

The rocks at the Fort des Poulains. Sarah Bernhardt in the centre, with her son Maurice and Reynaldo Hahn in the background

The "Sarahtorium" at the Pointe des Poulains. Sarah is on the right, with Maurice

CHAPTER XXXVII

SARAH BERNHARDT'S PRIVATE LIFE

MY grandmother's activities did not slacken after her return from Germany. She produced, successively, at the Théâtre Sarah Bernhardt: *Théroigne de Mericourt*, by Paul Hervieu; *Werther*, by Pierre Decourcelles; *La Légende du Cœur*, by Jean Aicart; *Jeanne Wedeking la Sorcière*, by Victorien Sardou; *Bohemos*, by Miguel Zamacoïs; *Varenne*, by Lenôtre and Lavedan; Victor Hugo's *Angelo*, and Racine's *Esther*. In 1905 she went to America, returning six months later to produce, in Paris, *La Vierge d'Avila*, by Catulle-Mendès and *Les Bouffons*, by Miguel Zamacoïs. In 1907, having been appointed lecturer at the National Academy of Elocution, she also gave a new version of *Adrienne Lecouvreur*, written by herself, and of *La Belle au Bois Dormant*, by Jean Richepin and Henri Cain. In 1908 she played Cléonice in the play of that name by Michel Carré and *La Courtisane de Corinthe*, by Bilhaud. In 1909, *La Fille des Rabenstein*, by Paul Rémon, and lastly *Le Procés de Jeanne d'Arc*, by Émile Moreau, which brought her, with de Max, a great and stirring success.

I remember my grandmother perfectly in some of those plays and I remember the insuperable stage-fright which made her hands go cold before each first night.

"My God, my God! If only the theatre would burn down!" she would exclaim an hour before having to face her audience.

Sarah Bernhardt never knew that calm of mind that certain actors feel, a calm of which, incidentally, she disapproved. Once, when she described her stage-fright to a well-known comedy actress, the actress laughed and said: "Really, Madame Sarah, I don't understand you. I am never frightened myself."

"So much the worse for you!" my grandmother replied quietly.

In April 1906 there was fresh trouble in the home. At that time my parents lived in the Boulevard Lannes. People whispered in corners, or came in and left mysteriously; mama wept, and my grandmother telephoned to us all day. Following an article on Sarah Bernhardt which had appeared in *La Vie Illustrée*, my father had sent his seconds to Monsieur de Wendel, who, however, retracted and apologized.

For a year now my mother had been suffering from the kidney disease which was to carry her off four years later. She seldom left the house and spent her days in bed. As for my father, neither his daughters, nor his wife's illness, nor his work as Assistant Director of the Théâtre Sarah Bernhardt prevented him from showing his own mother the same attentive and affectionate devotion as he had always done.

However, my grandmother's friends were frankly censorious of Maurice Bernhardt's wandering habits, his laziness and his extravagant amusements.

"Money," said Clairin. "Hold on to your money, Pretty Lady!"

"You ought to save up money for your future," Louise Abbéma told her quietly.

"Children cost a lot of money," said Geoffroy, going one better. My grandmother shrugged her shoulders.

"You're a lot of old egotists. Leave me in peace!"

My sister and I used to lunch every week in the Boulevard Pereire, and this was always a great treat for me. I never grew tired of that smell of citronella that assailed your nostrils as soon as you passed through the door, nor of the huge wapiti killed—or not killed—by my grandmother, nor of the studio in which I was allowed to browse after luncheon. Ah, that studio! What a jumble of curios, what a profusion of chairs, what piles of furs, and what a collection of weapons, pictures, masks and ivories! A precious glory-hole! The show-cases fascinated me: imagine a lot of shelves coated with clay and, stuck into the clay, bits of coral and semi-precious stones all carefully arranged and labelled. And three or four dogs which I used to fetch from the courtyard and which romped with me on the divan, without a thought to the cushions or my frock. My mother always expected me to return from the Boulevard Pereire all dirty and in holes. She was quite used to it. One day she wanted to send me along in a pinafore, but my grandmother protested indignantly. What she would really have liked was for my sister and myself always to be dressed in velvet or silks.

"Your daughters look as though they were attending a charity school," she reproached my mother. Nothing escaped her keen eyes, neither our hair, nor our clothes, nor our shoes.

My memory of old Madame Guérard is confused and rather vague. I do, however, remember the two pug-dogs which stank abominably and which she used to walk about the Boulevard Pereire. I remember also that my grandmother, tired of seeing Madame Guérard always dressed in black, wanted to buy her a new dress.

"Very well, Sarah, but choose me a dark woollen one in which I can take my dogs for a walk in the morning."

My grandmother shrugged her shoulders and ordered the dear old lady a blue taffeta dress with black lace flounces.

When my grandmother asked me questions at luncheon, which she never failed to do, she and I used to play a regular game of hide-and-seek behind the flowers, the china, the candlesticks and the glass. However, my grandmother soon put a stop to that. Her grand-daughters were no longer relegated to the far end of the table, and it often happened that I sat next to the principal guest. So it was that at various times I came into close contact with Sardou, Catulle-Mendès, Richepin, Pierre Loti, Harancourt, d'Annunzio, Edmond Rostand and many others. My grandmother, seated in her throne-like chair and always dressed in white, dominated us all. Often, after coffee was served, I would ask to be allowed to remain, fascinated by the conversation which sparkled like fireworks. Of course I did not always understand very much but I wanted to remain in my seat. Then my father, who was a stickler for convention, would sign to me to leave the room. And I would go in search of my friends the dogs and parrots. Incidentally, after the birth of her grand-daughters, Sarah had given up pumas, which she considered too dangerous, and her monkeys, which she thought were too "exhibitionist".

Our weekly visit took place on Thursday. As soon as her guests had gone, my grandmother would go up to her boudoir-dressing-room and devote herself exclusively to us for an hour. She questioned me about my studies, my companions, my games. Sometimes, on the days when Pitou was in a bad temper, I helped her to rehearse a new part or to tidy up her papers. I told her the plots of the plays I was going to write for her when I grew up; one day I burst into tears, because when I was explaining the most dramatic episode of one of them she began to weep. But she was only pretending. And to make up for it she kissed me fondly and commissioned me to write a poem about her dog, for which she paid me a louis. On another occasion, when I was about eight, she asked me what I was going to be when I was older. Without hesitation, I replied:

"I'm going to be an oculist, so as to be able to see what's the matter with your knee." I had got mixed, of course, between the profession and the organ. This time, it was my grandmother who really wept.

Simone and I often drove with her in her carriage. There was nothing to compare, for me, with those drives in the Bois de Boulogne. I was intoxicated with pride and happiness. Afterwards Sarah would take us back to the Boulevard Lannes, where she would embrace her daughter-in-law and then return to her work.

In 1909, the Thursday luncheons gave place to classic performances at the Théâtre Sarah Bernhardt, where a stage box holding twelve would be reserved for us: the children of Georges Feydau and of Carolus-Duran, the Rostands, etc., used to join us there. After the matinée we had tea in my grandmother's dressing-room. It was a happy band that invaded the three rooms of which Sarah Bernhardt's apartments at the theatre consisted. In an overheated atmosphere, among baskets of heavily-scented flowers and electric lamps and pervaded with the smell of incense, a table would be set up, loaded with pyramids of cakes. The children made short work of the sandwiches, moka cakes, babas and brioches and my grandmother was always delighted with this invasion. My little friends' mothers were not nearly so pleased. They had to cope with sleeplessness, nightmares, temperatures and even violent indigestion followed by purges.

In 1910 the performances took place of *Beffa*, by Benelli and Jean Richepin, and of *La Conquête d'Athènes*, by Albert Du Bois.

In the month of June of the same year my mother died. A few weeks later Sarah Bernhardt went to America for the seventh time. My sister Simone, who had been married for a year, took me to England, where I remained until my grandmother's return to France, in April 1911.

.   .   .   .   .

From that time onward I lived with my grandmother in the Boulevard Pereire, where I remained until the end of her life. I basked in the sunlight of her presence. I accompanied her on her European tours. She devoted herself entirely to me, and when my period of mourning was over she had me dressed, in accordance with her own taste, by dressmakers who did not usually have dealings with little girls of fifteen. But, although my frocks and my hats interested her enormously, the rest of my wardrobe did not concern her. If I said, "Grandmother, I need some new shoes . . . Grandmother, I need some underclothing," she would tell me, with a smile, to go and tell my father.

Very soon I was allowed to be present at the dinner-parties she gave in her house. I was no longer sent away after dessert. An unseen orchestra would often play in the round room, separated from the dining-room by a heavy curtain; there were usually about fifteen guests at these dinner-parties. It was at those parties that in about 1911 I met such celebrities as d'Annunzio, Henry Bauer, Eugène Brieux, Maître Busson-Billault, Léon Bailby, Marcel Boulenger, Tristan Bernard, the explorer Jean Charcot, Marie Carolus-Duran, the brothers Cassagnac, the Marquis de Castellane, Henri Cain, Paul Cambon, Paul Déroulède, Édouard Detaille, Maurice Donnay, Pierre Frondaie, Reynaldo Hahn, Paul Hervieu, Myron T. Herrick, Pierre Loti, Henri Lavedan, Robert de Montesquiou, Arthur Meyer, Madame Catulle-Mendès, Mary Marquet, the Comtesse Anna de Noailles, Professor Pozzi, Raoul Ponchon, Simone Porcher, Ida Rubinstein, Jean Richepin, Professor Charles Richet, Jean-Jacques Reinach and Miguel Zamacoïs, who was a neighbour of ours.

Another person who came was the "extraordinary little Sacha", as my grandmother called him, who in 1911 had already written more than twenty-five plays, almost one for every year of his life.

"You ought to find a subject for me, my little Sacha!"

Later, Sacha Guitry wrote a lovely play for Sarah Bernhardt but, alas! she was never able to produce it. In 1912 she fell seriously ill and had to abandon the rehearsals of *Un Sujet de Roman,* and I well remember her sorrow and disappointment.

"Little Sacha's play has no luck!" she said.

.　　　.　　　.　　　.　　　.

"Do something with your ten fingers," my grandmother said to me one day. "It doesn't matter what, so long as it is something."

"Oh!" I replied, rather taken aback.

She could not bear people to twiddle their thumbs; if you were doing nothing she said you were an idler, and she could not understand that her own boundless energy was sufficient distraction, occupation and sometimes even work for those around her.

So I took lessons in the piano, in drawing and in elocution. The first never took me further than Grieg's *Spring Song*; the second enabled me to make portraits of dogs which lined the staircase walls; and the third gave rise to lively scenes between my father, who was shocked at the idea of my becoming an actress, and my grandmother, furious at the idea that he should object. When she gave me lessons (and how patiently!) we were obliged to shut ourselves up so that papa, who was a bit of a snob, should not overhear us.

In the end, I took to writing short stories. The reason I put all this on record, and I apologize for it, is because I ended where I ought to have begun. Later, at the age of eighteen, I was appointed Sarah Bernhardt's principal secretary. But I was unable, any more than was my father at that age, to retain such an honourable post. Not that I abused my grandmother's confidence. But when I opened her mail and went through the list of requests addressed to her I wanted to answer them all. "Give them to Pitou, give them to Pitou!" she would say. But I myself knew that Pitou would, with sublime contempt, throw most of the letters into the waste-paper basket. I thought that this was too unkind to the writers, and I decided to attend to them all individually. Accordingly one morning, on the beautiful grey-edged notepaper with the motto "Despite All", I made appointments for all the applicants for the following Monday.

"I'll see these people myself," I told my grandmother, "and I'll ask them each for five francs for a photograph of you, and I'll give the money to your fund." (The money received from these photographs went to the Actors' Orphanage.)

"They won't give you a farthing," replied Sarah, "and look out for thieves."

Having other things to worry about, she thought no more about the matter. And on Monday, at two in the afternoon, Émile came in, frantically scratching himself, and announced:

"There are a dozen beggars at the door asking for Madame Bernhardt's secretary."

And in the space of half an hour a couple of dozen hoboes appeared at the Boulevard Pereire house. I got out of this predicament by giving each of them five francs and explaining that there had been a mistake. My grandmother laughed heartily at my discomfiture, and after that I decided not to interfere with Pitou's procedure and returned to my own personal work.

The nice quiet Félicie had been pensioned off and now two maids looked after my grandmother. They were both Italian: Dominga, and her niece Romilda. I do not know what their wages were, but I know that my grandmother hated paying her servants. If she owed one of them three or four months' wages she would buy them something, a watch, ear-rings, or something which cost quite as much as their actual wages. The wages themselves would come later, in part or fully, with something extra, for Sarah was generosity itself.

The butler and the footman might remain for quite a long time, but, on the other hand, she changed her cook and her kitchenmaid twice a month.

I have already noted how much importance my grandmother attached to the pleasures of the table. When a new cook entered her service my grandmother used to summon her to her room at dawn and make her sit at the end of the bed and greet her as an old friend. Rather embarrassed, the good woman would look around her and listen with only one ear to Sarah Bernhardt's instructions, "Monsieur Maurice's steak must be grilled, red, and slightly burned." Everything went well for five or six days and then in the sky of this morning idyll faint clouds would begin to appear; my grandmother wanted dishes such as the characters of Corneille insisted upon having, "just as they should be". She ate very little herself, but she had very definite ideas of how food should be prepared, and if, unfortunately, a dish appeared with a brown sauce instead of a white sauce or provided with a "roux" flavoured with thyme instead of with tarragon, she would fly into a fury. Even though my father protested that it was "exquisite", the storm broke with a peremptory,

"Ask the cook to come up." The cook, whose name nobody ever knew, owing to the perpetual changes, appeared and gave notice in a mixture of indignation and terror.

On the following morning Pitou would go through her accounts with his tongue in his cheek, Émile would go on scratching himself with embarrassment and a Marie would replace a Célestine, or vice versa.

CHAPTER XXXVIII

BELLE-ISLE-EN-MER

In 1911 my father sent his seconds, Messieurs Geoffroy and Marcel Boulenger, to Monsieur Georges Pioch, editor of *Gil Blas*. The duel never took place.

In the same year the Théâtre Sarah Bernhardt gave *Lucrèce Borgia*, followed by *La Reine Elisabeth*, by Émile Moreau (1912). And lastly, in 1913, after an eighth American tour, Sarah Bernhardt played the name-part in *Jeanne Doré*, a play by Tristan Bernard, with, as her leading man, the son of the author, Raymond Bernard, who is today one of our best producers.

My grandmother's right leg had become so painful that at times she could hardly move. The fact had to be faced that the tragedienne, whom Rostand had dubbed "the queen of posture and gesture", was becoming a cripple. Yet for three more years she lied to herself at the cost of prodigious efforts; thanks to her fierce energy she carried on with her work "despite all".

Authors who wrote plays for her arranged that her parts should entail as little action and fatigue as possible. Until her death, by scenic effects, by her profound knowledge of her art, by the strength and grace of her arms, she played these parts, thus preserving intact the crowns of laurel earned during her long life of struggle and glory. But it may be said that, after 1913, mutilated in soul and in body, in her desire to remain the idol of the Beloved Monster she added to her laurels a martyr's palms.

． ． ． ． ． ．

On March 6, 1914, my grandmother received the Cross of a Chevalier of the Legion of Honour from President Poincaré. This belated distinction was the occasion of her receiving great masses of flowers and countless congratulations, postcards, letters, telegrams and cables. Émile kept up the morale of over-loaded postmen with glasses of white wine. I helped to cope with this voluminous correspondence, the majority of which began with the words, "At last!" Yet the enrolment of Sarah Bernhardt into the ranks of the Legion of Honour did not prevent that year from being a disastrous one from every point of view.

We had a habit in the family of saying that things went wrong "all of a sudden". Now, "all of a sudden" is not merely an adverbial phrase, it is also the title of a play by the brothers Cassagnac. Though *Jeanne Doré* brought in a tidy sum of money, *Tout à coup* merely had a *succès d'estime*. So my grandmother took it off after a month's run and, being anxious to earn some money before her holidays, she pronounced the fateful words:

"I think I shall go on a little tour!"

After a great deal of hesitation my grandmother had changed her carriage for a Berliet motor-car, and into this we piled one fine morning with Switzerland as our destination. The term "to pile in" is disparaging but correct. There were seven people in the limousine: Sarah Bernhardt, Suzanne Seylor,

Dr. Marot, Pitou, Sarah's maid, the chauffeur and myself. To say nothing of two dogs and all the luggage, among which was Sarah's private bag, which had swollen with importance since the Rio de Janeiro episode. In the boot was crammed my grandmother's bed, her sheets, the Mongolian rug, her five pillows and a silver wash-hand basin. Nor was this last utensil merely a whim on Sarah's part. Even though hotel crockery was seldom lucky enough to please my grandmother, the silver basin always had another use. At night Sarah used to balance this expensive accessory on a chair, which in turn stood on a trunk set on end against the closed door of her room.

"Why all this formidable edifice?" I asked her the first time I saw it.

My grandmother withered me with a look.

"If anyone touches my door," she explained, "the basin falls down and acts as an alarm."

One morning, in Geneva, I heard the devil of a din in the early morning: I rushed in to see what had happened. Sarah Bernhardt, sitting up in bed, was pointing a service revolver at the door. The basin had fallen to the ground.

"Who's there?" she demanded, in a loud voice.

"Telegram," came the answer from the other side of the door.

"Idiot!" retorted my grandmother, replacing the revolver in its holster and going to sleep again. My father often tried to make her replace that dangerous weapon by a small automatic, but he never succeeded in persuading her to do so.

After Switzerland came Belgium. Our journey would have been delightful but for Sarah's unfortunate knee, which one could not touch except with infinite care. Dr. Marot, who had succeeded Dr. C——, massaged it each morning, thus procuring temporary relief for his patient.

We arrived in Brussels on the day on which Albert I received a visit from the King of Denmark. Yes, barely three months before the war we were in that attractive city where life was simple and food was good and beer flowed in rivers on the café terraces.

But it was also in May 1914 that my grandmother had to stop acting.

One evening her right knee-joint refused to bend at all. Sarah's eyes filled with tears.

"I can't . . . I can't walk at all!"

She was feverish with pain, her hands were burning and perspiration stood out on her forehead.

"We must break it to the audience," said someone.

These words produced a magic effect on Sarah. With her features twisted by pain she stood up.

"No!" she said. "I'm going to try."

Supported by her fellow-actors, she made her way to the wings of the theatre.

That evening I witnessed a real miracle of will-power. Sarah Bernhardt played right through *Jeanne Doré*, walking about the stage in short steps, leaning on all the furniture. When the pain was too sharp she would stop, and Jeanne Doré, the mother of a murderer, horrified at the fate in store for her child, would recover her breath and try with one hand to suppress the beating of her heart. Fever obscured Sarah's sight but she went on playing all the same,

200

not daring to sit down during the intervals for fear of not being able to rise again.

On the following day we left for Dax, in the Landes district, via Paris, where Dr. Doyen wanted to perform a surgical operation. But Pozzi, for his part, insisted upon a cure, followed by the immobilization of the leg in plaster of Paris; if mud-baths did not bring her relief then afterwards they would probe the stiffness of the knee. That was the last resort.

At Dax, Sarah Bernhardt and her poet, who lived at Cambo, quarrelled over a film of *L'Aiglon*. It was an astonishing quarrel. My grandmother and Edmond Rostand fought each other with flowers and fruit and telegrams and protestations of friendship. *No human power can make me defend myself against Madame Sarah Bernhardt*, the poet wrote to his lawyer. *I relinquish to her all my rights in these cinematographic rights which are worrying her. I gratefully kiss her fingers between which a writ has for me the grace of a lily.*

I refuse to accept the two hundred thousand francs, replied Sarah Bernhardt. *I have never wanted anything from Edmond Rostand. I hereby give notice to my illustrious lawyer, Maître Clunet, that I do not want to send any more blue lilies to my poet.*

It was at Dax, too, that we heard of the assassination of Franz-Ferdinand of Austria and of his wife.

"More Archduke trouble," observed my grandmother, thinking of *L'Aiglon* and her skirmishes with Rostand.

At the end of June the cure was finished and we left for Belle-Isle-en-Mer.

•   •   •   •   •

Here is a short history of the property of *Les Poulains*,[1] situated in the Morbihan department of Brittany.

In 1893, my grandmother, wanting to rest far away from the stares of the curious, went to Brittany and crossed over to Belle-Isle-en-Mer at about an hour's distance from Quiberon. This island, which was about fourteen miles long by seven miles deep, enchanted her with its rugged outline and its steep cliffs, by the cool shade of its fig-trees, by the pines growing in the interior of the island, by its vast stretches of gorse and heather (not to be picked, the heather!), by its charming valleys aromatic with fennel and wild mint, reached by sunken paths hedged on either side by gorse and blackberry bushes; by its deserted shores with their silvery sand or red sand like powdered rubies; by its smell of dried seaweed and iodine; by its huts in which the shepherd shared his charges' litter; by its little white houses where the Breton women with their velvet fichus scrubbed the windows of their homes; by the boats with their flower-coloured sails; by the children with their sea-green eyes who shuffled along on their bottoms on the white dust of the narrow roads.

In the north of the island, called Pointe-des-Poulains, Sarah acquired an old fort belonging to the Government, together with six hundred square yards of land. She paid two thousand francs for the lot. Some years later my father expressed a desire to spend his holidays there with his family; so my grandmother had a bungalow built, and called it *The Five Continents*. My nurse and I lived in Asia, my father in Africa, my mother in America, my sister in Europe and the maid in Oceania.

[1] The Foals.

And that was not all. I was baptized in the little village of Sauzon, in Belle-Isle-en-Mer, and, so that my godfather, Georges Clairin, should be able to paint at his ease, a studio was built for him beside *The Five Continents*. And Sarah Bernhardt bought another six hundred square yards from the Government.

Then she bought horses for the family and a farmyard from which to feed them. And this meant putting up stables and making a chicken-run on this new land. Very soon Sarah's friends wanted to see this famous estate and, to facilitate that, the Villa Lysiane was built to house them.

And Sarah bought another six hundred square yards from the Government.

All the shopping had to be done nearly six miles away, so, in order to get butter, eggs, milk and chickens more easily, my grandmother pushed out the boundaries of her estate still further and included in her property the Penhoët farm. Lastly, our neighbour, Baron Duhousoy, a delightful man, who lived a few hundred yards from *Les Poulains*, died, and my grandmother learned that the local council wanted to turn the Penhoët manor house into a tourist hotel.

"A hotel? How awful!" she cried, and she bought the Baron's property.

This estate swallowed up a great deal of money. Considerable sums had to be spent each year for the proper upkeep of Penhoët, of its houses, its staff, its gardens, its proprietress and her family, guests and animals.

Sarah Bernhardt would not have been Sarah Bernhardt if she had been content to own a charming house and to cultivate her corn- and wheat-fields, her potatoes, maize and wild oats, the latter growing with tufts of samphire even among the rocks veined with white marble. The first work put in hand by Sarah Bernhardt in 1898 was to have flights of steps built. Since she was lucky enough to have three beaches at her disposal, she must have means of gaining access to them. When the masons began to fix the concrete steps into the rocks of the Point the mayor came to call on his illustrious citizen.

"Madame," declared the good fellow apprehensively, "your flights of steps constitute a national danger."

"And may I ask in what way, monsieur?"

"You are making it easier for the enemy to land."

"But what enemy, monsieur?"

"The English fleet."

Sarah smiled, then she confided to the mayor of Sauzon her projects and plans. But the mayor continued to shake his head.

"A garden? A kitchen garden? But, madame, how are you going to water your flowers and your vegetables? You will not find a drop of water at Penhoët, or at *Les Poulains* or at Deux Bords.'"

"I'll find some somewhere. Do you see that little blue mark on my plan? That is where I'm putting my waterfalls. Yes, monsieur, my waterfalls!'"

And, indeed, a year later water began to gush from pumps and waterfalls fell with a joyful tinkle into artificial pools. This miracle was the work of Edouard Geoffroy, who, in addition to his status as "Mr. Grumpy", as my sister's godfather and as one of my father's seconds, was also a water-diviner.

Many incidents occurred during those visits to Belle-Isle. For instance, the incident when Edmond Haraucourt, like a Titan, held off the rock that was about to crush Sarah Bernhardt, and the incident when a guest, at the beginning of the holidays, had rashly picked some heather, with the result that on the following day my grandmother twisted her ankle, Suzanne Seylor put out her knee playing lawn-tennis, my father got mussel-poisoning, and I fell off my horse.

An Englishwoman, an old maid, had been invited to Belle-Isle. My grandmother was not particular as to whom she asked. She would often say:

"You must come to see me at *Les Poulains*!" and would immediately wish she could eat her too hasty words.

So, when this English lady suddenly announced that she was arriving one August morning, my father began to shout, Clairin began to rage and Geoffroy became purple in the face.

"I've got an idea," exclaimed my grandmother. "I can't avoid having her, now that she's on her way, but I'll tell her that one of my cousins, who is a lunatic, is living with us. You, Clairin, will be the lunatic."

And when the unfortunate lady saw Clairin gesticulating and screaming from his studio window, between Geoffroy wearing a keeper's cap and my father dressed as a hospital attendant, she left the next day.

One of my grandmother's main activities during her holidays was to make all the butter used at *Les Poulains* with her own hands. At the time of which I am speaking we did not possess a churn. So my grandmother, Geoffroy and any of the Little Court who happened to be there beat the milk with a fork. Their efforts were not always crowned with success; the milk had a habit of turning into cream cheese which the more sycophantic of our friends used to eat with an ecstatic look on their faces.

Another task consisted of pickling tiny melons, gherkins, onions and fennel; of making blackbird pies and of stuffing teal with larks.

But fishing was always the main occupation and preoccupation of the inhabitants of Penhoët; in the morning we took in the nets; in the afternoon, if it was misty, we would trawl. In the evening we set the seine-net, and at night, after dinner, we would pull it in with a ceremonial of torches, lanterns and shouting which entranced me.

And the fantastic prawning expeditions during the spring tides! Oh those lovely fat sand-coloured prawns, rare in our parts, but succulent and all pink after being cooked in sea-water with pepper and seaweed! I always watched for the moment at which my grandmother calmly entered the water up to her waist, clad in a white cloth bathing-costume with a long skirt, shoes and silk stockings, as though this costume was the ideal one for ferreting out the beady-eyed prawns who darted hither and thither among the rocks.

Every animal on Belle-Isle had its own degree of importance. In the stables lived a dozen dogs, two carriage-horses named Cassis and Vermouth, Pélagie, the mare belonging to Émile's trap, and two saddle-horses. A sheepfold contained some two-score sheep, from whose fleeces was woven a material the colour of hemp. The farmyard and buildings were full of chickens, rabbits, pigs and pigeons; there were a few cows in the byre. As for the bull, ever since the day when he had charged Louise Abbéma, who had wandered into his field dressed in a smart red linen coat, his pasturage was changed daily so that he should not interfere with the destination of our walks.

A great horned owl, a bird of prey called in French a grand duke and actually given to Sarah by a real Russian Grand Duke, lived alone in a cage and ate a young rabbit a day. Goldfish swam in ponds covered over with wire netting to protect them from sea-hawks and buzzards. Frogs, sent from Paris in boxes, croaked as they pursued their amorous adventures in the artificial streams in the garden. I have seldom seen a more repugnant sight than when the boxes containing these frogs were opened; at least one-third of them were dead; the others leaped into our faces or stretched their legs on the grass, hopping about everywhere except into the ponds provided for their activities.

And now for the story of Joseph. During the first few summers that Sarah Bernhardt spent in Brittany she had great difficulty in getting shrubbery to grow on the Pointe-des-Poulains, buffeted on three sides by the sea and the wind like the prow of a ship; the spindrift and the spray made it almost impossible to grow anything there. My grandmother refused to be defeated. After planting hedges of tamarisk and sea-purslane, she tried to grow a fig tree. From a height of a few inches, the little Joseph, as it was called, grew bigger from summer to summer, sturdier and stronger. One year, when it had reached a height of about five feet, a storm broke during the night and my grand-mother roused Geoffroy and asked him to go out at once to put Joseph's straw shirt on. Fuming, struggling against the wind and making progress with difficulty, Geoffroy, lantern in hand, stopped before the fence enclosing the little tree. Horrors! It had disappeared! My sister's godfather went back to bed grumbling and early next morning he went to look for the wicked Joseph, which he found ten yards away, roots in the air. My grandmother was appalled. She first blamed her old friend for his thoughtlessness and then hastily sent for the gardener to replant the erring fig tree. Joseph was surrounded with the most touching care and a strong wooden fence. It soon recovered from its ordeal and grew strong again. But my grandmother, going to admire it one day, discovered in the newly turned earth a tiny sprig of heather.

"Pull it out! Pull it out quickly!" she cried to Geoffroy.

At last, three years later, Joseph gave birth to three figs and, as we were admiring them, my grandmother ate them all.

Here is a day in Sarah Bernhardt's life on Belle-Isle-en-Mer towards 1912.

At nine o'clock in the morning she reviewed the staff in her room. Then my father came in and she ordered sole or skate or red mullet from him, as though her beloved son, lording it over the denizens of the deep, could at will decide upon what fish should flounder into his nets. After an interminable bath containing either fennel or seaweed, my grandmother, either on foot when her leg allowed it, or in a donkey-cart, made a tour of the houses on her property, accompanied by Pitou, who made copious notes.

At midday she took up a position by the dining-room window, and watched, through her field-glasses, for the return of my father with his fish-baskets. After luncheon a siesta in the "Sarahtorium", a square plot of grass strewn with poppies, in the shade of the tamarisks. Between three and four o'clock, especially on Thursdays and Sundays, clashes would nearly always occur with tourists; they used to enter the property, walk about, pick the flowers and take photographs. Geoffroy's face used to grow purple, Clairin would shut himself in his studio, my father would suggest setting the dogs on them, my sister brandished a stick and I was forbidden to meddle at all.

Then came lawn-tennis, on the blue-coloured concrete court; we played with red balls which got lost in the tamarisk hedges, in spite of the ball-boys and girls who came up from the village. As she was unable to run, my grandmother used to play at the net; she hated losing and always accused everyone of cheating.

We would often take our food with us in the morning and picnic under an awning, either in the interior of the island or on one of the western beaches. Dinner was at eight, and the evening was spent in various ways: if Reynaldo Hahn was there, we would listen to him singing and playing old songs, or we would play dominoes or Pope Joan or poker and, after the war, bridge, followed by strenuous arguments and discussions.

Each summer, before returning to Paris, my grandmother organized a "head-dress dinner", for which everyone prepared with the greatest secrecy, except my father, who hated this sort of entertainment and always appeared in a Breton hat which he removed as soon as the soup appeared. The evening always ended with fireworks, whose damp fuses refused to obey Émile, and by a chorus in honour of Sarah composed by Georges Clairin and which went something like:

> We are at Pretty Lady's place,
> By the side of the Ocean wide.
> Our souls are full of happiness,
> Our joy we cannot hide.

At the end of June 1914, Sarah Bernhardt, my father, my sister Simone and her husband Eddie Gross and their two children, Terka and Bernard, and myself, were all gathered on Belle-Isle-en-Mer. Geoffroy and Clairin were already there and we were at any moment expecting Professor Pozzi, who was coming to try to loosen Sarah's knee, as the Dax mud-baths had proved to be useless.

As soon as she arrived at *Les Poulains* Sarah Bernhardt set to work. Ever since she had been condemned to immobility she had been working on an idea, namely to make models of four statues destined to surround her tomb; this was to be erected on a rock near the fortress (a rock which was, in any case, inaccessible and would have to be connected with the mainland by an iron bridge). The four statues were meant to bear the features of my father, of my mother, of Simone and of myself.

In spite of the clouds gathering over Europe, our Breton sky remained calm and clear. The month of July passed as it had done in other Julys, in pure delight. We were now living in the Penhoët manor house, a brick building, ugly but comfortable, built, as I have already said, by our late neighbour the Baron Duhousoy.

And we were there when general mobilization was proclaimed.

CHAPTER XXXIX

1914

AUGUST 1, 1914, was a radiantly beautiful day. The sea was like oiled silk adorned with arabesques. Fishing-boats with sails full set, profiting by a light north-westerly breeze, rounded the Poulains cape and returned to harbour after the morning's fishing. Dotted about the sea were brown-sailed boats from Concarneau, others, with pale blue sails, from Lorient, and others again from Quiberon and from Vannes. In the distance tunny-boats glided slowly along with their lines out on either side, like antennae.

In her sunlit room Sarah, with her leg in plaster, listened to the news read to her from the previous day's Parisian papers by Suzanne Seylor, who went through them methodically from beginning to end, her blue eyes moving to and fro behind her lorgnette.

On July 23 Austria had sent an ultimatum to Serbia. On July 28 she had declared war on Serbia. What would France do? On the day of the Austrian ultimatum Raymond Poincaré was still on the high seas, on his way back from Russia with René Viviani, the French Prime Minister.

"We've been threatened with war for the past ten years," said Sarah, interrupting Suzanne. "People in France forget quickly. They forget the Kaiser's landing at Tangier, the Casablanca incident, and the incidents with Serbia, Russia and Austria, and finally the grave warning in 1911: Agadir! That word still rings in my ears! However, we cannot fight merely because the Archduke Franz-Ferdinand has been assassinated! Logic refuses to recognize in this incident a cause for another war. Where's Émile? Where are today's newspapers? Where's my son?"

"Maurice is out fishing with his daughters and Eddie. Émile isn't back from market yet."

"Naturally. He gets later and later every day. And I am just left here to eat my heart out."

"There's Émile!"

The trap came bowling along between the gorse-bushes bordering the main drive, grinding the white gravel beneath its wheels. My grandmother's steward always caused a sensation on his daily return from the market; the family, the guests and the staff all crowded round the trap, between the shafts of which the mare Pélagie stood steaming and pawing the ground. Then from beneath the seats would appear, all mixed up with the day's provisions, odd acquisitions and small purchases of which a list had been handed to the major-domo. Émile, the best fellow in the world, had three incurable habits: drinking white wine, scratching himself, and indiscriminate expenditure. Attracted by this or that, he would bring back on the same day a calf's head, a leg of mutton, a loin of pork, sausages, dozens of lettuces, masses of carrots and two or three different kinds of dessert. The result was that half these provisions went bad. I have already mentioned that the pleasures of the table were, for my grandmother, a matter of major importance. One day on Belle-Isle my father, smelling his beefsteak, declared that it was "peculiar". The steward was immediately sent for.

"Émile," cried Sarah, "this meat is putrid!"

"I know, madame," replied Émile calmly. "But the cook insisted on grilling it. When it is as far gone as that, a steak should be provided with a Madeira sauce to hide its taste."

"Murderer!" screamed my grandmother, as tragic as Lucretia Borgia. "You're trying to poison my family!" And three hunks of bread hit Émile hard on the head.

Émile merely returned to the kitchen shrugging his shoulders and scratching his head.

But I am digressing. That morning, when Pélagie's ears appeared after the Deux Bords rise, we eagerly awaited Émile's appearance. We were not interested in the flowers, or in the parcels, or in the food. Simone and I, who had come up from the beach with my father, took the *Figaro* and the *Gaulois* from the pocket of the phlegmatic steward and brought them straight to our grandmother.

"Russia has mobilized," read Simone aloud. Soon my sister's voice became anxious and her pretty face grew more serious. In spite of all attempts at mediation, a bloodthirsty Fate was egging on the old European nations to start killing each other once more.

"My God!" muttered Sarah. "Why is it that civilization recedes like this? Each war, even if won, is a fresh defeat for our intelligence."

·　　·　　·　　·　　·

That day luncheon at the manor of Penhoët was a gloomy affair. No one was grateful to Émile for the special Nantes cake which he provided as a surprise; our morning catch, which included some fine soles and a thornback with lovely white flesh, did not call forth their usual compliments. Eddie Gross, my sister's husband, tried in vain to engage my grandmother in a political argument; she, who was very fond of her grandson-in-law, refused to be drawn.

"My children," she said, after luncheon, "take the car, go down to Le Palais and ask the mayor if he has any fresh news."

As soon as we had finished our coffee, Simone and I abandoned the delights of the "Sarahtorium" to go to the little town fortified by Vauban. Sarah embraced us fondly.

"Come back as soon as you can."

But we were forced to disobey her.

We drove through five miles of narrow roads, bordered by gorse and quickset hedges beyond which lay expanses of heather, until the magnificent fig trees of Le Palais appeared. The town harbour presented an unusual aspect. The port was crowded with men standing in solemn silence, while here and there appeared the white head-dresses of the women. In front of the town hall the town crier gave a roll on his drum and announced, "By decree of the President of the Republic, the mobilization of the land and sea armies is hereby proclaimed."

Simone and I left the car and approached the municipal building: a man was already pasting the mobilization order on its wall.

"It's no use bothering the mayor now," said Simone. "Let's go back."

"Is that Madame Sarah Bernhardt's car?" asked a policeman.

"Yes."

"I will come with you. We will go to Bangor, to Lok-Maria and to Sauzon, to put up the mobilization orders."

It was not so much a request as a requisition, and we started off on our melancholy circuit. At each hamlet our appearance spread consternation: at the roll on the drum the inhabitants came to the doors of their low-built houses. The men shook their heads solemnly. The women crossed themselves and wept. Their head-dresses fell forward like white birds wounded in full flight.

"How terrible! Holy Mother! How terrible!"

The sailors, with their child-like eyes, clenched their fists.

It was nearly five o'clock when we had carried out our mission. The policeman and the town crier accompanied us to the manor house, where Émile offered them some of his best white wine. I hurried to the studio, where my grandmother was writing. I must have worn a strange look, because she stared at me in silence.

"General mobilization has been proclaimed," I said, and I told her of our gloomy pilgrimage.

"Two wars in one lifetime! And to be able to do nothing: to be old and ill!"

In those fateful hours of August 1914 she must have thought of 1870, of her ambulance, of the Odéon, of all her activities at that time; tears rolled slowly down her cheeks.

"General mobilization doesn't necessarily mean war," observed my father.

Sarah Bernhardt shook her head.

"It is war all right. And it is only forty-four years since the last one. But," she went on in a firm voice, "we will recover Alsace and Lorraine! Let us go to Paris, my children. I don't want to remain shut up on this island."

.   .   .   .   .

On August 1, 1914, Germany declared war on Russia, on August 3 on France, and on August 4 Great Britain ranged herself at our side.

For those who still remember it, the month of September 1914 remains a tragic and a magnificent one. As blow succeeded blow, the French people began to realize the gravity of the situation: the retreat of the French armies, the invasion of French territory, the removal of the Government to Bordeaux, and the German advance on Paris. Between September 6 and 9 everyone waited for the communiqués with intense anxiety; enemy cavalry was patrolling the Compiègne forest, less than fifty miles from Notre-Dame.

On our return to Paris from Belle-Isle we all lived in the Boulevard Pereire: my father, my sister, her husband and her children, Suzanne Seylor and the domestic staff. We combined in order to simplify the material details of daily life and to present a united front of mutual affection against pessimism and

At Edmond Rostand's country house at Cambo, 1902. Sarah, Rosemonde
Rostand, Edmond Rostand, and S. Grancher

Sarah Bernhardt in her studio at Belle-Isle-en-mer
Left to right : E. Geoffroy, Reynaldo Hahn, Sarah Bernhardt, Mme. Grau,
Georges Clairin

The Fort des Poulains, Belle-Isle-en-mer

anxiety. One September afternoon, Edmond Rostand, the Comtesse Anna de Noailles, Professor Pozzi and Henri Cain were discussing the latest news with Sarah Bernhardt when Émile came in with a long face and interrupted the conversation.

"A gentleman from the Ministry of War to see madame."

Messimy's messenger was brief and to the point, but he made me think of an undertaker's assistant come to arrange the details of a funeral; everything about the man was black, from his badly shaved chin to his elastic-sided boots. He spoke in a low monotone. T——, a friend of my grandmother's who was in Messimy's cabinet, begged Madame Sarah Bernhardt to leave Paris. Her name, it appeared, figured on a captured list of hostages: if the Germans reached the capital, Sarah Bernhardt must expect the worst. We never knew the truth of this but, when the man left, we were dazed. At first Sarah would not hear of going, but she gave in to my father's entreaties. The next question was where to go? Henri Cain suggested Arcachon; he himself owned a house there: it would be easy to find a small villa near his own.

"Here's for the Arcachon basin," said grandmother, resignedly. "We'll go there tomorrow by train."

The order against taking heavy luggage was being strictly enforced, and our hand luggage was soon packed. But, on the following morning, Émile, becoming more and more dramatic, informed us that no ambulance was available to take my grandmother to the railway station. He had telephoned everywhere, and everywhere he had received the same reply. It must be remembered that France was on the eve of the Battle of the Marne and was expecting, from day to day, to see the first German detachments at the gates of Paris. What was to be done? It might be possible to take my grandmother to the station in a taxi: her leg made it impossible for her to walk.

"But there aren't any taxis!" cried Émile, hopelessly.

"Well, there were plenty at the stations yesterday. They cannot have vanished into thin air. I'll go and find one myself," cried my father, angrily.

Sarah Bernhardt, her maid, Suzanne Seylor, Émile and I, with our light refugee luggage, waited in the hall. At the end of three-quarters of an hour Sarah declared furiously that she would not go away at all. She had her famous bag opened and began removing her cosmetics and scent-bottles and placing them on the floor. I prayed to God that He would grant my father a taxi and God must have heard me, for at that moment a motor-car drew up before the door. The bottles were all put back, my grandmother was hoisted into a red taxi, and the car moved slowly away.

"Chauffeur," said Sarah, "will you please go along the Avenue Wagram and down the Champs Élysées."

"But, madame, that isn't the way to the Quai d'Orsay station."

"Never mind, go that way."

We circled the Étoile and drove down the Champs Élysées. The sky was a pure, transparent blue. We met very few cars and no taxis. We did not try to conceal our forebodings. We all had the same idea. Would we ever see the Champs Élysées again? That Paris artery in which beats the life of the capital, that delightful but, alas, too feckless French life!

At the Rond-Point a policeman held us up. Smoke-coloured military lorries passed before us, carrying soldiers with their equipment and arms, packed close together. Our chauffeur turned in his seat.

"Look!" he said. "The Paris taxis!"

And, indeed, behind the lorries followed all the taxi-cabs in uninterrupted single file: they were taking to the front (as we learned later) all the soldiers in the Paris area who, under Gallieni's orders, were to contribute to the "Miracle of the Marne".

Catching sight of our taxi, an officer approached us and questioned the chauffeur.

"Why didn't you take your taxi to the mobilization point as the others did?"

The old man mumbled some complicated story, but the officer shrugged his shoulders and, addressing Émile seated beside the chauffeur, he said:

"I must ask you to get out. We need this cab."

Then he stopped, his eyes fixed on Sarah Bernhardt, who had been listening in silence, her poor leg stretched out before her. The officer brought his hand to his cap in a salute.

"I beg your pardon, madame. I did not know. Chauffeur, take Madame Sarah Bernhardt to the station and then come back to place yourself at our disposition."

Then he turned to my grandmother again.

"You have no need to fear, madame. They shall not pass."

Nor did "they" pass. Not that time.

CHAPTER XL

THE AMPUTATION

AT the beginning of 1915, Professor Pozzi came as far as Andernos to see his old friend. He removed the plaster and exposed the injured knee. But his hopes were doomed to disappointment. At first my grandmother experienced some relief, but a week later all the pain returned and she was deeply discouraged.

At Andernos, as at Belle-Isle, she devoted herself to her garden. Her passion for flowers seemed to increase as time went on. If a gardener passed our house on his way to market with a load of geraniums, nasturtiums or lilies, my grandmother would buy the lot.

But one February morning, even though Émile had told her of the arrival of a travelling seedsman and market gardener, Sarah turned a deaf ear and sent for us all to come to her room. All—that is to say my father, his second wife Marcelle, Suzanne Seylor, Pitou and myself; my sister and her husband had returned to London.

I immediately realized that something serious was about to happen. Sarah Bernhardt was wearing a sad little smile, her expression for solemn occasions. Her hair was carefully arranged, her nose was powdered and she was gaily dressed.

"Sit down, my children," she said. Then she turned to her son and addressed herself to him.

"Maurice, darling," she said, "I want to tell you the exact situation which has to be faced. My mind is made up: I am not going on suffering as I have suffered during these past four years. It is for you to choose: either I commit suicide or I have my leg off."

My father reasoned with her, pleaded with her, and tried to gain time or to make her change her mind about her draconian decision, but it was useless. My grandmother just went on smiling sadly.

"Don't try to deceive yourselves," she seemed to be saying. "You know perfectly well that I am incurable."

"I think you prefer the operation to the other solution," she said finally, looking fondly at my father.

And from that moment my grandmother recovered her spirits and her charm. She made enquiries about a surgeon, but it was not easy to find one, as most of them were on active service. Pozzi refused to accept the responsibility of amputating the leg of a woman of seventy-one whose general state of health was far from satisfactory. Dr. Doyen also refused: even though he had suggested an operation some months earlier, he certainly did not want to proceed to amputate in the present circumstances.

At length Major Denucé, of the Bordeaux hospital, agreed to perform the operation. My grandmother entered the hospital on February 11, 1915, to follow a very severe régime before undergoing the operation. That evening, when Simone and I returned to Andernos, we wept bitterly in the deserted villa.

On February 22, at nine in the morning, my father, Suzanne Seylor, Clairin, Geoffroy and I arrived at the hospital. On her way to the operating theatre my grandmother passed us, lying on a trolley.

"Come, my children," she cried to us, "cheer up! In any case it is not so hard to have an amputation at my age as at the age of our children out there." And she hummed the *Marseillaise*.

The operation took twenty minutes. After it was over Major Denucé came to reassure us. The amputation had been successful. The surgeon explained to us that, in view of the age of the patient and of her poor health, he had thought it wiser to cut the leg off well above the knee to avoid any risk of infection.

But what we feared most occurred on the ninth day; an attack of uremia set in. My grandmother fought against death with all her strength and all her vitality; she wanted to go on living; and she lived.

In March she became convalescent; in April she began to talk of her house at Andernos and the lilac which should be in flower; in May she was back in the Villa Eureka, where rosebuds were just beginning to appear on the walls and on the trellises.

When her wound was healed, Sarah, after a few attempts, flatly refused to wear an artificial leg. She realized that she would never have been able to walk again without limping pitifully.

"Not I! Not I!" she repeated.

She had a carrying-chair made of white wood and cane, narrow enough to be slid into a car or a lift. And during the last years of her life, that is to say from 1915 to 1923, Sarah Bernhardt was a familiar figure in her carrying-chair, both in the wings of the theatre and elsewhere.

•   •   •   •   •

In recovering ease of body, Sarah Bernhardt also recovered calm of mind. She immediately wanted to show herself to the public: what would it think? Eugène Morand wrote a play especially for her, *Les Cathedrales*. After acting in this play in Paris before an eager and appreciative audience, Sarah regained her confidence and devoted herself to another task: "The Army Theatre". She went to Châlons-sur-Marne and from there to Saint-Étienne-au-Temple, Tours-sur-Marne, Ay and Rheims, and I was fortunate enough to accompany her on all these visits.

(At the moment at which I write these words the first Germans are parading through deserted, tragic, sun-bathed Paris.[1] My own personal experience of 1914 is like a parade of wooden soldiers. At Châlons one heard the drone of German 'planes from time to time; in the distance in the Champagne skies one saw little grey clouds which burst like toy balloons. And yet this horrible war had already mown down so many young lives!

And today? We must not look out of the windows. We must not listen to the music, or to the fifes, or to the tramp of jack-boots in the streets of Paris. We must not try to think.)

Returning to 1916. My grandmother offered her services for the second

[1] Written in Paris on June 14, 1940.

time to "The Army Theatre". I have borrowed from Madame Dussane, the charming Sociétaire of the Comédie Française, a few lively and picturesque lines which she wrote on the subject.

". . . One day we were told that Sarah had expressed a wish to play to the soldiers.

"I had never met her before. I went to the Boulevard Pereire and, over the fire, in a white boudoir, I saw an extraordinary creature huddled in the depths of a low easy-chair; it consisted of thousands of folds of satin and lace surmounted by a reddish mop. It was an upsetting, rather depressing, sight; the great, brilliant Sarah seemed so small and helpless!

"But it was then, however, that I, as so many others before me, learnt something of her magic. For two hours she held forth, ordered tea, enquired about travelling conditions, got carried away, excited, amused; seeing everything, understanding everything, hearing everything. And all the time she never stopped scintillating.

"And now for our journey. Ah! The Gare de l'Est during the war, with our strange procession passing through it. Sarah, muffled in a striped coat with a large flowered hood, curled up in her little carrying-chair and smiling at everyone as if to dare them to pity her.

"We got out at Toul, the only civilian party on the train. The little chair reappeared; it was painted white and decorated with Louis XV scrolls; even the chair seemed to smile, and to wish to appear a whim and not a painful necessity. The townspeople looked at her with so much curiosity and excitement that they forgot to cheer or to applaud. Less than an hour later the cars came to take us to the scene of our first performance; a huge open market square in Commercy. There was a stage, with footlights and a curtain, but the place reserved for Sarah had no floor but the beaten earth; the stage could only be reached by a ten-rung ladder and the place was full of draughts. Sarah installed herself in her makeshift dressing-room and declared herself to be enchanted with everything.

"At last her turn came to appear. While she was being settled on the stage, behind the curtain, in a rickety armchair filled with cushions, and we grouped ourselves around her, one of the Company went before the curtain and announced to the three thousand lads packed together in the square that they were about to see Sarah Bernhardt, which was a complete surprise to them.

"The curtain rose, disclosing for us in the gloom beyond the bright light of the footlights first the stretcher-bearer musicians, then the wounded, whose white bandages riveted our eyes, and finally the multitude of eager-eyed faces. The ovation? It hung fire. There was a little applause, fairly warm but not unanimous and certainly not prolonged.

"Sarah felt a shudder go through her. This audience meant more to her than any audience at any big first night. She began to speak. I was there, quite close to her. I neglected my own part and I looked at her. I knew almost by heart what she was going to say. But she made me forget it. Everything seemed to vibrate and, in a rhythm that rose like a bugle-call, she sang of the martyrdom of Rheims and of Belgium. She conjured up all the glorious dead of our race and ranged them beside the men fighting France's battles at the moment; the rhythm of her speech rose in a constant crescendo. It carried us away with Sarah, and when, on the last cry of '*Aux Armes!*' the band broke into the *Marseillaise*, the three thousand French lads cheered her to the echo.

"This went on for three days; on a château terrace from which, in the distance, wrapped in mist but facing us, we could see the enemy positions at Woevre; in a hospital ward; in a ruined barn where the men even perched on the rafters. In all these places I witnessed Sarah's genius and her courage. No, we were never shelled. That was not the point. It was her courage as a cripple for whom will-power takes the place of all else, every hour of the day. We used to go out by car at about midday and return very late in the evening. Even when we stopped for meals we worked. Our dressing-rooms were casual hovels with straw-bottomed chairs or wooden trestles, the overpowering heat of a tent in the sun or the dampness of a cellar. On one occasion I found myself alone with her, and I had to help her to dress. She went from her chair to her dressing-table, leaning on me and hopping on her single seventy-year-old leg, which had the spareness of a bird's leg without its solidity. And she said to me, with a laugh:

" 'I'm like an old hen!'

"It was marvellous to see that pluck which ignored her disability, her victory over ever-growing weakness, and pity turned to admiration."[1]

[1] Dussane, in *Le Théâtre Illustré*, 1923.

CHAPTER XLI

GOOD-BYE TO THE UNITED STATES

In 1916 my grandmother signed a contract with the impresario Connor for another tour in the United States. After spending the summer with us at Boulouris, in the South of France, she embarked in September at Bordeaux on the steamship *Espagne*, of the Compagnie Transatlantique.

After a nine days' crossing, when she appeared on the gangway, carried by Émile and Pitou, New York received her with touching enthusiasm. In the eyes of the New World she was thrice blessed: she was French, she was an artiste, she was wounded.

Did she recall her first voyage in 1880? That suspicious curiosity of the American crowd, so soon to make way for affectionate fidelity? Did she think of the "fierce gentleman"? Did she remember Henry Smith, the whale-man?

"While they hoisted her little white chair into the car, Madame Sarah wept," one of the Company told me later.

Did she realize that she was now an old woman? And that the glamour of her name must thenceforward replace the magnetic attraction which formerly emanated from her?

Hardly had she arrived at the Savoy-Plaza Hotel before Dr. Marot, who was a sort of walking newspaper kiosk—in the sense that, mad on politics, he was always loaded with newspapers and magazines—read out to Sarah Bernhardt the latest news of the war.

"And about me?" asked Sarah. "What do they say about me, my dear doctor?"

"Well!" said the doctor, who was nervous and short-sighted.

"Well? Well?"

" 'The great Sarah, the oldest woman in the world, arrived in New York today.' "

"It's infamous! Infamous! Send for Connor at once! I'm not the oldest woman in the world. I'm only seventy-two! When I'm a hundred and three, I'll show them what it is to be an old woman!"

Connor, always perfectly correct, received these protests with complete calm; he smiled and kissed his star's hand, uttering the words which, to his mind, excused everything and explained everything.

"Publicity, my dear. Publicity!"

"At my age?" raged Sarah, contradicting herself. "Do I need publicity at my age? I warn you, my dear Connor, that I won't speak to any of your pressmen if your country continues to treat me like that."

"It would be advisable for you to receive the more important of them," replied Connor; "you must treat the American Press with respect; it has been kind to you for thirty-six years."

And immediately, as though they were only waiting for the word, the reporters crowded into Sarah's room at the Savoy-Plaza Hotel with their batteries of questions.

"Who is going to win the war? What do you think of the Kaiser? When will the war end? Have you seen any German prisoners? Are you a pacifist?"

Faced by these abrupt questions, Sarah smiled gently. She was no longer asked whether she liked cheese, whether she was a Catholic, if she made her hair curl with beer. It was war, nothing but war. Today, more than ever, she was the envoy of France. A Tricolor flag was spread out behind her and the ribbon of the Legion of Honour barred her white satin dress with its red line.

.   .   .   .   .

Some months passed and Sarah kept herself in touch with the daily communiqués. The warm welcome she received in each town consoled her for being far away from France, one quarter of which was invaded, battered, bombarded or destroyed. The submarine warfare round Great Britain, France and Italy was becoming intensified. But, although this submarine warfare put the Allies in a difficult position, it had its other side; the Americans were becoming incensed and American indignation rose as far as the White House; in peaceful homes the names of Washington and of La Fayette were on everyone's lips.

In February 1917 the United States began to consider intervening in the European conflict. Sarah Bernhardt was in Chicago; she grew impatient. *America must come to the help of Europe,* she wrote to us. *She must come quickly!*

When she received prominent American citizens, either at the theatre or in her hotel, she would hold their hands in hers and gaze into their eyes, in an effort to communicate her faith to them:

"Come in with us! We are exhausted over there! You are a great Democracy! If Democracy refuses to go on a crusade to put an end to such a struggle, what, then, is the meaning of the word Democracy in the mind of humanity?"

The Americans looked at her and shook their heads or bowed gravely to her.

The theatre management decorated the stage with French and American flags.

One evening the audience had been particularly moved. Sarah Bernhardt was playing *Les Cathédrales* and symbolized Strasburg: when she appeared in her white drapery the audience stamped their feet and cried, "Long live France!" When the play was over, prolonged applause kept Sarah bowing on the stage. She rose, supporting herself on the arm of her chair, as a vision of a battered country that refused to die. Pitou was already unfolding the white chair in the wings. But, profiting by a moment at which the curtain was down, Sarah Bernhardt sent her porters away and remained standing on the stage.

"Bring me a French flag," she commanded. "Quickly!"

The curtain rose.

The audience did not understand. What was that woman doing with a Tricolor flag spread across her chest? A speech? Yes, she was going to make a speech.

"Ladies and gentlemen," began Sarah in English, "I have something to say to you," she continued in French. And suddenly, in a firm voice, clear as a trumpet, and as measured as the rolling of a drum, she sang the first verse of the *Marseillaise.*

The audience rose as one man, breathless with excitement. Then Sarah signed for the curtain to be lowered. She had said what she wanted to say. The house roared:

"Long live France; America for ever!"

Some of the people in the stalls leaped on the stage.

Behind the curtain, Émile and Pitou lifted Sarah and bore her away in her little chair, still hugging her flag.

. . . . .

Indefatigable, travelling from town to town with her Company of twelve artistes, her impresario, her personal staff and fifty trunks, Sarah Bernhardt for the ninth time picked up a fortune in gold dollars. Perhaps she thought: "This is my last tour. When it is over I shall return home and live in peace." Perhaps. But fate decided otherwise. After a performance at Saratoga she fell ill; a fresh attack of uremia interrupted her contract and put an end to her marvellous energy. At the end of March my father received an alarming cable. The removal of one of her kidneys seemed inevitable. But a young American surgeon, Dr. Burger, operated immediately without removing the kidney, and his bold and difficult experiment was perfectly successful; for the rest of her life my grandmother carried a tube in the defective kidney. A week passed and suddenly "the Bernhardt" took a turn for the worse. She felt that she was about to die, far from her son, far from us, far from France. And a blood transfusion was considered necessary. Dr. Burger told us afterwards that an innumerable number of people offered themselves for this service.

Powerless, devoured by anxiety, all we could do, unfortunately, was to wait for news. Dr. Burger promised to cable us and I spent the day watching for the telegraph-boy.

On April 6, 1917, at about seven in the evening, a bicycle stopped on the Boulevard. A small ragged boy, employed by the post-office, rang the bell. What catastrophe was this piece of blue paper going to impart to us? My father's hands shook as he opened it.

The cable was not signed *Burger* but *Sarah Bernhardt*, and it just read *Hurrah!*

For it was on April 6, 1917, that America entered the war on our side.

. . . . .

In July 1917 my father, my stepmother Marcelle Bernhardt and I rejoined my grandmother, convalescent at Long Beach. We found her recovered, and full of hope. Connor had got out a new contract for one year from August 22 and Sarah asked me to remain with her in the United States. Death had brushed her so closely that she dreaded the idea of being "without a Bernhardt" in future. After a month, my father returned to Paris with his wife, to take on the management of the Théâtre Sarah Bernhardt. My grandmother reshuffled her Company and on August 23 we left in a private railway car, the *Mayflower*, to go to Atlantic City, Mendel, New London and Stanford. At Columbus we changed cars, abandoning the *Mayflower* for the *Boston*, a steel-constructed car, much more comfortable and more luxurious. My grandmother appeared twice a day, but only in a single act: *Au Champ d'Honneur*, *Le Vitrail*, one act of *Camille*. In every town she was given proof of amazing American hospitality. Sometimes, at daybreak, musicians would play the *Marseillaise* beneath the windows of the car, accompanied by cheers from the small crowd gathered to greet her. In spite of her age, my grandmother slept like a child. At first she appreciated these acts of courtesy and would greet her welcomers with sleepy smiles through the windows of her car: but she soon grew tired of this. At Hartford, the *Marseillaise* blared forth at five o'clock in the morning, waking Sarah with a start. She flew into a violent temper and after that we would keep the hour of our arrival secret.

This gipsy life, the three negroes with their boot-blacking faces who danced attendance on us, the daily change of towns seemed a marvellous adventure to me. When her morning toilette was finished Sarah Bernhardt would have herself carried into the dining-drawing-room where she worked, rehearsed, wrote or bickered with Pitou: if we remained in a station she would receive journalists, tradesmen, friends and casual visitors until luncheon-time. Moreover, she ate very little, tapping her plate with her fork and criticizing American food. In her opinion everything had been through a refrigerator, from chicken to peaches, and including bread, sweet corn and salad. After the matinée performance she and I would go for a drive seeing the town, the Central Park and the surrounding country. The evening brought the second performance, hullabaloo, applause, autographs, hysterics and smiles. And lastly, at one in the morning, we went quietly to bed, lulled by noise of the engines which we no longer heard, and rocked by the swaying of the train which we no longer felt.

I have forgotten to mention our three other companions: a Pekinese dog, an Airedale terrier and a lion cub. The lion cub was given to Sarah by a circus proprietor, and named by me Hernani II, with rather a lack of originality. I took it for walks in all the Central Parks of America; it was a magnificent lion cub which drank milk soup and gazed at me with sad, gold-flecked eyes. It grew larger week by week, clawed me to the bone and climbed up hotel curtains when we finally left the *Boston* for good. Soon Hernani II was eating raw meat, and loudly crunching bones while we lunched and while I tried, in spite of this rather disgusting sight, to eat *Tournedos Rossini* which my grandmother declared peremptorily to be "putrefied with cold"; it made enormous messes, always at luncheon time and always on the carpet. In short, at the end of six months and in spite of my protestations, Hernani II was returned to his circus because hotels refused to take us in.

In September, Sarah Bernhardt returned to New York and the Savoy-Plaza Hotel for a fortnight. After that we made for Chicago, taking in, on the way, Salem, Hartville, Portland, Bridgeport, Newhaven, Worcester, Springfield, Pittsfield, Albany, Port Huron, Saginaw, Flint, Lading, Battle Creek and Grand Rapids.

We stopped seven days in Chicago. A large number of people crowded into the matinées and evening performances at the Auditorium Theatre. No more cars or caravans or cabins; we were steeping ourselves in cosmopolitan life once more. My grandmother gave luncheons and dinners; Lou Tellegen and his wife, Geraldine Farrar, were among the guests. Sarah Bernhardt organized a charity matinée for the Art Union and, for the first and last time in my life, I was on the stage with her. I played the part of the French soldier in *Les Cathédrales*. I put on the infantryman's uniform which Sarah wore in *Au Champ d'Honneur*, and went on to the huge stage of the Auditorium Theatre. The curtain rose over what looked to me like a great black abyss. The only quality that I possessed in common with my illustrious grandmother was unconquerable stage-fright. I said my piece and, as I made the sweeping gesture introducing the Strasburg Cathedral (Sarah Bernhardt), the safety-pin which held up my sky-blue trousers gave way. What on earth was I to do now? I was completely at a loss; my grandmother prompted me with my words, but no sound issued from my lips. At last, in the sudden energy of despair, holding my trousers up with one hand and pointing with the other to the five Cathedrals lined up behind me, I roared out my words in a stentorian voice.

So that when Sarah Bernhardt's voice followed mine it was like listening to sacred music after a jazz band. Deafening applause. I turned to the audience. Sarah bowed and whispered to me:

"Your trousers, Lysiane! Hold your trousers up!"

And such was the beginning of a theatrical career which had no sequel.

From Chicago, we continued our journey across Illinois, Wisconsin, Minnesota, Indiana, Ohio. On November 24 we glided in sleighs over the frozen earth of Canada: Ottawa and Montreal. Then back to New York.

We spent Christmas Eve at the Savoy-Plaza Hotel, where my grandmother had invited a few friends: the Knoedlers, Miss Elizabeth Marbury, Lottie Yorska, etc. A Christmas tree sparkled in the sitting-room. It glittered with silver stars, tinsel, golden apples and artificial frost; and there were endless presents all round, to everyone's delight.

"If only I could embrace my Maurice!" said my grandmother.

.   .   .   .   .

On February 14, 1918, we left New York again in the S.S. *Sixaola* to go to Havana. It was many years since my grandmother had been to the West Indies: but when she arrived at Havana she tried unsuccessfully to find a "house surrounded by flowers" in which she had once lived. My grandmother told me that on her former visit the police used to escort her back to her hotel, owing to the evil reputation enjoyed by the suburbs. I could hardly believe her story as I looked at the straight, well-lit streets, the newly built houses and the carefully tended gardens.

We returned by way of New Orleans, which reminded me of a French Colony. Distance had no terrors for us. On July 21 we entered the beautiful land of British Columbia and had an ideal time in Vancouver. My grandmother hired a boat, in which we used to go fishing every morning. It was as though someone had poured blue- and green-tinted milk over the sea and along the whole coast. Even the sky was impregnated with it and we seemed to float in an atmosphere of sublimated pearls.

From British Columbia we returned to the United States: San Francisco, Oakland, and that little one-horse town which we just passed quickly through. Can you guess? Hollywood.

It was at that time that the American Government was energetically launching its "Liberty Bonds". Sarah Bernhardt was invited to take part in a parade at Los Angeles; she accepted, and asked permission of the authorities to take me with her. Dressed in white, we took our seats in a white victoria, decorated with white lilies, white roses and white carnations and drawn by white horses. The coachman and footman were also dressed in white!

A picturesque incident marked this parade. Some Los Angeles official, having rather tactlessly remembered that Sarah Bernhardt had formerly been married to a Greek, had our carriage escorted by a guard of honour composed of a dozen men dressed as Greeks: but a slight error in their uniforms turned them into Turks, and we were at war with Turkey! I looked at my grandmother, wondering whether she would laugh or be angry. She was neither. She just took control of herself and held her own counsel.

On leaving the American Riviera, we went to Denver, Kansas City, Cleveland. And then came the banks of the Hudson River and soon after Fifth Avenue and Broadway. The last performances in New York and in Brooklyn, and our wonderful tour was over.

Between August 22, 1917 and October 14, 1918, we played in ninety-nine different towns. The next ship was to take us back to France. Sarah made purchases, a vast number of purchases, before her departure. We were happy. It was too good to last!

The Spanish 'flu epidemic was at its height. People were dying like flies; the New York hospitals were full; patients overflowed into the passages; coffins waited their turn at the cemetery gates. One afternoon one of my grandmother's friends tied round my neck a strand of wool at the ends of which dangled two horrible little dolls.

"It's a mascot," she said. "Nénette and Rintintin. If you wear it you never catch 'flu."

That evening I had a high fever and Dr. Burger shook his head. My grandmother was frantic. Of course we missed the first ship leaving for France, and the second. At last, when I had recovered after a fashion, we left the United States, in November 1918, in the *Espagne*.

CHAPTER XLII

ARMISTICE, 1918

THE return voyage was without incident. The *Espagne* proceeded at night with damped fires, and two sailors were detailed to look after my grandmother.

"Do you imagine for one moment that I would allow those boys to bother about me if we were torpedoed? At my age!"

She made use of her age according to the way it suited her; sometimes she would declare that she had another thirty years to live and would become a great-great-grandmother and would nurse her great-grand-daughter, Terka's children; while at other times she would say, with a bitter smile, that she had lived too long.

Then she would attack the Empress Eugénie and the old Emperor Franz-Josef of Austria.

"How can one go on living when one has lost, as they have, one's husband, one's wife, one's throne?" she would cry furiously. "My own hope is that I may go before those who are dear to me."

(And yet she was fated to survive her oldest and most faithful friends: Pozzi, murdered by a lunatic in 1918, Rostand, Geoffroy, Clairin, Maître Clunet.)

I have said that the voyage back to France took place without incident, but, before the *Espagne* sailed, an American soldier insisted on greeting Madame Sarah Bernhardt. When asked his name, he said he was Robert Markero. And, as no one seemed to know the name, the soldier added, in French:

"Tell madame that I was born on the *Amérique* in 1880."

My grandmother embraced the godson whom she was seeing for the first time since his birth, and who was on his way back to Nevada, a State which we had omitted to visit. Robert Markero had returned from France, where, by a strange coincidence, he had had a leg amputated after a battle before Saint-Mihiel.

On November 11, 1918, at ten o'clock in the morning, the coast of France appeared on the horizon. Having been deprived of news for nine days, we were eager to hear the latest, and to know how the third phase of Marshal Foch's offensive was proceeding.

Before us the Gironde estuary slowly narrowed. We had already passed Pauillac on our right and Blaye on our left. Bordeaux was advancing to meet us; the Gironde married in the estuary and changed its name to the Garonne. We passed the Bacalan wharf and the Chartrons wharf. Another quarter of an hour and we would be alongside. In her cabin, seated in her folding-chair, my grandmother waited quietly for someone to fetch her and asked question after question.

"Have you seen your father? Do I look all right? Where is my Maurice?"

I ran up to the deck three steps at a time; a large crowd was standing on the Compagnie Transatlantique's wharf; people were shouting and gesticulating, making loud-speakers of their hands.

"Can you hear what they're saying?" I asked Dr. Marot.

"No," he replied, pulling at the eyelid of the more short-sighted of his eyes, as though he could hear better in that way.

I could not see my father anywhere, and I dared not go below again for fear of upsetting my grandmother. And I could not make out what was the matter with all these people.

"Perhaps we've won a great victory?"

Dr. Marot continued to pull at his eyelid and shook his head. Suddenly he paled.

"But . . . It's the armistice! They're shouting 'Armistice!' Can't you hear them?"

"Yes, yes! I must tell my grandmother!"

The ship had stopped and an immense roar rose from the quays of Bordeaux; it drowned the rattle of the anchor chain running out at our feet, and of the gangway which was being hauled into position.

"Armistice! Armistice! Armistice!"

I ran along the deck, jostled by the passengers, who were mad with excitement. Just as I was about to seize the handrail of the steep companionway a tall gentleman passed in front of me.

"Papa!" I cried.

He did not even hear me. My father, usually so meticulously polite, bumped into a steward and let out a lurid oath which reached my astonished ears. When I finally reached the cabin, the tall gentleman was holding my grandmother in his arms.

"Mama! It's the armistice! The war is over!"

Sarah Bernhardt wept. We all wept, because we were together again and because the war was over and our country was victorious. Yes, victorious on that November 11, 1918.

•   •   •   •   •

One or two years later Arthur Meyer had an excellent idea. He came to the Boulevard Pereire to tell the person mainly interested, and was received with some coldness.

Since her operation in 1917 my grandmother had often been ill; she had attacks of fever, uremia, kidney trouble and headaches. Neither diet nor nursing seemed to be able to get rid of this invalid condition. She would take no rest and was always making fresh plans. "Never stop, otherwise you die," was the watchword which she had given herself. Not that she was afraid of death, but she believed that her cup was not yet drained; a few of the sips had already tasted slightly of ashes, but others, luckily, still sparkled like champagne. God had granted her such an extraordinary life that her duty now was to go on to the end . . . "despite all!" She did not mind growing older, but she refused to be an old woman. And, when her debts were paid, the Théâtre Sarah Bernhardt put on its feet again and the Belle-Isle estate and its garden tidied, what would she have left? Enough to live like a moth in an old shawl. "No! Let me go on in my own way."

So, when Arthur Meyer told her his idea, which was to give on the same day, in France and abroad, a "Sarah Bernhardt Benefit" performance in every town in which she had played, she replied, with a smile:

"My dear friend, your idea is a magnificent one."

"It ought to bring you in enough money to put you and your family in comfortable circumstances."

"Naturally! But why don't you also offer me a room in a house for distressed ladies with a dressing-room and a little sitting-room?"

"But, my dear Sarah!"

"Let's forget about it. If I'm going to spend money, it must be money which I have earned myself, and I can still earn a great deal. I am maimed, an invalid and hard up, but not to the extent of having to sit on the pavement with a tin mug in my hand. Now don't look like that, my dear. Come and give me a kiss."

Arthur Meyer was distinctly annoyed with her. A few months later he came to the Boulevard Pereire with an air of mystery.

"My dear Sarah," he said, "I want to talk to you in private."

"Pooh! Lysiane won't listen. Whisper it to me. No, in the other ear, it's a better one."

As, at the third attempt, my grandmother still heard nothing, Arthur Meyer said in a loud voice that could be heard by anyone:

"The Prince de Ligne is dead."

"Poor Henri!" said Sarah Bernhardt in a soft voice, playing with her rings.

.   .   .   .   .   .

But Sarah mourned for her dear poet. Edmond Rostand died in November 1918 from what was called Spanish 'flu, and my grandmother was deeply moved by his death.

She had hoped that, after the war, her poet would be inspired to brilliant, tender or witty verses of which she, Sarah, would exalt the lyricism or the malice.

"He ought not to have gone before me!" she cried.

For a long time she had been wanting to play *Athalie*. So she gave several performances of that play, interpreting the part of Jezebel's daughter in a marvellous way, and endowing her with a more human and extremely emotional character. She followed this by a play at the Théâtre Sarah Bernhardt by Louis Verneuil, entitled *Daniel*. And on March 9, 1921, the young author of the play became Sarah Bernhardt's grandson-in-law.

My wedding to Louis Verneuil took place at the Church of Saint-François-de-Sales; as at my father's wedding, thirty-four years earlier, the guests and the sightseers even climbed on the holy-water stoups to see Sarah being carried along in her little chair with its scrollwork.

In 1921, under President Millerand, Sarah Bernhardt was promoted from a Chevalier of the Legion of Honour to be an Officer of the Legion, and afterwards she went on a Spanish tour with her grandson-in-law. Everywhere she met with the same reception, the same enthusiasm, but I imagine that a certain amount of pity and curiosity entered into the feelings of the people she met.

Then followed a play by Maurice Rostand, *La Gloire*, with Sarah Bernhardt symbolizing that great and pure allegorical figure.

In 1922, Louis Verneuil produced three scenes specially written for Sarah Bernhardt. She accepted *Régine Armand*, and the Beloved Monster came to the Théâtre Sarah Bernhardt to applaud her in the part of a mother and a great artiste. And that was her last creation.

At the age of seventy-six, certain things about Sarah Bernhardt still remained amazingly young: her voice, her gestures, the expression of her eyes, her hair: her hair remained the hair of an obstinate schoolgirl or of a coquette. Sometimes she had it dyed and sometimes she wanted it to retain its natural whiteness. "What can I do, Liseron? As a red-haired woman I look like a woman who refuses to grow old. As a white-haired woman, I look old !"

What could I advise her? Sarah Bernhardt had to be red-haired; my grandmother could be white.

. . . . .

I shall never forget my impressions on the day in October 1922, when we celebrated her seventy-ninth birthday. My grandmother was very ill, and a violent attack confined her to her bed. The greatest specialists, Professors Chauffard and Labbé, had been called to her bedside. Added to which, she was in a detestable humour, because Sacha Guitry had brought her a charming play, *Comment on écrit l'Histoire*, and she had been looking forward to playing in it with Lucien Guitry. Seeing his mother so ill, Maurice Bernhardt wanted to countermand the birthday luncheon, but Sarah fixed her faded eyes with their brilliant pupils upon him and said:

"Leave me alone ! I shall get up, despite all !"

At one o'clock she was carried into the dining-room. Her pale blue eyes, big with fever, shone like water. Her transparent complexion was heightened by a hectic colour which emphasized its fragility; she wore a long white dress on which was pinned a bunch of roses. Her hair, almost white, spread in a halo round her wasted face, triangular like that of certain modern young women. She had an unearthly beauty, her voice came in a far-off whisper, at the same time clear and feeble. Had Sarah's spirit already joined those of the heroines whom she had represented here below? All tortured souls, all women of different periods and with intricate and tangled feelings.

We, who ought to have been rejoicing on this festive occasion, remained silent, intimidated by our respect for Sarah, wrung by anguish and burdened by our love for her.

After luncheon Sarah Bernhardt was exhausted and went back to bed. Then my father begged her to give up, once for all, her work and all her various other activities, and to live the rest of her life in peace. Tired and heavy-eyed, Sarah promised vaguely and fell asleep.

In her dreams her parts appeared to her as fantastic personages moving among well-known scenery. And suddenly the vision became smaller and smaller and smaller, until all that was left was a marionette theatre, the last brilliant point in the midst of the sheet-iron and painted canvas scenery which threatened to collapse on to the frail cardboard edifice. This was the night-

The Apothecary's Grotto at Belle-Isle

Left to right: Georges Clairin, Terka Bernhardt, Maurice Bernhardt and Sarah

Sarah Bernhardt on her return from America, 1911, being met by her granddaughters Simone and Lysiane and Simone's husband Eddie Gross

mare which often used to haunt Sarah Bernhardt's sleep and of which she told me in her waking hours.

That afternoon, the image of the "fierce gentleman" came into her thoughts, suggesting fresh contracts. "Come to China, to India, to Japan." He became insistent, she felt his gaze fixed upon her and she opened her eyes. Émile was standing by her bedside.

"Madame," he said, scratching himself. "I wasn't sure whether you were asleep. There's an American gentleman asking for you. He says it is very important."

"Jarrett! Tell him to come in. But no, Émile, I'm not in my second child-hood yet. I know quite well that Jarrett is dead. What is this gentleman's name?"

"Mr. Abrams. He says he's from the cinema city, over there in California ... Hollywood." And Émile pointed to the Place Pereire.

Sarah Bernhardt patted her hair and then hesitated awkwardly, as she became aware of the fact that her son was looking at her anxiously and reproachfully.

"Don't be afraid, Maurice," she said. "It must be about making a film of *Adrienne Lecouvreur*; I know all about it. Go into my dressing-room."

She was lying to him, as she had done when he was a boy and she wanted to go for a trip in a balloon.

Mr. Abrams was surprised to find Sarah Bernhardt in bed.

"A slight attack of influenza, monsieur. Please excuse me."

She lied to him, too. Actually, she felt better: she could always listen to a Mr. Abrams. He suggested making a film of *La Voyante*, with her in the name part.

"You will not have to tire yourself at all, madame. The shots will all be taken in your own studio. I will bring the lamps, the studio hands and the artistes; my Company has empowered me to sign a contract with you."

"He is going to offer me untold gold," thought Sarah.

Perhaps not that, but all the same Mr. Abrams offered her a considerable fee.

Suddenly Sarah signed to him to lower his voice. In the next room her son was pacing up and down. And she had promised him that she would not work any more. Sarah and Mr. Abrams talked in whispers, and she signed the contract with a smile, like someone who has just got into mischief.

CHAPTER XLIII

THE GOLDEN VOICE IS SILENCED

ON March 15, 1923, I arrived at the Boulevard Pereire to be present at the filming of part of *La Voyante*.

"Madame is not at all well," said Émile, shaking his head.

I entered the studio, which Mr. Abrams's workmen had transformed into a battlefield. All the furniture had gone. Networks of scaffolding supported the cameras, the mercury lights and the spotlights; lamps shed their fierce light on everything; the atmosphere was stifling. In one corner of the room was laid the scene of a fortune-teller's den; my grandmother was seated behind a table. She looked preoccupied and terribly tired. Yet she smiled at Mary Marquet who worked with her and for whom she had a great regard. The make-up on Sarah Bernhardt's face sat ill upon her tired features, and made the expression of her pale eyes more elusive than ever. That clear sky-blue, that charming blue that one used to see in them, was gone for ever.

Sarah Bernhardt put on her dark glasses. Abrams was afraid of tiring her by making her wait, but one of the lamps had burned out and a new one had to be fitted. Sarah did not complain, knowing that the cinema is a game of patience. In front of her, a dummy window opened on a scene representing Montmartre; Abrams stepped over the cardboard Sacré-Cœur, went up to his star and arranged her dress; she thanked him.

"Shoot!"

Sarah was absorbed in her part, the light shone in her eyes, she picked up the fortune-telling cards and went through her movements without hurrying.

"Cut!"

Sarah Bernhardt had crumpled up and her eyes were closed, and this fainting-fit was not in the scenario.

"Doctor!" cried Abrams.

Dr. Marot, who was reading the newspapers behind the sky of the Sacré-Cœur, dashed up and there was momentary confusion. My grandmother was laid on the divan in the round room. Her forehead was bathed in perspiration, but she soon recovered consciousness and a wan smile contracted her face. "The more's the pity," she seemed to be saying to life and to her work. While she was being taken up to her room in her little chair, she signed to me to come close.

"Make my apologies to Abrams," she said.

·   ·   ·   ·

The attack lasted several days, with ups and downs, but on March 20, Professor Chauffard declared that there was no hope. The poison had entered her system; she grew weaker, suffered from constant sickness and could not take any nourishment. At first she was in despair at not being able to act in Sacha Guitry's play and having let Abrams down, but she soon resigned herself to accept her illness, and this resignation gradually became torpor. Then we knew that our Sarah was going to die.

The doctors visited her twice a day, interspersing their observations with Latin words, leaving prescriptions as a matter of form, as though to justify their presence. But Sarah Bernhardt was still in possession of her faculties; she talked quietly, fixing her pale eyes on us.

"Have you been out today, Maurice?"

"No, I prefer to remain with you."

"Don't be afraid. I won't go without kissing you good-bye. Go and get me a strawberry ice. Go on! My diet is no longer of any importance."

From statements like this one we realized that she was quite aware of the seriousness of her condition. Then she said:

"Are there any journalists down below?"

For the past forty-eight hours pressmen had been seated, night and day, on the bench in the Boulevard Pereire facing her windows. They asked no questions, they just waited. In the editorial offices, the obituary notices were dug out and brought up to date, as in 1915 and in 1917. She smiled.

"The Press has tormented me enough all my life. I can certainly plague it a little by making it kick its heels now."

Those were her last words and her last smile. My father, my stepmother Marcelle Bernhardt, Simone and I remained near her, either in her room or in her boudoir where her old friends were gathered: Madame Maurice Grau, Louise Abbéma, Madame Normand, Madeleine Porée, the Peronnets and her two grandsons-in-law.

On the morning of May 25 Sarah Bernhardt looked at us in a strange way. That was, perhaps, the moment at which the soul left her body, because it was no longer a look of suffering or anguish but a look of one who is free from the troubles of this world. She shut her eyes: never again would we see their pale irises. Her breathing was calm: she was lying in the midst of her five pillows, her hair spread over the pillowcases embroidered with her motto, "Despite All".

In the afternoon she received Extreme Unction. The telephone was cut off, but the carriage entrance remained open. Émile kept callers informed of the latest news. A continuous stream of people came and went. On the bench on the Boulevard Pereire three men dozed with their coat collars turned up. They were waiting; they had still to wait all day on the 26th. "I can certainly plague them a little," she had said.

On March 26, at eight o'clock in the evening, while my father was dozing in an easy-chair, overcome by weariness and grief, Simone beckoned to me to draw near to the bed. Our grandmother's breath was coming in gasps; her chest rose and fell spasmodically. I placed my hand on her heart; through the white silk of her nightgown I felt it flutter softly, so softly, like a wounded bird trying to fly away. And then nothing. Nothing more.

That great heart was stilled. It would no longer beat proudly for Art, for her son, for France or for the so-greatly Beloved Monster.

People entered and fell on their knees. Someone opened a window. Dr. Marot leaned out.

"Gentlemen," he said, "Madame Sarah Bernhardt is dead."

I could hear scurrying footsteps. The Press was dashing off into the night.

PARIS, 1940.

THE END

INDEX

PRINTED IN GREAT BRITAIN BY THE ANCHOR PRESS, LTD., TIPTREE ESSEX